THE TRANSLATION
OF THE BIBLE INTO CHINESE

Studies in Chinese Christianity

G. Wright Doyle and Carol Lee Hamrin,
Series Editors

A Project of the Global China Center

www.globalchinacenter.org

Previously published volumes in the series

Carol Lee Hamrin & Stacey Bieler, eds., *Salt and Light: Lives of Faith That Shaped Modern China*, volume 1

Carol Lee Hamrin & Stacey Bieler, eds., *Salt and Light: More Lives of Faith That Shaped Modern China*, volume 2

Richard R. Cook & David W. Pao, eds., *After Imperialism: Christian Identity in China and the Global Evangelical Movement*

Carol Lee Hamrin & Stacey Bieler, *Salt and Light: More Lives of Faith That Shaped Modern China*, volume 3

Lit-sen Chang, *Wise Man from the East: Lit-sen Chang (Zhang Lisheng)*

George Hunter McNeur, *Liang A-Fa: China's First Preacher, 1789–1855*

Eunice V. Johnson, *Timothy Richard's Vision: Education and Reform in China, 1880–1910*

G. Wright Doyle, *Builders of the Chinese Church: Pioneer Protestant Missionaries and Chinese Church Leaders*

Jack R. Lundbom, *On the Road to Siangyang: Covenant Mission in Mainland China 1890–1949*

Brent Fulton, *China's Urban Christians: A Light That Cannot Be Hidden*

Andrew T. Kaiser, *The Rushing on of the Purposes of God: Christian Missions in Shanxi since 1876*

Li Ma & Jin Li, *Surviving the State, Remaking the Church: A Sociological Portrait of Christians in Mainland China*

Linda Banks and Robert Banks, *Through the Valley of the Shadow: Australian Women in War-Torn China*

Arthur Lin, *The History of Christian Missions in Guangxi, China*

Linda Banks and Robert Banks, *They Shall See His Face: The Story of Amy Oxley Wilkinson and Her Visionary Work among the Blind in China*

Wayne Ten Harmsel, *The Registered Church in China: Flourishing in a Challenging Environment*

THE TRANSLATION OF THE BIBLE INTO CHINESE

The Origin and Unique Authority of the Union Version

ANN CUI'AN PENG

PICKWICK *Publications* · Eugene, Oregon

THE TRANSLATION OF THE BIBLE INTO CHINESE
The Origin and Unique Authority of the Union Version
Studies in Chinese Christianity

Pickwick Publications
An Imprint of Wipf and Stock Publishers
199 W. 8th Ave., Suite 3
Eugene, OR 97401

www.wipfandstock.com

PAPERBACK ISBN: 978-1-5326-7566-9
HARDCOVER ISBN: 978-1-5326-7567-6
EBOOK ISBN: 978-1-5326-7568-3

Cataloguing-in-Publication data:

Names: Peng, Ann Cui'an, author.

Title: The translation of the Bible into Chinese : the origin and unique authority of the Union Version / Ann Cui'an Peng.

Description: Eugene, OR: Pickwick Publications, 2021. | Studies in Chinese Christianity. | Includes bibliographical references and index.

Identifiers: ISBN 978-1-5326-7566-9 (paperback). | ISBN 978-1-5326-7567-6 (hardcover). | ISBN 978-1-5326-7568-3 (ebook).

Subjects: LCSH: Bible—Chinese—Versions. | Bible translation. | Chinese Bible. | Christianity—China.

Classification: BS315 C59 P46 2021 (paperback). | BS315 (ebook).

04/21/21

To
Unknown Chinese scholars and assistants
who labored along with the missionary translators
whose names are in
the Book of Life

To
All who made sacrificial efforts
to provide the Union Version
for the Chinese people

Contents

Illustrations and Sources

All are courtesy of the Yale Divinity School Library, New Haven, Connecticut, with the exception of figure 3, which is courtesy of the American Bible Society Library, New York, and figure 1, which was designed by the author.

Preface

AFTER COMPLETING MY MA at the University of Birmingham in 1991, I attended a one-month course in the Holy Land. One day, we visited a church where, according to legend, Jesus' mother Mary had visited Elizabeth. On the wall of the surrounding churchyard, the Magnificat, Mary's song of praise, was written in forty-seven languages. Our tutor asked us, a group of twelve people from seven different countries, to find our own language version of the Magnificat and read it aloud in turn. I quickly scanned the various languages on the wall, doubting that I would see Chinese. I was thrilled when my eyes were caught by some Chinese characters. I had learned the Magnificat before ever attending seminary; I could have recited it by heart, and I even knew how to sing it. To my surprise, as I stared at the Chinese characters, I realized that I could not read them easily. "Is this really the Chinese version?" I wondered as I stuttered over the words. This was my first experience reading biblical verses in a classical style.

A few months later, on my way back to China from England, I had the opportunity to visit the American Bible Society library in New York. Although I am a third generation Christian, I had been unaware that there were other versions of the Chinese Bible besides the Chinese Union Version until I saw the *Wenli* (classical Chinese) version in the library. I was surprised to learn that there are in fact many Chinese versions of the Bible. "How did the Bible come to China and become Chinese?" I wondered. At that moment, my desire to study the formation of the Chinese Bible began.

This desire continued to grow during my time as a theology teacher and Director of the Commission on Bible Publication at the China Christian Council. I dreamed that one day I could do more scholarly research to explore the origin of the Chinese Bible. The more I read the Chinese Bible, the stronger this interest grew, especially as I became involved in revising the section headings of the Union Version. Finally, in 2001, I had the opportunity to return to Birmingham University to fulfill my dream. The present study is the result of that long-cherished aspiration.

As 2019 recently marked the 100th anniversary of the Chinese Union Version of the Bible, I have been encouraged to make a contribution to the celebration by updating my research on the subject. In honor of those who dedicated their lives to the task of creating the Chinese Union Version, I undertook this project.

Acknowledgments

MY HEARTY GRATITUDE GOES first to Dr. G. Wright Doyle and Dr. Carol Lee Hamrin for their understanding of my research, scholarly comments, consistent encouragement, invaluable advice, and warm fellowship and friendship.

I would like to thank those who made their archives available to me, especially the British and Foreign Bible Society Library, in Cambridge; the American Bible Society Library in New York; the library at Regent's Park College in Oxford; the School of Oriental and African Studies in London; the Orchard Centre Library of the University of Birmingham; and the Day Mission Library at Yale Divinity School in New Haven, Connecticut.

I want to express my appreciation to Laura Mason, and to Stephanie and Kittie Helmick who helped with English style and patiently edited my work.

Finally, I wish to acknowledge my thanks to members of my family who are in China, and to brothers and sisters in Christ, near and far, for it is they who instilled in me the tenacity of spirit, and sustained me with their constant prayers that has helped me to achieve my goals. But to no one do I owe more than to my dear husband, Yading, for his understanding, patience and love, which encouraged me and supported me throughout this study. It is sufficient to say that he has been even more delighted than I am to see the task completed. So, for that, as for so much more, I am deeply grateful.

Note on Language

THE SYSTEM FOR ROMANIZING Chinese characters known as *pinyin* has been employed in italics throughout this study, except for proper names. In the case of quoted materials, older variants have been retained.

A few place names, because of their common usage in English, have not been rendered into *pinyin*; notably, Hong Kong, Macao, Mongolia. Names like "Peking" (Beijing) and "Nanking" (Nanjing) remain in the old style in this historical study about the nineteenth century in China. The English translations, if not noted otherwise, are by the present author.

Abbreviations

Bible Versions

CNET	Chinese New English Translation Bible
CCB	Chinese Contemporary Bible
CCV	Contemporary Chinese Version
CSB	Chinese Standard Bible
KJV	King James Version
LZV	Lü Zhenzhong Version
MUV	Mandarin Union Version
NCV	New Chinese Version
PV	Peking Version
TCV	Today's Chinese Version
UV	Union Version, Chinese Union Version

Missions, Bible Societies, and Others[1]

ABCFM	American Board of Commissioners for Foreign Missions
ABS	American Bible Society
ABU	American Bible Union
BFBS	British and Foreign Bible Society
CCC	China Christian Council
CMS	Church Missionary Society
HKBS	Hong Kong Bible Society
LMS	London Missionary Society

1. For more missions, see "Institutions" on http://www.bdcconline.net/en/institutions.

NBSS	National Bible Society of Scotland
SBF	Studium Biblicum Franciscanum
TSPM	Three Self Patriotic Movement
UBS	United Bible Societies
WBS	Worldwide Bible Society

Frequently Quoted Documents

Records 1877	*Records of the General Conference of the Protestant Missionaries of China, Held at Shanghai, May 10–24, 1877.* Shanghai: Presbyterian Mission, 1877.
Records 1890	*Records of the General Conference of the Protestant Missionaries of China, Held at Shanghai, May 7–20, 1890.* Shanghai: Presbyterian Mission Press, 1890.
Records 1907	*Records: China Centenary Missionary Conference, Held at Shanghai, April 25 to May 8, 1907.* Shanghai: Centenary Conference Committee, 1907.
Recorder	*The Chinese Recorder* 1 (1867)—44 (1912)
Repository	*The Chinese Repository* 1 (1832)—20 (1851)

Introduction

THIS STUDY EXAMINES IN detail, through the history of Chinese Bible translation, the origin, development, influence, and uniqueness of the Chinese Union Version (UV). It explores the reasons for its being the version most accepted by the Chinese Church worldwide, and its contemporary challenges. It argues that, with the unique authority that history has bestowed, the UV will remain in use, and its dominant status will last until the appearance of the best possible translation of the Scriptures, one that is both more accurate and elegant and that satisfies the expectations of Chinese Christians.

Part I traces the history of Chinese Bible translation. The study critically evaluates the different phases of translation work in the light of historical developments and different Christian traditions. It identifies the significant contribution of Western Protestant missionaries in this field and evaluates the role of Chinese assistants as well.

Part II investigates the principles underlying the UV translation. The case studies demonstrate the nature of these principles. It explores the most heated, unresolved debate among the missionaries, i.e., the Term Question (the debate about which Chinese name for God is most appropriate) and observes its present resolution by Chinese Christians. Various efforts to revise the UV and their latest results are outlined.

Part III identifies the uniqueness of the UV as the most outstanding achievement of Western missionary Bible translation in China, and as a pioneer in the New Culture Movement, where it played a significant role in the reform of Chinese language and literature. It assesses the contemporary challenges to the UV from a historical perspective and concludes that the unique authority that history has given to the UV remains the same and will continue to be indelible.

This study offers a comprehensive history of Protestant Chinese Bible translations, excluding versions in various dialects and in the language of Chinese minority groups, as background to a discussion of the unique characteristics of the UV and the challenges it currently faces. By critically examining the original records of the history of Chinese Bible translations and correcting erroneous assertions, it presents a reliable resource for further research. As well as clearly stating the significant contribution of Western missionary translators, I include an evaluation of the roles and work of Chinese assistants. My advantage in being Chinese is that I am able to work with Chinese characters, contribute a reference list of those assistants that are known, and make suggestions concerning those that are at present unknown for further study and identification.

The history of Chinese Bible translation was first recorded by missionaries Muirhead (1890), Wherry (1890), Broomhall (1934), and Garnier (1934), followed by a Chinese author, Cheng Zhiyi (1947). They give accounts of the history of Chinese Bible translations from the earliest period up to their own time, including versions in the languages of ethnic minority groups in China. Since the 1960s, the specific topic of Chinese Bible translation has drawn more and more interest and concern from a variety of authors in Taiwan, Hong Kong, and mainland China. There are a number of articles and books written on this subject, such as those published by Yang Senfu (1968), Li Shiyuan (1977), Xu Mushi (1982), Luo Xurong (1988), Wang Weifan (1991), Wen Yong (1992), and I-Jin Loh (1995).

From the 1960s and up to the 1980s, three representative collections reflected the concerns of different periods: (1) *Shengjing Hanyi Lunwenji* (Collection of articles on Chinese Bible Translations), edited by Jia Baoluo (R. P. Kramers), consists of articles on the revision of the Chinese Bible, i.e., the UV and the developments of modern Bible translations in the post-UV era.; (2) *Yijing luncong* (Study Series on Bible Translation), edited by Liu Yiling (1979), comprises several publications concerning the UV that debate new translation issues; and (3) *Shangdi de ai* (The Love of God), primarily edited by Xiao Min (1981), is a collection of articles, papers, and reviews on the Today's Chinese Version (TCV), which represent the opinions of Chinese Christians who support the re-translation of the Chinese Bible, especially the publication of the TCV.

From the 1980s to the 1990s, the most scholarly studies referring to the UV were Thor Strandenaes's dissertation, "Principles of Chinese Bible Translation" (1987), Zhao Weiben's dissertation, *Tracing Bible Translation*

(1993), Jost Oliver Zetzsche's study *The Bible in China: The Culmination of Protestant Missionary Bible Translation in China* (1999). Writing at approximately the same time as Zetzsche, Irene Eber published *The Jewish Bishop and the Chinese Bible* (1999).

Strandenaes compares five mainstream versions from 1814 to 1984, namely Morrison's version (1823), the Delegates' version (1854), the UV (1919), *Studium Biblicum* (1968), and Today's Chinese Version (1979), to discover the main guidelines used in translation. His dissertation contributes to the linguistic understanding of Chinese Bible translation, but the history of Bible translation is not his major focus. Zhao analyzes the history of modern Chinese Bible translations, tracing some earlier history as well. He explores the historical background of Bible translation work, covering the conflict and cooperation between Chinese Roman Catholics and Protestants in translating the Scriptures. His work only focuses on five selected versions published in the twentieth century, however: the UV, *Studium Biblicum*, and Today's Chinese Version, as well as The New Chinese Bible (New Testament, 1976) and the Interconfessional Version (Luke, 1986). Zetzsche provides information on archival material regarding the history of Chinese Bible translation, which none of the previously mentioned works emphasized. As a historian, Zetzsche reveals the conflicts, doubts, and criticisms of the translators and missionary societies that were usually deleted from official reports written for public consumption. His work details the intricacies of Protestant Bible translation work, including full-length biographies of some significant translators who were involved in Bible translations before and during the UV translation. Because he focuses on the history of the UV, Zetzsche only provides a list of versions translated by Chinese Christians after the publication of the UV in the appendices, however. Irene Eber narrates the life and times of Samuel I. J. Schereschewsky, a fascinating figure in the history of Chinese Bible translation. Based largely on archival materials, missionary records, and letters, the book also includes the controversial Term Question and Schereschewsky's techniques of translating the Hebrew text.

First published in April 1919, the UV now has one hundred years of history. To this day it is still the authoritative version accepted by the majority of Chinese Christians. How can one explain the pre-eminence of the UV among the various translations of the Chinese Bible in the last century? This question was neglected until the year 2000, when the first systematic scholarly studies by Zhuang Rouyu from Hong Kong appeared. Using a method called Descriptive Translation Studies, she broke new ground with a masterpiece entitled *A Study of the Phenomenon of Authoritativeness in the Chinese Translations of the Protestant Bible*.

These academic publications demonstrate an increasing recognition of the significance of Bible translation in China. Each study has its own specialization and emphasis concerning Bible translation in China; taken together, they provide a rich resource and much relevant material for my present research and analysis. I acknowledge a general dependence on all the previously mentioned works.

This volume explores the uniqueness and contemporary challenges of the UV in the context of the history of Chinese Bible translation, a topic that is attracting more and more attention. I have several advantages in conducting this research. Like the majority of readers of the UV, I grew up in mainland China. When the UV went through a severe, historic ordeal along with its readers, I was there to witness the UV comforting those who were suffering under persecution. I once participated in Chinese Bible revision with a group under the auspices of the United Bible Societies. I was Director of the Commission on Bible Publication at the China Christian Council and Chief editor of the UV concise annotated version, published in 1998. These experiences have provided me with first-hand knowledge of the context for research and analysis.

The UV resulted from decisions made by the Protestant Missionary Conference held in Shanghai in 1890. At the conference, it was decided that "One Bible, Three Versions" should be the goal of the union version project. The UV, originally known as "The *Guanhua*/Mandarin Union Version," was one of the three versions. The other two were "The *Wenli* Union Version" and "The Easy *Wenli* Union Version."[1] Why did only the Mandarin Union Version become the standard Bible commonly used by Chinese Christians? The catalogue compiled by H. W. Spillett (1975) was based on Darlow/Mould's, —the most exhaustive list of Chinese versions and editions published thus far, showing that there is no lack of versions

---

1 "Mandarin" refers to standard Chinese. It is a term used first by Jesuit missionaries in the 16th century as the equivalent of the Chinese term *Guanhua* (language of the officials). *Guanhua* was replaced with *Guoyu* (national language), which is still used in HK and Taiwan, and with *Putonghua* (common language) in the mainland. The term *Wenli* (principles of literature or writing) was coined by the 19th century missionaries to describe a high form of classical Chinese and Easy *Wenli* (or Low *Wenli*) for a lower form of classical Chinese. These terms were used only within missionary circles. Sinologists outside Christian circles commonly use *Wenyanwen* for classical Chinese and *Baihuawen* for the colloquial form.

for Chinese Christians to choose from.[2] Nonetheless, since the UV appeared in 1919, it has been accepted as the standard translation by Chinese Protestants worldwide, for all their different cultural experiences, levels of education, and denominational backgrounds. This is still true to this day, despite many criticisms.

The UV has dominated the religious life of Chinese Protestants by serving multiple functions. As the Word of God, it helps Chinese Christians in times of need. It is used not only for Sunday services and personal devotions, but also in various group meetings, such as women's prayer meetings, youth groups, senior gatherings, and Bible studies. More and more people, men and women, young and old, are seeking to know the value of life through the Bible. It is a common and highly treasured gift at ordinations, baptisms, and weddings. Zhou Lianhua, biblical scholar and translator, once commented on the UV's multiple functions:

> For sixty years, the UV has led many people to believe in Jesus, has comforted many who were broken-hearted or in sorrow, and has guided numerous lost sheep as well. This Bible has been read from the pulpit in church, used as a teaching material in classrooms, read carefully in studies and used also as devotional reading in the living room, the dining room and the bedroom. It has accompanied soldiers to war; it has been placed by the side of a bed to comfort the sick and also it has been put into many coffins of those who rest in the Lord. . . This is a best-selling book and also is the only book that is read by someone every single day.[3]

The UV has been pored over by a high proportion of Chinese Bible readers over a long period of time. It has enjoyed the longest period of acceptance in the Chinese churches. When the UV came into being, Protestant Bible translation had taken place for over a hundred years, with various versions in circulation. The emergence of the UV ended the practice of using multiple versions as it rapidly became and continues to be the most widely used Protestant Chinese Bible. Twelve years ago, my survey of Chinese Bible readers showed that the UV was favored by the majority. Now, although many new versions have become available, it is still the UV that enjoys the highest number of sales.

---

2. Darlow/Moule is short for *Historical Catalogue of the Printed Editions of Holy Scripture in the Library of the British and Foreign Bible Society* I-II, 181–255, edited by Darlow, T. H., and H. F. Moule, published by BFBS in 1903.

3. Zhou, "Jieshao *Xiandai Zhongwen Yiben*," 17.

Why was the UV accepted as a unifying and standard version by the Chinese Church? How did it come into being? Why has the UV played the role of an "authorized" version since it emerged? What was the contribution made by missionaries and their Chinese coworkers to Chinese Bible translation? What is the uniqueness of the UV among the various versions? Could post-UV translations in modern Chinese become its rivals? To answer these questions, it is necessary to study the history of the UV.

In this study, the history of Chinese Bible translation is divided into four periods, involving translators of different Christian traditions: 1) the Nestorians in the seventh century; 2) Roman Catholics in the thirteenth and from the sixteenth to eighteenth centuries; 3) Protestant missionaries from 1807 to 1919; and 4) Protestant Chinese from 1920 onwards. For the first two periods, only a brief account is given in Chapter 1, since my research focuses on a Protestant Bible translation, the UV. Chapter 1 analyzes the reasons why these early Christian missions failed to achieve a lasting position in Chinese society. The history of Chinese Bible translation dates back to the introduction of Christianity to China in the seventh century. It was not until the nineteenth century that the first major Chinese Bible translation activities began, however. Chapter 2 investigates the translation strategies, theoretical issues, and practices of Protestant missionaries during the nineteenth century. Although Roman Catholic translations have developed in parallel to the Protestant translations since the nineteenth century, they receive no further detailed discussion. In China, the Roman Catholic and Protestant traditions are distinct from each other not only in church structures, doctrine, creed, and liturgy, but also in their Bible translations.[4] Chapter 3 focuses on the union version project. Since Robert Morrison of the London Missionary Society, the first Protestant missionary to live and work in China, published a complete Chinese version of the Bible in 1823, various translations have emerged. Some have been produced by teams of missionaries, others by individual translators. The existence of multiple versions created a demand for union. The union version project was the product of the demand. Through over a hundred years of arduous labor, Western missionaries, with the aid of Chinese assistants, finally presented to the Chinese people the Union Version, the most successful and satisfying outcome of the project. The above three chapters make up Part One.

---

4. In China, people refer to the Roman Catholic and the Protestant churches as two entirely different religions. They themselves live and work in mutual isolation and their names are different, viz., *Tianzhujiao* and *Jidujiao*.

Chapter 4 investigates the principles of translation. When translating the Bible, the translators obviously followed certain principles in their work, whether consciously recognized or not. The nature of these principles is illustrated through a case study. Ascertaining the nature of the principles of translation is important for understanding past missionaries' experiences of Bible translation and may give valuable suggestions for the present and future task of the Chinese church. The chapter explores, in detail, the most heated debate among missionaries: The Term Question, caused by their translating "God" into Chinese "*Shen*" or "*Shangdi*," and discovers that this unsolved question left by the missionaries is no longer a question for today's Chinese believers. Chapter 5 discusses various efforts at revising the UV. In the late twentieth century, there had been much debate over whether the UV should be revised or whether a new translation was needed. These are issues worthy of attention in this research, as they help with exploring the unique characteristics of the UV. The UV, translated almost a century ago, could not be without any mistakes and inaccuracies. It is an excellent translation but not perfect in every way. Results from textual and archaeological discoveries, most prominently the discovery of the Dead Sea Scrolls, and the development of the Chinese language in the last hundred years have revealed that the UV contains many major and minor inaccuracies. When the Bible moved from the edge to the center of Chinese expectations in the late twentieth century, here and there increasingly arose calls for revision and re-translation. At that time, the UV stood alone; it was the sole Scripture in common use and was recognized as the Chinese authorized version. As a result, revision became an almost impossible endeavor and further translation efforts encountered opposition and strong criticism. The English Revised Version (1885), the blueprint on which the UV translation was based, has itself gone through many revisions, the latest being the New Revised Standard Version published in the late 1980s. In 1988, the UV was revised but only with respect to punctuation, some proper names, and pronouns. The Revised Chinese Union Version of 2010 is the result of twenty-seven years of effort. The work was entrusted to over thirty Chinese Biblical scholars from mainland China, Hong Kong, Taiwan, Malaysia and Singapore, beginning in 1983, with the entire project completed in 2010. It was planned first by the United Bible Society, then the Hong Kong Bible Society. Chapters 4 and 5 are the core of Part Two.

Part Three is comprised of Chapter 6 and Chapter 7. Chapter 6 examines and analyses the unique characteristics of the UV. The UV is a marvelous culmination of nearly a century of missionaries' efforts in the field of translating the Bible into Chinese. Generally speaking, after the 1920s, the Chinese Church began to emphasize its desire to be indigenous, self-governing, self-supporting, and self-propagating. Why then has the version translated mainly by missionaries been more accepted than the versions done entirely by Chinese? Why has the UV, which was published at the beginning of the New Culture Movement (1917), and the subsequent May Fourth Movement (1919), not been replaced by modern translations? Why did the UV quickly supersede the various versions that existed before it, and why has it never been supplanted by the various versions that came after it? What gives it such a firm position in the hearts of Chinese Christians? Will revision undermine its "authorized" position? Does the history of the King James Version provide a parallel to that of the UV? The findings of this research offer a fresh interpretation of the uniqueness of the UV with respect to historical development, political movements, religious sentiment, and social influence. Chapter 7 assesses the contemporary challenges to the UV from the perspective of historical development. The UV marks the pinnacle of Protestant missionary Bible translation in China, and it also signals the end of their mission of translating the Bible into Chinese.

The task of Chinese Bible translation has shifted from Western missionaries to the Chinese church. Several Chinese versions of the Bible, or parts thereof, translated solely by Chinese, have been published since the UV, such as the ones by Wang Xuanchen, who also assisted with preparing the UV. He published a New Testament version in 1933. Lü Zhenzhong's version, in a tentative edition that appeared in 1946, followed by the entire Bible in 1970, not only challenged some of the UV's interpretations of the Greek text of the New Testament, but also aimed at employing more idiomatic Chinese. From the 1970s to the 1990s, three teamwork versions have been published, all regarded by their translators as versions in modern Chinese, namely: The Chinese Living Bible (1979), Today's Chinese Version (1979), and The New Chinese Bible (1992).

In the twenty-first century, advances in computer technology have opened new doors for Bible translation. Several efforts at Chinese Bible translation have achieved their aims. More than 5 translations or revised versions have appeared within the last ten years. None of these versions have had as wide a circulation as the UV, nor do they seem to have enjoyed the same acceptance by the majority of Chinese believers as was given to the UV, however. Chinese Bible translation is moving from the stage of having one "authorized" version, the UV, towards that of multiple versions. Nowadays, digital Bibles are becoming popular, allowing easy access to a variety of translations, even the original text, just by clicking a button. The UV went through a process from diversity to unity, from multiplicity to union. Will people soon get lost in various new versions and appeal for a UV II? Will history repeat itself? These questions are worthy of further study. So far, these versions are taken just as supplements to the UV, with the UV remaining dominant. Although the UV is imperfect, its pre-eminent position has not been affected by recent translations or by the revision of the UV itself. The conclusion summarizes the findings of this research with a historical analysis of the uniqueness and the contemporary challenges of the UV, and then considers a new chapter of history of Chinese Bible translation made by Chinese. This study is one attempt to explore the unique authority and current challenges of the UV in the context of the history of Chinese Bible translation. It offers a study in the realm of Chinese Bible translation and creates an agenda for further research. On the 100th anniversary of the UV, I present it as a contribution in honor of those who dedicated their lives to the production of this unique version.

The bibliography includes sources both in English and Chinese; the Chinese sources will be provided in *pinyin* Romanization instead of characters.

Studying archival material in Chinese presents a problem when dealing with Western missionaries in China because most of them had adopted Chinese names, not transliterations of their English names. This makes identification difficult. To avoid confusion, I append an English-Chinese list of those involved in the translation of the union version project.

Part I

A Historical Survey
of Chinese Bible Translation

1

The Beginnings of
Chinese Bible Translation

WHEN DID THE BIBLE come to China? When was it translated into Chinese? These questions are closely connected with the beginnings of the Christian mission in China. A beautiful legend has it that St. Thomas, one of the twelve disciples of Jesus, reached China from India. In China, he preached the gospel and saw many conversions to Christianity. Many Chinese Christians are still convinced that this is true. There is nothing inherently impossible in the idea of Thomas in China. He might have travelled, as Paul did, around the Mediterranean, but also gone on through Asia to India, or even further to some place in China. Possibilities do not make history, however. Moreover, there is no mention that Bible translation was involved. So, while these stories may preserve an authentic tradition, in the absence of reliable concrete evidence, they will have to remain a legend. There is no certain proof of the existence of Christianity in China until the Tang dynasty (AD 618–907). In this chapter, the discussion of the beginnings of Chinese Bible translation falls into two subsections: 1) The Nestorians and Lost Translations, and 2) The Roman Catholics and Their Endeavors.

The Nestorians and Lost Translations[1]

The Nestorians in the Tang Dynasty

The first direct evidence of Christian missionary activity in China is that of Nestorian missionaries who travelled along the Silk Road and arrived at Chang'an (now Xi'an), the capital of China, at the beginning of the Tang dynasty in the seventh century.

The Tang dynasty in Chinese history was an era of glory and splendor. In the eyes of the Chinese, it stands for the "golden age" of China. The "men of Tang" once became a proud title for the Chinese. To this day, "China town" abroad is known in Chinese as "the street of the men of Tang," for this name recalls the time when China was a world power.

Tang dynasty China was cosmopolitan and tolerant. Emperor Tai Zong (AD 626–49) was the most illustrious figure of the Tang dynasty and one of the greatest men who ever sat upon the throne of China. During his reign, international trade flourished between China and the lands to the west. Visitors were to be found from many distant parts of the world. The missionaries of a variety of faiths were hospitably received. It was under these circumstances that the Nestorian missionary, Alopen, made his way to China. He came from a country named Daqin and arrived in Chang'an in AD 635. Emperor Tai Zong paid him great honor, sending one of his chief ministers to receive him. He was directed to the palace, and there the Christian books that he had brought with him were translated. Later, as a result of the emperor's decree, Nestorians were given the right to propagate their faith and a monastery was built in the capital. Yet, all historical traces of such an event have been lost in the dim mists of antiquity and were completely forgotten until 1625, with the unearthing of a stone monument known as the Nestorian Tablet.

---

1. The term "Nestorian" is used simply by convention. Many scholars now employ the term, "Syrian Church of the East" instead, since that is the name used by these Christians, who were separated by geography from the churches in the Roman Empire. Furthermore, "Nestorianism" was condemned as a heresy. That charged was dropped in 1994, when the Roman Catholic church and the Assyrian Church of the East issued a "Common Christological Declaration." See Charbonnier, *Christians in China*, 39–51. See also Moffett, *History of Christianity*, 301–314, and Covell, "Confucius," 20–35.

The Tablet and the Naming of Jingjiao

The Nestorian Tablet was discovered in a town about thirty miles east of Xi'an, when workmen were laying the foundations for a building.[2] It is a single block of fine-grained limestone that stands some nine feet high, about three and a half feet across, and a little less than one foot thick. The date of its erection was AD 781. Despite having been long buried, the stone, with its inscription, is almost in perfect condition. Chinese characters arranged in neat, vertical columns covered the broad face of the Tablet. At the bottom of the inscription, on both the left and the right sides of the slab, there was a long list of names in Syriac and Chinese, which refer to the clergy of that time.[3]

The main inscription includes a heading, a statement of Christian doctrine, an account of the Apostolic Age, the story of Alopen's arrival in China, the edict of the emperor, and the history of Nestorian missionaries during a period of 150 years of the Tang dynasty. The inscription ends with a statement of who set up the stone and when. All of this was written in about 1,900 characters, in both prose and verse, and composed by Adam Jingjing, a monk of the Daqin Monastery.

The crown of the Nestorian Tablet is richly carved with a cross and the title of the inscription reads: "The Tablet of the Spread of the Daqin Luminous Religion in China."

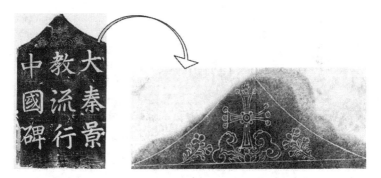

Figure 1: The crown of the Nestorian Tablet
(This combined diagram was designed by the author.)

---

2. For different stories about the finding of the stone, see Moule, *Christians in China*, 28; Saeki, *Nestorian Monument*, 27.

3. The Syriac portions were translated by J. Terrenz in about 1629, which is still of value in revealing the existence of Syriac names on both sides of the stone.

When Christian missionaries arrived from Persia and first set up monasteries, "Persian Religion" was taken as the name for this "new" religion. In 745, an imperial edict was issued that the official Chinese name for the Christian monasteries be changed from "Persian" to "Daqin." The edict reads:

> The Luminous Religion of Persia was originally started in Ta-Ch'in [Daqin]. It is a long time since this religion came to be preached here. Now it is practised by many, spreading throughout the Middle Kingdom. When they first built monasteries we gave them the name of "Persian Temple" (because of their supposed origin). But in order that all men might know the (real and true) origin of what are commonly known as "Persian Monasteries" in the two Capitals, (the names) are henceforth to be changed to the "Ta-Ch'in Monasteries." Let those also which are established in all parts of the empire follow this example.

The reason for such a change might be that it was necessary to distinguish the "Luminous Religion" from some of the other Persian religions which were also active in China at that time, such as the Zoroastrians, or the Manicheans, or the Muslims. The Nestorian Tablet also records how the Nestorians were given the name "*Jingjiao*" or "Luminous Religion," thus:

> This ever True and Unchanging Way is mysterious,
> and is almost impossible to name.
> But its meritorious operations are so brilliantly manifested
> that we make an effort and call it by the name of "The Luminous Religion."[4]

Chinese naming is always meaningful. The name presents the nature and character of its bearer. "We make an effort and call it by the name. . ." which is enough to suggest that the name of "*Jingjiao*" or "Luminous Religion" had been carefully chosen to suit it. Wang Weifan, professor at Nanjing Union Theological Seminary, with his profound knowledge of Chinese culture, states that "Jing" means blessed, auspicious, propitious, peaceful, harmonious in Chinese.[5]

Thus, the name "*Daqin Jingjiao*," which appears on the Nestorian Tablet, has been known to this day as the name of Christianity in the Tang dynasty.

---

4. The edict and this quote were translated by Saeki, *Nestorian Documents*, 457.
5. Wang, "Shengjing Yiben," 63.

Evidences of the Impact of Translation

The Nestorian Tablet is the earliest evidence of the coming of Christianity to China and of the translation of the Scriptures into the Chinese language. This history is inscribed on the Tablet thus:

> When Tai Zong, the polished Emperor, was beginning his prosperous reign in glory and splendour with light and wisdom ruling the people, there was in the land of Ta-ch'in [Daqin] one of high virtue called A-lo-pen, who, auguring by the blue clouds, carried the true Scriptures; watching the harmony of the winds, hastened to meet difficulties and dangers. In the ninth Cheng Kuan [Zhen Guan] year (635) he came to Ch'ang-an [Chang'an]. The Emperor sent the Minister of State, Duke Fang Hsuan-ling [Fang Xuanling], to take an escort to the west suburb to meet the guest and bring him to the palace. When the books had been translated in the library and the doctrine examined in his private apartments, [the Emperor] thoroughly understood their propriety and truth and specially ordered their preaching and transmission.[6]

Alopen was received with honor by the emperor, translations of the sacred books were made in the imperial library, and the emperor himself studied the religion and found it excellent. He acknowledged that it meant the salvation of creatures and the benefit of man and was worthy of being spread over all the empire. Thus, he gave orders for its propagation. It was an auspicious beginning. Three years later, in AD 638, a monastery was built in the capital and twenty-one monks were appointed there as a result of the emperor's edict. The edict stated on the Tablet:

> The way has no unchanging name, sages have no unchanging method. Teaching is established to suit the land, that all living may be saved. The man of great virtue, A-lo-pen of the land of Ta-ch'in [Daqin], bringing books and images from afar has come to offer them at the upper capital. If we carefully examine the meaning of the teaching it is mysterious, wonderful, full of repose. If we look at the fundamental principle it fixes the essentials of production and perfection. In its speech there is no multitude of words; in its principle there is [perfect accomplishment,] forgetting the means. It is the salvation of living beings, it is the wealth of men. It is right that it should have free course under the sky. Let the local officers

---

6. Translated by Moule, *Christians in China,* 38.

therefore build a Ta-ch'in monastery in the I-ning quarter at the capital with twenty-one men as regular monks.[7]

In the edict, it is said that Alopen had "brought books and images from afar." The "books" refer to the Bible and the "images" refer to portraits of the figures in the Bible which were preserved until at least the ninth century. When Ibn Wahab, an old Christian from Arabia, visited the capital of China, he was shown the portraits of Noah, Moses, Jesus and his disciples, and had an interesting conversation with the emperor. The Bible brought by Alopen comprised "the Old Law as it was declared by the Twenty-Four Sages" and "the Scriptures, left in twenty-seven books." The "Old Law" refers to the Old Testament. The "Twenty-Four Sages" refer to the authors of the Old Testament and "twenty-seven books" refer to the New Testament.[8]

Tai Zong's toleration made the Nestorians' success possible. In the eulogy that forms the principal part of the inscription, there is a record of incidents during the reign of Tai Zong. It states: "They translated books, they built monasteries." One question which concerns us here is, how much of the Bible was translated?

Wylie asserts: "From these various notices, preserved to us in the durable records of a stone tablet, we gather with much confidence the impression that the New Testament, at least, was translated into Chinese during the first half of the seventh century."[9]

The important discoveries of Nestorian manuscripts by Paul Pelliot at the Dunhuang grottoes in 1908 seem to confirm Wylie's assertion. Among them, the *Zunjing* (Honored Sutra) is in reality a listing of names and books. Moule gave a more suitable title: "Honoured Persons and Sacred Books."[10]

Among the list of twenty-two saints and holy men, seven of them are reckoned as follows:

- *Yuhannan*: John

- *Lujia*: Luke

7. Ibid., 39.

8. Moule, *Christians in China*, 77. Wang Weifan ("Shengjing Yiben," 62) believes that "Twenty-Four Sages" refers to the Old Testament prophets of which Moses is the first. No satisfactory explanation has yet been given as to why the orthodox Western canonical number of twenty-seven is used for the New Testament instead of the Syriac canonical number of twenty-two. Yang Senfu (*Zhongguo Jidujiao*, 358) believes it is because *Jingjiao* was independent of the Syriac Church.

9. Wylie, *Chinese Researches*, 89.

10. Moule, *Christians in China*, 55.

- *Mojuci*: Mark
- *Mingtai*: Matthew
- *Moushi*: Moses
- *Duohui*: David
- *Baolu*: Paul

Among the thirty-five Sacred Books ten are identified as follows:

- *Duohui sheng wang jing*: The Psalms of David
- *A si qu li rong jing*: Evangelion/Gospel
- *Hun yuan jing*: Genesis
- *Chuan hua jing*: The Acts
- *Baolu fawang jing*: Pauline Epistles
- *Shan he lu jing*: Zechariah
- *Moushi fawang jing*: Exodus
- *Efulin jing*: Ephesians
- *Wu sha na jing*: Hosea
- *Qi zhen jing*: Revelation[11]

This shows that not only parts of the New Testament, but also some of the Old Testament books were translated into Chinese in the seventh century. The above list may also give some indication of the liturgical and theological priorities of the Nestorians missionaries.

These are the first Chinese translations of the Bible. It is regrettable that none of these early translations survived. It could be that the purpose of their translation was for the examination and understanding by the ruler rather than for dissemination and evangelization. Meanwhile, we should bear in mind that the art of printing was not practised at that time in China. The Nestorian Church completely disappeared from the stage of church history in China when the mighty Tang dynasty collapsed in AD 907. Not a building which the Nestorians erected, nor a Bible portion that they had translated into the Chinese language, has been preserved, not even in oral tradition.

11. Yang, *Zhongguo Jidujiao*, 350–52.

Reasons for Lack of Permanent Influence

The reasons why the first Christian mission to China failed to achieve a lasting position in Chinese society have been much debated. No one has yet given a completely satisfactory answer. In days past there have been those who attributed the failure of the Nestorian Church to its "heretical" basis, as it was banished from the Roman Empire at the Council of Ephesus in 431. This assertion runs counter to history, which shows that the Church of the East, as the Nestorian Church preferred to call itself, was the most successful church between the seventh and eleventh centuries.[12] J. Foster also argues that this attitude needs to be corrected. He writes: "The significance of Nestorianism lies rather in its freedom from connection with the Roman Empire than in any marked difference of faith. It was only because of such freedom that it was possible for the Church of the East to undertake such widespread missionary work."

Latourette, however, believes that there could be a further reason for the failure: the Nestorian Church appears to have compromised its message. He states: "To the average Chinese, Nestorianism may have appeared to be another of the Buddhist sects that were so flourishing under the Tang .. . The Nestorians, in other words, in trying to clothe their faith in dress familiar to the Chinese, may have sacrificed in part its distinctiveness and defeated their own aim."

His suggestion seems to be supported by the unearthed Nestorian documents discovered at Dunhuang in 1908, which show that the author of the Nestorian inscription was also a translator of Buddhist sutras. Some of the documents suggest a degree of syncretism; others reveal a creative use of Taoist and Buddhist terminology to serve Christian ends. This strategy can also be seen in the figure on the crown of the Tablet. As Saeki points out: "Beneath the Cross, —i.e., supporting the cross—, there is the cloud, which the Chinese describes as a "flying cloud" or "white cloud." The cloud is the characteristic symbol of Taoism. Underneath this cloud there lies a lotus-flower, the characteristic emblem of Buddhists. The design was doubtlessly used to denote that 'the three Religions are one.'"

Such a mixture seems closer to syncretism than to missionary contextualization. It can be argued, however, to the contrary, namely that the three symbols show that the Nestorians attempted to adapt their message to the Chinese context and made the Cross superior to the other two symbols.

12. Whyte, *Unfinished Encounter*, 40.

The most common cause given for the disappearance of the Nestorian Church in ninth century China was religious persecution. The church had first encountered hostile voices from Buddhists during the reign of Empress Wu (624–705), who declared Buddhism the official state religion in AD 691. After this attack focused mainly on Taoism, the most severe opposition arose in AD 845 when Wu Zong (814–46), the emperor of the time, came under the influence of the native Taoist monks, and launched an attack on Buddhism that embroiled all foreign religions. The Christian monasteries, together with those of the Buddhists and Manicheans, were suppressed.

Another popular belief has it that the Nestorian Church never became Chinese but remained a church of foreigners. With the expulsion of the foreign missionaries as the result of the edict in 845, the church simply vanished since it lacked the native leadership and strong Chinese following necessary for its survival.

Moffett believes that the decisive factor was none of those previously mentioned, "but rather the fall of an imperial house on which the church had too long relied for its patronage and protection."[13] Is this the only reason? The experience of the Church in China in the twentieth century speaks of a different kind of historical influence. New political power replaced the old with a complete rejection of Western imperialism and the expulsion of all foreign missionaries, but this time the results were different: The Church did not disappear but remained. Persecution alone was not sufficient to explain the Nestorian failure. During the Cultural Revolution (1966–76) there was severe persecution, but the Church did not vanish; on the contrary, it grew stronger and greater.[14] There were two important factors which were present in this later period but absent in the Nestorian period: 1) the Church, no longer foreign, had sunk its roots into the Chinese soil and become Chinese, and 2) the whole Bible had been translated, widely distributed, and widely read, which attests to the fact that the Bible's translation into vernacular language is very important to mission and to churches' survival in their trials.

---

13. The argument points of the scholars in this section are excerpted from their works: Foster, *Church of the Tang Dynasty,* 24; Latourette, *History of Christian Missions,* 59; Saeki, *Nestorian Documents,* 26; Moffett, *History of Christianity,* 313.

14. There were about four million Chinese Christians (including Roman Catholics) when the missionaries left China, but after the Cultural Revolution the number grew at least 4 times.

So, all of the above tentative conjectures are reasonable but no single one can be considered definitive.

The Roman Catholics and Their Endeavors

Franciscans in the Yuan Dynasty

The history of Chinese Bible translation now takes a leap of some four hundred years, during which time little to nothing is known of Christianity. This brings us to the powerful Mongol or Yuan dynasty (1271–1368).

In the midst of the thirteenth century, a new page in the history of Chinese Bible translation was opened by Roman Catholic missions when Franciscans, travelling by land and sea routes, came from the West to the Mongol Court at Khan-baliq or Cambulac, the Mongols' name for Peking.

New Testament and Psalms by Montecorvino

The honor of being the first Roman Catholic Chinese Bible translator belongs, as far as we know, to an Italian Franciscan, John of Montecorvino (1247–1328). In 1289, Friar John, then forty-two years of age, was sent by Pope Nicholas IV to the court of Khubilai (1215–94). When he arrived in Cambulac in 1294, Khubilai had recently died. The friar presented the pope's letter to the new emperor, Timur (1265–1307), who courteously received it.

In 1299, Friar John was allowed by the emperor to build his first church in the capital. Making converts steadily, he had, as he said in his second letter home, baptized about six thousand converts by 1305.[15] In the same year, he began to construct a second church near the gates of the Imperial Palace. For many years, Friar John labored alone. He had heard nothing from the pope or the Franciscans in Europe for twelve years. In 1307, Clement V appointed John as Archbishop of Cambulac and Patriarch of the East. His life had been both eventful and courageous. Latourette spoke highly of him:

> He had, almost single-handed, established the Roman Catholic faith in the capital of the mightiest empire of his time and to do so had journeyed farther from his home than ever any missionary of any religion is known to have done before him. When measured by

15. The letter was reprinted in *The Mongol Mission* ed. by Christopher Dawson New York 1980, [1955].

the effect of his life upon his contemporaries and the succeeding generations, he is by no means the greatest of Christian apostles, but for single-hearted devotion and quiet persistence he deserves to be ranked with the foremost pioneers of all faiths and times.[16]

Friar John never returned to Europe and died at his post around 1328, when he was over eighty years of age.[17] He was the first Roman Catholic archbishop in China.

Our knowledge of his Bible translation is derived from one of John's own letters written from Cambulac and dated January 8, 1305, in which he wrote: "I have an adequate knowledge of the Tartar language and script, which is the usual language of the Tartars, and now I have translated into that language and script the whole of the New Testament and the Psalter and have had it written in beautiful characters. And I bear witness to the Law of Christ and read and preach openly and in public."[18]

The "usual language of the Tartars" would have been Mongolian, the language of the court during the time of the Yuan dynasty. This was the first Mongolian translation of the Bible in China—New Testament and Psalms. Like the Nestorian translation, this manuscript was lost and ceased to exist, along with the Franciscan mission, which ended in 1368 when the Yuan dynasty collapsed. Today, no known portion of this work exists. With the expulsion of the Mongols, Christianity vanished from China even more completely than it had after the fall of the Tang. This was the second disappearance of Christianity in China. When Ricci and his Jesuit companions reached China two centuries later, they could find no trace of the ancient Christians among the inhabitants, not even a memory.

Again, as with the Tang period, the question arises, why did the Christian communities disappear so utterly? Why did the Franciscan mission have so little effect upon the Chinese? It is difficult to judge. Here are some probable causes of their failure: 1) The long distance and the dangers of the journey made survival difficult, many missionaries never reaching their destination. Friar John had to work alone for twelve years before he received any reinforcements. 2) Roman Catholic missions seem to have been very much a "foreign mission," for they received their church orders from outside China and used a foreign language in their liturgy. 3) The Mongol overlords of the Yuan dynasty, on whom the missionaries and their

16. Latourette, *History of Christian Mission*, 71–72.

17. The date of his death is variously given as 1328, 1329, 1330, and 1333.

18. Dawson, *Mongol Mission*, 227.

converts were dependent, were themselves foreigners. So, to the Chinese, Christianity appeared as a foreign religion protected and supported by a foreign government. When the native Chinese Ming dynasty won its way to the imperial throne, an anti-foreign reaction wiped out all that was foreign. It is no surprise that the church fell with the old dynasty.

The Jesuits in the Late Ming and the Early Qing Dynasty

When the Yuan dynasty was overtaken by the Ming in 1368, and the second wave of Christianity had totally vanished from Chinese history, there was a long period of absence during the fourteenth and fifteenth centuries. It was in the late sixteenth century when Christianity again entered China. This time, it was in the form of the Jesuits, later followed by the Dominicans and the Franciscans.

Matteo Ricci and the Jesuits

Matteo Ricci (1552–1610), an Italian Jesuit, was one of the outstanding missionaries of the Church in China. In 1582, he arrived in Macao and began to study the Chinese language. The following year, he moved to Zhaoqing, China, along with Michele Ruggieri (1543–1607), and there they set up the first Chinese base of the Society of Jesus. Ricci immersed himself in the culture of China. He shaved off his hair and beard, wore the dress of a Buddhist monk, and identified himself with Chinese ways. He later adopted the dress and manners of a Confucian scholar.

After nineteen long years of visiting cities all over China, with avid and intense study of its language, history, and culture, Ricci entered Peking in 1601. He lived there for the rest of his life, dying in 1610 at the age of fifty-seven. During his twenty-eight years of labor in China, he achieved a considerable reputation and was much respected by the literati and upright officials. He succeeded in winning a number of converts, among them a man of distinction in official circles, Paul Xu Guangqi (1562–1633).[19]

In 1584, when he and Ruggieri wrote their first catechism in Chinese, *Zuchuan Tianzhu shijie* (Ten Commandments of Lord of Heaven), Ricci had

---

19. Xu, the strong supporter and defender of the early Roman Catholic Church in China, served as a Ming court official from 1610 until his death. He collaborated with Ricci and other Jesuits to translate Western mathematical and scientific works into Chinese and polished or rewrote most of Ricci's writings in Chinese.

his first experience of wrestling with the critical problem of finding suitable Chinese words for expressing Christian ideas. He noted Chinese names for the Deity: *Shangdi* (Supreme Ruler) and *Tian* (Heaven). For instance, *Tian*, an ancient term indicating a transcendental power and originally used by scholars to denote a somewhat non-personal Being, could be personalized to "Heavenly Lord," thus becoming Christian in content. Believing the new faith would certainly seem less strange if familiar words could be employed to express its leading concepts, Ricci adopted the controversial method of adapting to Chinese culture and used *Tianzhu* (The Lord of Heaven) for God. Among his other labors, he wrote the famous apologetic work *Tianzhu shiyi* (*The True Meaning of the Lord of Heaven*) in 1603.

In 2001, Pope Paul II praised Ricci in his speech for the Fourth Centenary of the Arrival in Peking of Father Matteo Ricci, saying, "Ricci forged a Chinese terminology for Roman Catholic theology and liturgy, and thus created the conditions for making Christ known and for incarnating the Gospel message and the church within Chinese culture."[20]

In the late Ming dynasty and the early Qing dynasty, Ricci and his Jesuits developed an approach to evangelization which was unique in their time, one based on an understanding of, and respect for, Chinese civilization. They used their knowledge of mathematics, astronomy, and mechanics to win the respect of the educated, while attempting to adjust the Christian faith further to its Chinese environment. They even found it possible to adjust themselves a little to the Chinese reverence for ancestors. From this accommodation arose the bitter "Rites Controversy" (involving the term to be used for God), which lasted for more than a century and involved the pope, the emperor, and the various Roman Catholic orders in China. Noteworthy, however, is that in 1704, Pope Clement XI announced his approval of *Tianzhu* for God, but prohibited the use of *Tian* alone, and also that of *Shangdi*.

The news reached Emperor Kangxi (1662–1723) that a foreign power without first-hand knowledge of the Chinese language and culture had settled the controversy. This he interpreted as an infringement of his sovereignty and he became suspicious of the political aims and ambitions of the missionaries. As a result, in 1721, the emperor issued an edict banning Christianity. In 1724, Emperor Yongzheng (1723–36) banned all Europeans

---

20. *Message to the International Conference Commemorating the Fourth Centenary of the Arrival in Beijing of Father Matteo Ricci* (Oct. 24, 2001) by John Paul II http://www.vatican.va/holy_father/john_paul_ii/speeches /2001/October/documents. See also Zhao, *Yijing Suyuan*, 12.

from China except those employed by the court because of their scientific expertise. Such an incident is a salutary reminder to future revisers of the Chinese Bible of the difficulties involved in settling Chinese questions.

The issues raised by the whole lengthy controversy during the Jesuit period deserve further consideration. For instance, we may ask why the proposal made by Paul Xu Guangqi for Ricci to translate the Bible came to nothing. Ricci excused himself from the task of translation because of other duties, pleading pressures of work, the difficulty of the task, and the need to secure papal approval before commencing.[21]

We have to remember that in China, as in other regions of the world, the liturgy was celebrated in Latin; to say Mass in the vernacular, permission had to be obtained from Rome. In 1615, Pope Paul V permitted Chinese translations of the liturgy and Bible, as requested by some Jesuits working in China. However, this permission was never officially sent to China for practical action because the religious superiors in Macao believed the task to be too difficult, dangerous, boring, and unnecessary. This may be considered the main reason why Jesuits did not dare translate the Bible or publish translations already completed.

Obviously, Bible translation was not the center of mission at the time. The Jesuits preferred to write Chinese catechisms (such as "Ten Commandments of the Lord of Heaven"), general introductions to the Christian faith (such as "The True Meaning of the Lord of Heaven"), Scripture explanations (such as "A Direct Explanation of the Holy Scripture" by Emmanuel Diaz in 1636), and narratives of Jesus's life (such as "Short Record of the Words and Deeds of God's Incarnation" by Giulio Aleni in 1635), etc. These contained Bible passages but were not full translations of any books. They can hardly be called Bible translations. We need to look further at these difficulties.

Early Unpublished Translations in the Eighteenth and Nineteenth Centuries

Translation by Basset

Jean Basset (ca. 1662–1707) a French Catholic missionary, arrived in Canton in 1689. From 1702 on, he was a missionary in Sichuan. He translated the first part of the Small Catechism, which was very useful to the mission. He also translated parts of the New Testament, from the Gospels to the first

---

21. Standaert "Bible in Early Seventeenth Century China," 37–38.

chapter of the letter to the Hebrews. It was only in 1945 that a manuscript in the British Museum was identified with Basset's translation by Bernward H. Willeke, a Franciscan missiologist. The proof was found in the diary of Andrew Ly (1692–1774), a Chinese priest from Sichuan, who may have been Basset's helper in his work. In the diary, published in the day-by-day journal of a Chinese Roman Catholic priest in Sichuan in 1924, Ly clearly referred to Basset's translation: "Father Joannes Basset had translated . . . also the New Testament from the Latin into the Chinese idiom, beginning with St. Matthew, up to the first chapter of the Letter of St. Paul to the Hebrews. Prevented by death, he was unable to finish the wonderful work he had undertaken."[22]

In 1738, the Englishman, Hodgson, who worked for the East India Company, found a Chinese manuscript containing the New Testament in Canton, where Basset died in 1707. Hodgson had a copy of this manuscript made and presented it to Hans Sloane (1660–1753) of the Royal Society in London; the latter, in turn, donated it to the British Museum. This manuscript, which includes a harmony of the Gospels, the book of Acts, the Pauline Epistles, and the first chapter of Hebrews, is today known as "Basset's version" or "Sloane Manuscript #3599."

Basset's version later became essential for the history of Protestant Bible translation as Robert Morrison, with the help of Yong Sam-tak, a Chinese from Canton, had a new copy made of this text when he left for China in 1807, and it became a reference for his own translation.

Translation by Poirot

A complete translation of the New Testament and a partial translation of the Old Testament were made by the French Jesuit Louis de Poirot (1735–1813) who arrived China in 1770 and worked as a painter and translator at the court in the service of the Qianlong Emperor. He adopted the Chinese name He Qingtai. The translation he made, also based on the Vulgate, consisted of 29 books in 42 volumes, and was entitled *Guxin Shengjing* (Old and New Holy Scripture). It contained the whole Bible with the exception of the Song of Songs, Jeremiah, Lamentation, Ezekiel, and the Minor Prophets.[23]

---

22. Translated from Latin by Willeke, "Chinese Bible Manuscript," 451.

23. Zhao, *Yijing Suyuan*, 14–15; Camps, "Father Gabriele," 56.

According to the decree of *Propaganda Fide* in 1655, any printing of books by missionaries without written permission was prohibited.[24] Poirot reported his translation to officials of the *Propaganda* in 1803; his passion for translation was praised but his request for publication was denied. This manuscript was never printed in his time, and it was stored in the Beitang library in Peking, where it was destroyed in 1958. Fortunately, a copy had been made for the Xujiahui (or Zikawei) Library in Shanghai but was lost for a while.[25] With the changes of regime and several political movements, it was unaccounted for until it was dramatically found in 2011. In 2014, it was edited into nine books by two scholars, Li Shixue (Taiwan) and Zheng Haijuan (Beijing), and published by Zhonghua Shuju, Beijing. Poirot's *Guxin Shengjing* was banned by Roman Catholic authorities. About two centuries later, it has been published outside of Roman Catholic jurisdiction, and entitled *Guxin Shengjing Cangao* (Old and New Holy Scripture Incomplete Manuscripts, or Remnant Old and New Holy Scripture). Since then, Poirot's translation has become a popular research topic in academic circles as it is reckoned as the earliest Bible translation so far in vernacular— *baihua* style.

Translation by Others

During this early period, there were three other Roman Catholics who started to translate the Bible or parts thereof into Chinese. They were the Portuguese missionary, Joaquim Alfonso Goncalvez (1781–1841), who lived in Macao from 1814 and translated the New Testament. Two Chinese priests are also known to have translated parts of the Bible: The Gospels (1875) and Acts (1883) by Thomas Wang (Wang Duomo), and at around the same time, the four Gospels by Francis Xin (Xin Fangji). Wang and Xin's manuscripts are stored in *Xujiahui* library.[26]

These are the translations which never saw the light of day. Thus, up to the middle of the nineteenth century, the Roman Catholic church in China did not possess a printed version of the Bible in the Chinese language.

---

24. *Propaganda Fide*, in charge of all mission areas, was established in 1622.

25. Both the Beitang and Xujiahui Libraries were original to the earliest Jesuit missionaries. The Xujiahui Library, donated by Paul Xu Guanqi, was a part of the Jesuit mission complex begun in 1847. Now it is a unit of the Shanghai Library.

26. Bondfield, "Bible in China," 468.

Later Published Translations in the Nineteenth and Twentieth Centuries

The origin of the first entire Chinese Roman Catholic Bible is intimately connected with the life and work of Father Gabriele M. Allegra (1907–76). Allegra was born in San Giovanni la Punta, Sicily, in 1907 and joined the Franciscans at the age of 16. He arrived in Hengyang, China in 1931 and at once set to work. Aided by Chinese teachers, he had finished a rough draft of the Old Testament by 1936. In 1945, Allegra, together with a team of Chinese Franciscan priests, founded the *Studium Biblicum Franciscanum Sinense* (SBFS), and by 1947, the first printings of the Psalms and wisdom literature were published. The SBFS was transferred from Peking to Hong Kong in 1948; there, book after book of the Bible was translated. It took another twenty years for the whole Bible to be printed. A. Camps states, "the translation was well received not only by Roman Catholics but also by many other Christians, especially students in the various Bible colleges and seminaries."[27] In 1968, this translation had its first edition containing all the books of the Bible in one volume, which is known as *Sigaoben Shengjing* (Studium Biblicum Version). Roman Catholic Bible translation differs from that of Protestants in terminology, transliteration, and number of books.[28] Before the entire Chinese Roman Catholic Bible appeared in 1968, some other attempts on parts of the Bible were made. They are classified into four categories: date and place of publication, translator, scripture, and base text.

A List of Roman Catholic Bible Translations

Date, Publication Location	Translator	Scripture	Base Text
1892, Hong Kong	J. Dejean	Four Gospels, with Comments	Vulgate
1897, 1905, Shanghai	Laurentius Wenyu Li	Gospels & Acts	Vulgate
1922, Hebei	Joseph Xiao Jingshan	New Testament	Vulgate
1923, Hong Kong	Pierre Bousquet	Epistles and Revelation	Vulgate

27. Camps, "Father Gabriele," 64.

28. See Appendix 1.

Date, Publication Location	Translator	Scripture	Base Text
1927, Hong Kong	M. L. F. Aubzac Feng Jialu	Epistles of St. Paul and other Apostles	Vulgate
1949, Shanghai	Ma Xiangbo	World-Saving Gospels	Latin Glaire (1904)
1946, Shanghai 1949, H.K.	John Wu Jingxiong	Psalms, New Testament	French Crampon (1905), others
1949 Beijing	G. Litvanyi, R. Archen, E. Peti, Xiao Shunhua	New Testament	Greek text
1953 Shanghai	Xujiahui zong xiu yuan	First Draft of a New Translation of the Gospels	Greek text
1946–53 1957–61 1968, H.K.	Gabriele Allegra, SBFS	Old Testament New Testament Revised one-volume Bible	Masoretic text, Septuaguint, Vulgate, Greek text, others

The above list of Roman Catholic Bible translations shows that:

- Only in 1922 was the first complete Chinese Roman Catholic New Testament published.

- Before 1949, translations were mainly done by one-man translators and based on the Latin version.

- Only the New Testament, or parts thereof, was translated before 1946; in that year, the Psalms were the first part of the Old Testament to be translated.

- The first complete Chinese Roman Catholic version to be published was translated by a team at the SBFS. The translation project began in the 1940s, but the entire Bible in one volume was completed only in 1968.

It is clear that the Roman Catholic church has a long history of mission work in China, beginning in the thirteenth century; it only began to publish parts of the Bible during the nineteenth century, however. Obviously, circulation of the Bible in Chinese was not given prominence in their mission until the twentieth century. It is noteworthy that during the nineteenth century, several versions of the Bible had already been translated by Protestants. This reveals a significant difference between the policy and practice of the Protestants and that of the Roman Catholics. What is the Protestant approach to Bible translation? Were Protestants influenced by the earlier Roman Catholic translations? What contributions did the Protestants make to Chinese Bible translation? The answers to these questions are the subject of the next chapter.

Summary

Chinese Bible translation began with the first Christian presence in China — the Tang dynasty. The Nestorian monk Alopen took Scriptures there and introduced the new faith as "The Daqin Luminous Religion." In the beginning, Nestorians found great favor with the emperor. Under these favorable circumstances, they were able to build churches, establish monasteries, and translate some parts of the Scriptures. Before long, they had to face the challenge of other religions. During the two centuries of its existence in China, the Nestorian church had periods of persecution alternating with peace, depending on the varying favors of successive emperors. With its dependence on the imperial house, however, it could not survive in the chaos at the end of the Tang dynasty. When the dynasty finally collapsed, the Nestorian church, without native leadership and lacking multiple copies of Biblical texts as a support for a persecuted remnant, also disappeared and left only some traces in the Dunhuang documents and the Nestorian Tablet, silent evidence telling of the brilliant history they once had in China.

The unearthed Nestorian Tablet and documents discovered in the Dunhuang caves demonstrate that the Nestorian missionaries were willing to make the attempt to adapt to a Chinese setting and to employ Chinese concepts to express their faith. However, the line between distortion and adaptation or contextualization is difficult to define. This, perhaps, contributed to their failure. Here, in the earliest days of rendering the Bible into Chinese, we find the struggle between syncretism and contextualization, an issue which every Bible translator has to face.

The second arrival of Christianity was during the Yuan dynasty. We learn from a Franciscan missionary's account of his work, which survives, that the New Testament and the Psalms were translated. Unfortunately, the translations were lost; nothing remains except for some traces in the historical record.

When Roman Catholics entered China again, in the form of the Jesuits, it was in the late sixteenth century. At that time some of the substance of the Gospels was translated and printed for general use. Because Roman Catholics emphasized the importance of catechetical teaching and sacramental practice more than that of Scripture reading, translation activity was not much encouraged. The whole of the Scriptures was translated, yet it was never printed until 1968. Different New Testament translations made by different men only appeared in the late nineteenth century. In the practice of Scripture translation, they experienced the difficulty of choosing a suitable Chinese word by which to render "God." The Jesuits adopted the term *Shangdi* for God, but now we have only *Tianzhu* for the word in all their translations and writings. The Term Question they raised became a heated debate which was later inherited by the Protestant missionaries.

2

The Early Protestant Translations

The Beginnings of Protestant Translations

It was Protestant missionary activities of the nineteenth century that gave the entire Bible in Chinese to China. The honor of actually beginning Protestant Bible translation must be divided between Joshua Marshman in Serampore, India and Robert Morrison in Canton, China. Their translations of the entire Bible into Chinese appeared almost simultaneously, Marshman/Lassar's version in 1822 and Morrison/Milne's version in 1823.

Marshman and His Translation

The English Baptist Joshua Marshman (1768–1837) was sent to Serampore, India by his mission in 1799. In 1800, he founded a church there with William Carey (1761–1834) and William Ward (1769–1823). The three of them became known as the "Serampore Trio." They made the whole of Asia their province, translating the Bible into several of the Eastern local languages. Marshman was assigned to translate the Bible into Chinese. Before going to Serampore, Marshman had been a teacher in a Bristol school; there he read the Classics and studied Hebrew and Syriac. He did not have the opportunity to learn Chinese until 1806, when he was taught by a young Armenian, Joannes Lassar, who was born and educated in Macao. Lassar was employed in 1804 by Claudius Buchanan (1766–1815), vice-provost of

33

the Fort William College, with the special task of translating the Bible into Chinese. The first two publications of the Chinese Bible by Lassar were a few pages from the first books of the Old and the New Testaments; these publications appeared in the same year. Later, Lassar moved to Serampore to participate with Marshman in the translation project.[1]

In his letter to the British and Foreign Bible Society (BFBS) of December 1813, Marshman described their translation work in some detail:

> The first step, as I have told you, taken in the translation, is that of Mr. Lassar's sitting down at my elbow (where he sits from month to month and year to year), and translating from the English, assisted by his knowledge of the Armenian. For a long time, he and I read over the assigned portion together . . . . In due time follows the correcting verse by verse; when, with Griesbach [the Greek text of J. J. Griesbach] in my hand, I read over every verse in Chinese, and suggest my doubts relative to the force of particular characters, rejecting some, and suggesting others. When a whole chapter is thus done, which sometimes takes three or four hours, I give him the Chinese, and read Griesbach into English very slowly and distinctly, he the meanwhile keeping his eye on the Chinese Version. It is then copied fairly, and sometimes (that is, when any doubt remains), it is examined thus a second, and even a third time. It then goes to press, and here it undergoes a fresh ordeal. A double page being set up with our movable metal types, I then read it over with another Chinese assistant who is ignorant of English. He suggests such alterations as may seem necessary to render the language perfectly clear. It is then corrected, and a clean proof given, or two or three, if they be required, to be read by different persons. This done, I sit down alone and read it, comparing it with Griesbach again, and occasionally consulting all the helps I have. This is to me the closest examination of all. Here, as I have two Latin Chinese Dictionaries by me, I make it a point to examine them for every character, of the meaning of which I do not feel quite certain . . . Having written in the margin of the sheet every alteration my mind suggests, and everything that seems a discrepancy, I then consult Mr. Lassar and the Chinese assistant together, sitting with them till every query be solved and every discrepancy adjusted. This done, another clear proof is given, which, when read, I give to my son John, that he may examine for himself, as his knowledge of the Chinese idiom is perhaps greater than my own . . .[2]

---

1 Broomhall, *Bible in China*, 51.

2. BFBS *Report* (1815), 471–73.

This letter shows that Marshman relied on Griesbach and compared the translation with it three times at different stages. Different people proofread Marshman's version many times before it was finally printed, including his son John Clark Marshman (1794–1877). We learn also that there was another Chinese assistant involved in this project. Unfortunately, his name was not mentioned.

Four years later, in 1810, the Gospel of Matthew was published as the first fruit of their labor. The New Testament was finally published in 1816, with the exception of Luke and Acts.[3] In 1822, the first complete Chinese Bible was printed in Serampore in five volumes with the title *Xinjiu Yizhao Quanshu* (Completed Old & New Testamentary Edict). It was presented in May 1823 by Marshman's son John at the annual meeting of the BFBS in London.

The translation, made outside of China, was necessarily rough. It was criticized in 1890 for being ungrammatical, crude in its style, with narrow vocabulary and glaring infelicities, all of which were due to the translator's shortage of Chinese terms to express Biblical and Christian ideas.[4] Marshman's son, the official historian of the Serampore Mission, later expressed some strong objections to his father's translation: "The translation was necessarily imperfect; indeed, considering the great disadvantages under which it was executed, it could not have been otherwise, and it is now valuable chiefly as a memorial of his missionary zeal and his literary perseverance."[5]

It was never extensively circulated except in some of the early Baptist missions. The Baptists preferred Marshman/Lassar's version not only because of Marshman/Lassar's denominational ties, but also because of their translation of the Greek term *baptizo*. Marshman/Lassar followed the tradition of all Bible translations from the Baptist mission of Serampore, which according to their doctrine had a translation meaning "baptism by immersion." They found that the term *zhan* (to dip) differed from *xi* (to wash), which was adopted by Morrison/Milne.

Marshman/Lassar's version was of some help, however, in the preparation of later Baptist translations.

---

3. Zetzsche attributes the omission to Morrison's publishing these same two books in 1810 and 1811.

4. Wherry, "Historical Summary," 48.

5. Marshman, *Life and Times*, 244.

Morrison and His Translation

Robert Morrison (1782–1834), a Presbyterian, was appointed as a missionary in 1804 by the London Missionary Society (LMS). He was the first Protestant missionary to enter China, and his major purpose was to give the Scriptures to the Chinese in their own language. During Morrison's preparation for this mission, William Moseley, a Congregational minister in Northamptonshire, discovered a Chinese manuscript labeled *quattuor Evangelia Sinice in the British Museum.* This manuscript, examined carefully by several Sinologues, was a transcript made in Canton in 1737 from the translation by Jean Basset, a Roman Catholic. It is now known as the Basset manuscript, or "Sloane MS #3599." Moseley longed deeply for the conversion of China. Believing that the Scriptures might penetrate where the preacher could not go, he had called as early as 1798 for the establishment of a society for Bible translations into the languages of the most populous Oriental nations. When he found this Chinese manuscript, he believed that they should print and circulate a sufficient number of copies. He first approached the Church Mission Society about printing it, then the Society for the Promotion of Christian Knowledge and the British and Foreign Bible Society, but they all felt unable to proceed and turned it down because of the cost of the project and the impossibility of distributing the books in China, which was still closed to missionary work at that time.

It was Moseley who introduced Morrison to Yong Sam-tak, a Chinese man from Canton who had just arrived in England to study English. With the aid of Yong, Morrison made copies of the Basset manuscript and also of a Latin-Chinese dictionary lent to him by the Royal Society. During Morrison's time of preparation, Yong also acted as his first Chinese teacher.

In 1807, Morrison arrived in Canton, China, where he found himself in a difficult situation. The historian Marshall Broomhall (1866–1937) identified three problems:

> In Canton all foreigners were confined to a limited area . . . and they were only allowed to reside there during the trade season. When the fleet sailed, they had to depart for Macao. Further, in Canton the East India Company was ill-disposed to missionary ideals, and in Macao the Roman Catholic bishop and priests were hostile to all Protestants. Again, the Chinese Government forbade, under penalty of death, any native to teach his language to the

despised foreigner. The teacher Morrison secured actually carried poison on his person, with a view to suicide should he be detected.[6]

For six years, Morrison was to carry on the enterprise alone. Morrison's path was hedged with difficulties on all sides. With the help of the Basset manuscript and a Latin-Chinese Dictionary, he made great progress with his translation, however. His translation of Acts was published in 1810, followed by the Gospel of Luke in 1811, and Paul's epistles in 1812.

Morrison's translation of the New Testament profited a great deal from the Basset manuscript. He himself recognized this quite frankly. In a letter accompanying a set of the completed New Testament sent to the BFBS from Canton, January 11, 1814, Morrison wrote: "[T]he Gospels, the closing Epistles, and the Book of Revelation, are entirely my own translation. The middle part of the volume is founded on the work of some unknown individual, whose pious labors were deposited in the British Museum. I took the liberty of altering and supplying what appeared to me to be requisite; and I feel great pleasure in recording the benefit which I first derived from the labors of my unknown predecessor."[7]

Morrison's letter implies that he regarded "the middle parts" of his version to be a revision of Basset rather than his own independent translation. This may be the reason why Morrison was able to work so efficiently on the New Testament translation. When William Milne (1785–1822), also of the LMS, joined his translation efforts in 1813, Morrison had already completed the New Testament.

Milne worked on translating the Old Testament. He completed ten books from Deuteronomy to Job (except Ruth) and died in 1822 at the age of thirty-seven, one year before the entire Bible was published. Considering that during his short life of thirty-seven years, he devoted nine years to translation work in China and lost his wife, we can better understand why he once said with some humor: "To acquire Chinese is a work for men with bodies of brass, lungs of steel, heads of oak, hands of spring steel, hearts of apostles, memories of angels, and lives of Methuselah."[8]

Besides his great achievement in aiding production of the first Bible in Chinese, Milne is also responsible for mentoring the first Chinese Protestant evangelist—Liang A-Fa in 1816.[9]

---

6. Broomhall, *Bible in China*, 54.

7. BFBS *Report* (1815), 333.

8. Broomhall, *Chinese Empire*, 371.

9. See McNeur's biography of Liang A-Fa at https://wipfandstock.com/liang-a-fa.

Thus, the entire Bible by Morrison/Milne emerged from the Malaccan printing press in 1823 as twenty-one volumes bearing the title *Shentian shengshu.*

Summary

The history of Protestant Chinese Bible translation began with two "horses" from Britain.[10] They both spent sixteen years completing their great task of rendering the entire Bible into Chinese. Both of them completed their work almost simultaneously, but Marshman, with his better facilities for printing, was the first to get his work through the press. His Bible was printed with movable metallic type. Morrison's was printed from wooden blocks.

Marshman/Lassar's version and Morrison/Milne's version, as now commonly named, are identical to a great extent, especially in the New Testament, which demonstrates that they are both based on the same source—the Basset manuscript. Some scholars, like Zetzsche, believe Marshman adapted this indirectly, via Morrison. Marshman received copies of the Basset manuscript from Morrison in 1810, and in the following years he also obtained copies of Morrison's translation. We can conclude, therefore, that the Protestant Bible translations were indebted to Catholic activities. This fact, as Zetzsche points out, has been largely ignored.[11]

Of these two translations, only Baptists preferred Marshman/Lassar's version. Morrison/Milne's version was more successful and more generally adopted. Most historians have considered it the foundation of Chinese Bible translation. In the British and Foreign Bible Society records, Marshman/Lassar's was the first fruit, but most scholars, like Xu Mushi, would count Morrison's work the beginning of Protestant Chinese Bible translation history. The reasons for according priority to Morrison/Milne's work are: 1) It was the first translation done in China; 2) Morrison was the first Protestant missionary to enter China; 3) Morrison was the first to complete the New Testament translation; 4) Morrison played an important role in Chinese church history and continues to be revered as the father of Protestant missions in China.

---

html. See now also Song, *Training Laborers*, 2015.

10. The surname of their Chinese names, Ma Shiman and Ma Lixun, means "horse." That is why some writers humorously referred to these versions as *Er Ma Yiben* (lit. "two horses' versions"). See Xu, *Jing yu Yijing*, 131; Wang, "Shengjing Yiben," 66.

11. Zetzsche, *Bible in China*, 49–50, 56.

Besides Yong Sam-Tak, did Morrison have other Chinese helpers? A treasured picture of "Dr. Robert Morrison and Writers" indicates there are two Chinese working alongside Morrison, who was dressed in an academic gown. The photo's caption reads, "From painting of Chinnery, 1828. The gown is that of the Degree of D. D. conferred by Glasgow University, December 24, 1817. The writer sitting is Mr. Lee; name of one standing unknown, neither is Liang Ah-fa as sometimes stated." Since Liang Ah-fa, the first Chinese pastor, was Morrison's printer, he was easily mistaken for that unknown standing person. According to Broomhall in his book *Robert Morrison: A Master-Builder* (1924), the writer sitting was Lee Shigong and the standing person was Chen Laoyi, however (see figure 2).

These two translations, Marshman/Lassar's version and Morrison/Milne's version not only had a great influence in promoting the spread of Christianity among Chinese but also produced a foundation for the next generation to engage with Chinese Bible translation.

Figure 2: Morrison and His Two Chinese Assistants
The writer sitting is Li Shigong; the one standing is Chen Laoyi

The Development of Protestant Translations

Medhurst/Gützlaff's Version

Morrison/Milne's Chinese Bible had been in circulation for seventeen years before another version appeared in 1840. This version was produced by a group of four consisting of Walter Henry Medhurst (1796–1857), Karl Friedrich August Gützlaff (1803–51), Elijah Coleman Bridgman (1801–61), and John Robert Morrison (1814–43), a son of Robert Morrison. That is why some writers refer to it as *Siren Xiaozu Yiben* (four-man/tetrad version).[12]

Working Group

Medhurst, the main translator of the New Testament, arrived in Malacca in June 1817. He was close to Milne, who became his teacher both in theological knowledge and in the Chinese language. Medhurst was Morrison's chosen successor for revising and translating the Bible. Believing that Morrison would be the most competent man to launch the work, Medhurst did not commence revising Morrison/Milne's version until after Morrison's death in 1834, however. From then on, he was actively involved in several Chinese Bible translation projects and played an important role in the history of Chinese Bible translation.

John Robert Morrison took part in the translation work, although his official duties as successor to his father in his post as translator to the government of Hong Kong in 1834 required much of his time. He had little opportunity to be involved in Bible translation and could only correct the work of others.

Bridgman, the first American missionary to China, also participated in the translation work. The American Board of Commissioners for Foreign Mission sent him to Canton in 1830, where he learned Chinese from Morrison. After two years, he founded *The Chinese Repository*, a magazine that became the main resource for mission activities in China until 1851. His role in this new translation of the Bible was not a conspicuous one. Between him and the other translators, there was some disagreement about

---

12 See Zhao, *Yijing Suyuan*, 18; Zhuang, *Jidujiao Shengjing*, 12; Cai, "Zhongwen Shengjing," 225.

the principles of translation. This division, especially in terminology, became more severe in later translation projects.

Gützlaff, a Prussian agent of the Netherlands Missionary Society, was Medhurst's most active companion in the work on the new version. Medhurst translated the Old Testament up to Joshua, but Gützlaff translated the rest alone. Because they mainly produced the translation, this version became known as Medhurst/Gützlaff's version.

Publication and Reception

The New Testament was completed in 1835, revised by Medhurst in 1836, and published under the title of *Xin Yizhao Shu*, dated 1837. The printing had to take place in Batavia because a Chinese government proclamation of 1836 prohibited the distribution of Christian literature. The first edition of the Old Testament was published in Singapore in 1840. In the same year, an edition of the whole Bible was published under the title of *Shentian Xinjiu Yizhao Shengshu*, which was a combination of the titles of two previous versions. This translation became the version most commonly used by Protestant churches in China for the next twelve years.

The revision of Morrison's work turned out to be a new translation in which Medhurst touched for the first time on the rendering of the word for "God." Instead of *Shen,* he decided on *Shangdi,* a term used in the most ancient classics of the Chinese. According to Medhurst, *Shen* in the earlier translations meant "spirit," one person of the Trinity. Some authors highlight the translation of "Word" (*logos*) as *dao* (way) as the outstanding feature of the translation.

This version's influence on later translations was immense, especially relating to their terminology: for example, *roushen* (physical body), *endian* (grace), *zhenshi* (true) and *zhendao* (true way). It created the highest number of today's Protestant biblical transliterations. Wherry described the version as a "steppingstone" to later translations.[13]

While doing the Old Testament translation, Gützlaff also modified the translation of Medhurst's New Testament. The first edition was published under the title *Jiushizhu Yesu Xin Yizhao Shu* (The Savior Jesus New Testamentary Edict Book) in 1840.

Gützlaff's version may have become the most influential Bible translation in Chinese history, not because of its high value for the Chinese

13. Wherry, "Historical Summary," 50.

church, but because it was employed by the leaders of the Taiping rebellion (1851–62).

The Delegates' Version

After the Treaty of Nanking, in 1842, the five ports of Shanghai, Xiamen (then Amoy), Fuzhou (then Foochow), Guangzhou (then Canton), and Ningbo were opened to foreigners. It became possible for Protestant missions in China to establish work in the newly opened ports. The number of missionaries in China increased fourfold during the following fifteen years (1842–57), and this in turn increased the demand for a translation of the Bible that would be better adapted for general circulation than any hitherto published. As a result, Bible translation became the main field of cooperation between various missionary societies, both American and British.

Principles of Translation

In 1843, six meetings were held in Hong Kong, from August 22 to September 4, to consider the matter of a jointly translated Chinese Bible. Fifteen participants represented the London Missionary Society (LMS), the American Baptist Board (ABB), the Morrison Education Society (MES), the American Presbyterian Mission (APM), and the American Board of Commissioners for Foreign Missions (ABCFM)—see list below

Fifteen Representatives from Five Mission Societies

Representative	Mission society
W. H. Medhurst (1796–1857)	LMS
S. Dyer (1804–43)	LMS
B. Hobson (1816–73)	LMS
J. Legge (1815–97)	LMS
W. C. Milne (1815–63)	LMS
A. Stronach (1800–79)	LMS
J. Stronach (1810–88)	LMS
E. C. Bridgman (1801–61)	ABCFM
D. Ball (1796–1873)	ABCFM
S. R. Brown (1810–80)	MES

W. Dean (1807–95)	ABB
I. J. Roberts (1802–71)	ABB
D. J. MacGowan (1815–93)	ABB
J. L. Shuck (1812–63)	ABB
W. M. Lowrie (1819–47)	APM

The main decisions made during this meeting may be summarized as follows:

- That the *Textus Receptus* be taken as the Greek basis text for the New Testament.

- That any translation of the sacred scriptures into Chinese issued with the approval of the body of Protestant missions be in exact conformity to the Hebrew and Greek originals in meaning, and, so far as the idiom of the Chinese language would allow, in style and manner also.

- That terms for weights, measures, and money be rendered in corresponding Chinese terms, along with natural history names, as far as these could be ascertained.

- That passages occurring in different places, but expressed in the same way in the original, be translated in a uniform manner.

- That the interchange of noun and pronoun be allowed when deemed necessary by the translators.

- That euphemisms in the original be rendered by corresponding euphemisms in Chinese.

- That the work of revision be divided into five parts and translated by each station.

- That a General Committee be formed to appoint selected delegates for final revision and edition.[14]

These regulations laid a foundation for the principles of Chinese Bible translation and established a precedent for future collaboration work.

14. *Chinese Repository* (1843), 551–52.

New Testament Translation

Another decision made during the meeting was to divide the New Testament into five portions and assigned to five mission stations. Each station would translate its own portions and then submit to the other four for correction. The drafts would eventually be sent back to the original station for revising, thence the emendation would be submitted to the general committee for the final shaping.

Assigned Portions of Bible to Five Stations

Station	Assigned Portion	Chief Translator
Guangzhou/ Hong Kong	Acts, Hebrews to 2 Peter	Bridgman
Xiamen	Mark, 1 & 2 Corinthians	Stronach
Fuzhou	Luke, Romans, Galatians, Ephesians	Dyer
Shanghai/Ningbo	Matthew, Philippians to Philemon	Medhurst & Boone
Bangkok	John, the Epistles of John, Jude, Revelation	Dean

The general committee was to comprise the most experienced men sent by each station; regardless of the number of men it sent, each station had only one vote on each decision in the final revision. The revision went forward, not as the work of one party or another, but as the result of the combined efforts of the whole, and no part of the new translation was to be printed until finally revised by the general committee and approved by the Bible Society.

The first general meeting was supposed to be held in September 1846, but was postponed until June 1847, due to Guangzhou missionaries' not having finished translating the part assigned to them. The reason for this was that their mission work prioritized evangelizing and preaching, conversion and baptism.

Before the first general meeting took place, the Baptists withdrew, deciding later to produce a revised translation of their own, based on the work of Marshman/Lassar. The delegates eventually meeting in Walter Medhurst's house in Shanghai were William Boone, Medhurst, Elijah Bridgman, John Stronach, and Walter Lowrie.[15] Boone (1811–64), from the American Episcopal Church Mission soon retired from the group, however.

15. *Chinese Repository* (1848), 53.

Lowrie (1819–47) was killed by pirates while travelling back to Ningbo; W. C. Milne took his place.[16] For three years these men worked together in Shanghai. According to the report by Bridgman, the process of translation was as follows:

1848.5.30	Matthew
1848.7.26	Mark
1848.11.9	Luke
1849.1.18	John
1849.4.19	Acts

In 1850, the delegates published the four Gospels.

The Term Question

Debate about translation of the most controversial terms, "baptism" and "God," as well as "Holy Spirit," started at the very beginning of the translation project. At the meeting in Hong Kong (August 1843), the participants decided that each mission could choose which term it would use to render "baptism." Each mission could then publish its own edition, using the same translation except for the rendering of "baptism." Unfortunately, there was no agreement as to the best name for "God." The Term Question, as later commonly referred to in debate, was neither merely linguistic nor theological. Eber said:

> It raised a host of other questions, some having to do with Chinese monotheism, polytheism, and pantheism. It also brought up issues related to belief in Creation and the "idea of God," as well as questions regarding the nature and content of Chinese religion. By which name Chinese Christians addressed God, and what that name meant to them, what they thought and believed when uttering the name of God in Chinese, was the crucial problem.[17]

In the versions of Marshman and of Morrison, the word for "God" had been translated *Shen*. Some of the delegates, like Boone, were of the opinion that this was the best term to use in the new version, while other delegates,

16. Lowrie died at the early age of 28, the first Protestant martyr in China. See details in Broomhall, *Bible in China*, 68.

17. Eber, *Jewish Bishop*, 199.

like Medhurst, thought that such a term was open to misunderstanding and held that *Shangdi* should be used. The conflict over these terms continued to be one of the most crucial debates in the history of Chinese Bible translation. The history of the conflict will be discussed at length in Chapter Four.

Unable to solve the problem themselves, delegates referred it to the two Bible societies: the American Bible Society (ABS) and the British Foreign Bible Society (BFBS). The ABS adopted *Shen*, and the BFBS *Shangdi*. It took about three years of research for the Bible societies to obtain missionaries' consent to use the "Compromise Term," which would translate "God" with *Shangdi* and "Spirit" with *Shengling*.

Style of Language

The question and definition of style was another very controversial topic in the history of Chinese Bible translation. When the first missionaries were confined in their activities to Guangzhou and Macao, they did not have sufficient knowledge of matters of style. Later missionaries learned enough about the possibilities of Chinese to define different styles as a means of gaining influence in different groups of Chinese society. From their observation, the delegates for the New Testament classified the Chinese language under four types: 1) the antiquated style of the ancient classics; 2) the classical style, the chaste and correct style of the language; 3) the free style of the novels; and 4) the conversational style, called the Mandarin Colloquial. This classification demonstrates that the missionaries realized that there were varieties of style in the Chinese language. At this time, they still believed that the classical style was the best model for Chinese Bible translation, however, since they had noticed: "All the sects of religion in China employ this style in discussing doctrines inculcating deities; all foreigners attempting to introduce their religions thus into China, have done the same; witness the Jews, Mahometans, Nestorians, and Roman Catholics."[18]

Living among the Chinese as they did, the missionaries were also aware of the Chinese scholar's prejudice against familiar speech for high literature. Because the classical style was a scholarly style, delegates considered it the proper style for reaching out to the literati. "With this view," Zetzsche accurately observed, "they were very much in the tradition of the early Jesuit missionaries who had tried to gain influence in China through

18. Letter from Medhurst, Stronach, and Milne to the London Missionary Society of 13 March 1851.

contact with the literati."[19] The missionaries' limited understanding of Mandarin Colloquial was possibly due to their confined situation at that time.

In his letter to the ABS on March 2, 1848, Bridgman mentioned the Chinese assistants involved in the translation of the Delegates' version: "In addition to each member having its own [assistant], there are three others in attendance at the sessions of the Committee . . . These men, being from different provinces and of different habits and education, form a very respectable body of assistants. All of them are intelligent and well educated . . ."[20]

The value of Chinese assistants was recognized but their name was often ignored. Only the names of two assistants are known: Wang Changgui and his son Wang Tao. Wang Tao's high education and literary talents ensured that his main task during the first few months with Medhurst became the revision of the New Testament. Many commentators agree that Wang had a decisive influence on the style of the Delegates' version.

The completed New Testament, known as *Daibiao Yiben* (Delegates' New Testament), was printed in 1852.

The Committee of Old Testament Translation

When the delegates came to the Old Testament translation, general opposition arose to continuing the work of translating the Old Testament using the method adopted for the New Testament. This method required various groups to do the initial work of translation at their stations. The delegates found it impractical because it consumed much time and produced little benefit. Instead, they entrusted the entire translation work to a committee of delegates consisting of representatives working in Guangzhou, Xiamen, Fuzhou, Ningbo Shanghai, and Hong Kong. Each of these stations could send one or more delegates, but each station could have only one vote. The committee consisted of eleven people from seven mission societies.

This committee did not function well and split up before long. The delegates from Hong Kong and Fuzhou failed to attend any of the meetings in Shanghai; James Legge (1814–97) did not, in fact, take much active part in the translation. As a result, the actual committee comprised three British missionaries and four from American missionary societies. The divergence of views among the British and American missionaries soon became too

19. Zetzsche, *Bible in China,* 94.

20. Ibid., 91–92.

pronounced for cooperation to continue, however. The three representatives of the London Missionary Society, Medhurst, Stronach, and Milne, withdrew in 1851. They proceeded to work on the Old Testament translation alone in order to speed the process. They also wanted to avoid a situation where they would have to compromise their principles of translation practiced in the newly completed New Testament version. There were now two separate groups, divided by nationality, each working on the same task of revising the Old Testament.

The Old Testament translation of Medhurst, Stronach, and Milne, referred to by some as the "London Mission Version" or "Medhurst/Stronach's version," was completed in 1853 and published by the BFBS during the following year. This Old Testament version was published with the Delegates' New Testament in 1858. Together they became known as the Delegates' version.

Bridgman/Culbertson's Version

While the British missionaries proceeded from Deuteronomy 9, the point at which the committee had split, the American group started again from the beginning of Genesis. They decided to produce a new version of the entire Bible, which would be more in accordance with their view of what a translation ought to be. Along with the translation of the Old Testament, the Americans revised the New Testament of the Delegates' version in order to correspond with the principles they were following in their own Old Testament version. The ABS published the completed New Testament in 1859 and the Old Testament in 1863. Since this version eventually turned out to be the work of only two men, it was given their name and became known as Bridgman/Culbertson's version. Unfortunately, neither of them lived to see its publication. Culbertson finished the Old Testament alone in 1862 as Bridgman had died in 1861, shortly before the completion of the entire task. Culbertson died in August 1862, a year before the Old Testament was published in Shanghai in 1863.

The Bridgman/Culbertson's version never received the high esteem accorded the Delegates' version, although it circulated for almost the same length of time. As expected, it differed from the Delegates' version in the terminology employed: *Shen* was used for "God" and *Shengling* for "Spirit" (instead of *Shangdi* and *Shen*).

It is generally agreed that, if the Bridgman/Culbertson's version is inferior to the Delegates' in regard to style, it is superior to it in the matter of fidelity to the original. As Wherry stated, "This Bible is a valuable aid to the theological student or to the preacher who wishes to get at the exact mind of the Spirit and is a safer basis on which to build a textual discourse than the previous translation." Cheng Zhiyi agreed with the opinion of Wherry when he commented, "This version [Bridgman/Culbertson's] was hard to understand and confusing for readers not acquainted with the Bible. However, it was a great aid to theology students and pastors who desire to learn the meaning from the original text."[21]

According Cheng, the Bridgman/Culbertson's version was adopted and largely circulated by the ABS until the early days of the 1940s.

Goddard's Version

From the beginning of Protestant Bible translation in China, there was a difference of opinion with regard to the translation of "baptism." The delegates split at the beginning of the translation of the Delegates' version for this very reason. For a long time, the Baptists continued to use Marshman's version, in which "baptism" was translated *Zhan* (to dip), instead of *Xi* (to wash), although the publication of more recent versions caused them to realize the necessity for a revision of Marshman's version. The American Baptist Josiah Goddard (1813–54), who had been in Bangkok since 1840, undertook this task. He only completed the New Testament revision and had to leave the Old Testament almost untouched, to be finished by others. Nevertheless, the whole work is still known as Goddard's version.

Goddard and New Testament Translation

Goddard arrived in Shanghai in 1848 and moved to Ningbo in 1849. He set himself at once to the task of a Baptist translation of the New Testament, beginning with its revision. With the assistance of W. Dean (1807–95), separate portions were published from time to time either in Ningbo or Shanghai: Matthew appeared in 1851, the four Gospels and Acts in 1852, and the completed New Testament in 1853.

---

21. Wherry, "Historical Summary," 53; Cheng, "Shengjing zhi Zhongwen Yiben," 11.

Goddard planned to finish the translation of the entire Bible, but he had only completed translations of the first three books of the Old Testament when he died in 1854. From a letter to his mission society dated 6 September 1850, it appears that Goddard worked from the original Hebrew texts. He usually translated during the day; then, in the evening, he examined the Hebrew of the portions of Scripture for the next day's translation.[22] The letter shows that Goddard relied so much on his Chinese teachers that, if they were absent, he spent the day preparing the next part of Scripture and did not take up the work of translation himself. This may be the reason that Wherry commended this version when he said it "succeeds in a manner, often remarkably happy, in obtaining an easy and agreeable flow in published Chinese."[23]

Goddard's New Testament version was revised by Edward Clemens Lord (1817–87), the founder of the Baptist mission in Ningbo, who arrived there in 1847. Lord's revision was published in 1872 by the American Bible Union. It uses *Shen* for "God," as in Marshman's, but *Shengling* supplants *Shengfeng* for Holy Spirit, and *Jin* (to immerse) replaced *Zhan* (to dip) for baptism.

Lord's revision was reprinted, with references by H. Jenkins, at Shanghai in 1883. Because Wherry only mentioned the 1883 version in his historical summary, it was mistakenly believed by some authors, such as Garnier (1934), Cheng (1965) and Xu (1983), that Lord's revision first appeared in 1883 instead of 1872.

Dean and Old Testament Translation

Unlike other authors mentioned above, Zetzsche believes it was Dean, not Lord, who continued to work on the translation of the Old Testament in Bangkok. Dean had returned to the U.S. in 1853, the year when the New Testament was published. He retired from the American Baptist Missionary Union (ABMU) in 1857. In 1863, the ABMU reappointed him to its mission station in Bangkok. Soon after arriving there in 1864, he started to translate the Old Testament. Four years later, in 1868, he published his completed Old Testament with Goddard's New Testament in one volume, under the title *Shengjing Xinjiu Yizhao Quanshu* (Old and New Testamentary

22. To report his translation work in the letter, Goddard copied a week of entries from his diary. See Zetzsche, *Bible in China*, 116.

23. Wherry, "Historical Summary," 54.

Edict Complete Holy Script). The publication of a revised New Testament in two volumes followed in 1870. The American and Foreign Bible Society published these translations and revisions.

Because it was a denominational version, few people knew or used it outside Baptist circles, and most historians were not familiar with it. Zetzsche was the first to clarify Dean's role in Goddard's version. The translation of the Old Testament was not done, as Garnier stated, "by Lord, in association with Dean," but was entirely Dean's work.[24]

Up to this point, we have been concerned solely with versions produced in *Wenli*, the literary style. In the next stage, the missionaries adopted another style: Mandarin.

The Mandarin Versions

Mandarin refers to the Chinese term *guanhua*, that is, the spoken language of officeholders. It can be divided into Southern (Nanking) Mandarin and Northern (Peking) Mandarin. It is also the language of the common people, spoken in daily life by a large number of the population, especially in the North.

When the missionaries were confined to a few ports in China with exposure to many radically different dialects, they were unable to recognize that Mandarin was the speech of the vast majority of the Chinese people. They only realized it was an opportunity for their mission work when the missionaries extended their endeavors into the interior of China as well as into Peking and Tianjin after the Treaty of Tianjin (1858) and the Convention of Peking (1860).

Realizing that Mandarin as a written style of language was no longer understood merely in its spoken form, but that it had become used increasingly as a literary style on its own. A. Williamson (1829–1900), the agent of the Scottish Bible Society in China, strongly urged that efforts should be made to push Mandarin, in believing that Mandarin will eventually become a uniform language among different dialects.[25]

The missionaries discovered that the benefits of employing Mandarin in Bible translation were, first, it could be understood better when read aloud, and second, that it could avoid the problem of relying too much on the Confucian terminology of classical Chinese.

24. Garnier, *Chinese Versions,* 32.

25. *Recorder* (1877), 225.

The Nanking Version

When they arrived in China, the missionaries focused on learning the Chinese classical style and the local spoken dialect. Therefore, it was not easy to find someone who was capable of Mandarin translation. Even more than when learning spoken Chinese for preaching purposes, missionaries could not undertake the preparation of a written text in idiomatic Chinese without the aid, indeed the close collaboration, of Chinese co-workers. Medhurst and Stronach supervised a native of Nanking when they made the first attempt to translate the classical Chinese of the Delegates' version New Testament into Mandarin. This version is known as Medhurst/Stronach's version or the Nanking Mandarin Version. The name of the Chinese man is never mentioned. A record left in the American Bible Society catalogue says only: "Translated from the High *Wenli* Delegates' version by a Chinese under the supervision of W. H. Medhurst and J. Stronach." 50,000 copies of the New Testament were published in 1857.[26]

The first Mandarin version does not seem to have been a success. Opinions vary as to its value, however. Critics do not acclaim this version as being a very accurate or good translation. It lacked fidelity to the Greek. Wherry criticized it, saying, "[T]he style, though idiomatic, is by no means of a high order," and it is "well interspersed with localisms, and is injured by undignified and unworthy expressions."[27]

Despite that, this defective version went through many editions and served to show the need for a translation of the Bible in the spoken language.

As the first Protestant Mandarin translation, it is considered a pioneer version that influenced the course of Chinese Bible translation.

The Peking Version

A committee in the capital, Peking, made the next attempt at a Mandarin New Testament.

After the opening of Peking to foreigners in 1860, the northern missionaries, who had been feeling the need for a Mandarin version,

26. Spillett, *Catalogue of Scriptures*, 119. In *Catalogue*, this entry includes a note, "Wylie's *Memorials* gives 1856 as the date of this version." Zetzsche (*Bible in China*, 143) dated it 1856 according to the letter from Medhurst to London Mission Society on Sept. 6, 1855. The unknown Chinese must be Wang Tao, who had been hired by Medhurst for LMS since 1849 and was involved in the Delegate's version.

27. Wherry, "Historical Summary," 55.

commenced correspondence on the matter. The Peking Translation Committee, constituted in 1864, consisted of J. Edkins (1823–1905) of the London Missionary Society, J. S. Burdon (1827–1907) of the Church Missionary Society, S. I. J. Schereschewsky (1831–1906) of the American Episcopal Church Mission, H. Blodget (1825–1903) of the American Board of Commissioners for Foreign Missions, and W. A. P. Martin (1827–1916) of the American Presbyterian Mission. All of these men were distinguished by outstanding ability and character. Bishop Burdon came to Peking as the chaplain of the British legation, while Bishop Schereschewsky's official status was interpreter for the American envoy. Dr. Edkins was an eminent Sinologue. Dr. Blodget was a man in "whom nature, grace, and culture combined to form a model missionary," and Dr. Martin was "a man of massive mind and comprehensive scholarship," as Broomhall described.[28]

All five of these talented missionaries had been in China for some time and had acquired an excellent command of Chinese. They came to Peking one after another, shortly after 1860, to translate the New Testament into northern Mandarin in harmonious cooperation. This version became commonly known as the Peking Mandarin Version. Based on the publication dates of different parts of the New Testament, their translations proceeded as follows:[29]

1865 Four Gospels and Acts

1867 Romans

1869 Romans to Philemon

1870 Romans to Revelation

1872 Revised New Testament, divided into six parts.

The committee adopted a method of work generally similar to the method employed for the translation of the Delegates' New Testament. The books of the New Testament were assigned to individual translators to make their first draft. Their work was then circulated among the other members of the Committee for criticisms and corrections. Then the original translator examined these suggestions and sent around another draft with his reactions to the work of the other members. The Committee then met for discussion, with two or three native teachers present to assist; a majority decided in cases of disagreement.

28. Broomhall, *Bible in China*, 83.

29. Darlow and Moule, *Historical Catalogue*, 211.

This working method was not the unique invention of the Peking group. The Delegates' version translators used similar procedures of cooperative work. "What does seem to have been unique to the Peking group was," as Eber points out, "its open and tolerant spirit and the close collaboration among participants. Differences of opinion, which surely arose never reached the point of impeding the work, as had been the case when the Delegates' version translators began their translation of the OT."[30]

When the question of translating "God" once more arose, the group did not break up. In addition to the terms *Shen* and *Shangdi*, the use of *Tianzhu* was advocated by Burdon. *Tianzhu* was the neologism adopted by the Jesuits in seventeenth century China and employed by Chinese Roman Catholics ever since. The Peking group believed the term might confuse Protestants with Catholics, but that this was not as great a problem as it had once been made out to be. Schereschewsky argued that this term had never been used in "an idolatrous sense," since none of the Chinese gods were referred to as *Tianzhu*. He rejected *Shangdi* because it was associated with so much of China's cultural fabric that its use would obscure the meaning of "an absolute personal living God."[31] He disagreed also with the use of *Shen* because its meanings were too manifold in Chinese to stand for the one, true God. Although all members of the Peking Translation Committee were in favor of *Tianzhu* and believed that it was the most suitable term for "God," in the end, no agreement on the term was reached among the Bible societies. When the final revision of the New Testament was published in 1872, it appeared in three editions. The British Foreign Bible Society published two of them: one using *Shangdi*, and the other using *Tianzhu*. The ABS published an edition which employed *Shen*. It is a great pity that no agreement was reached concerning a common term for rendering "God." Had there been agreement, Chinese churches today would not have found it necessary to print the Bible in "*Shangdi*" and "*Shen*" editions. Also, Protestantism and Catholicism would not be considered two different religions in China.

In his letter to the ABS of February 21, 1871, Blodget reported, "with very good Chinese scholars present at our discussions to aid us, we have had access to all the versions of any value which have been made into the

---

30. Eber, *Jewish Bishop*, 110.

31. Ibid., 220, 222.

54

written language from Marshman and Morrison to that by the Russian Archimandrite Gouri [Gury], which is the most recent."[32]

This demonstrated that they used a variety of Chinese versions rather than relying on only the Nanking Version, as some have suggested.

The success of the Peking Version was far greater than the translators had hoped. Even the Peking Translation Committee "could not have anticipated a success so immediate, so wide, and so permanent as fell to the lot of their work," says Wherry. "Almost immediately in one half of the empire the new Mandarin Testament supplanted the *Wenli* in the family, the classroom, the street chapel and the Church services of the Sabbath and has held its place securely ever since."[33]

The success of this translation may be due to its being the collaborative work of a joint Committee of outstanding English and American missionaries, each assisted by a highly accredited Chinese scholar as his personal teacher. The names of the Chinese scholars were still not mentioned, however.

Schereschewsky's Mandarin Version

After a committee completed the New Testament Mandarin Version, Schereschewsky produced a one-man-version: The Old Testament Mandarin translation. He was to become one of the most fascinating figures in the history of Chinese Bible translation.

Samuel Isaac Joseph Schereschewsky was born into a Jewish family in Taurage in Lithuania. Through reading the New Testament, he became a believer in Jesus as the Messiah while a youth. In 1854, he migrated to the United States; in the following year, he entered Western Theological Seminary in Pittsburgh. He was soon offered a professorship but refused it as he had a strong desire to go to China and translate the Bible. Having later joined the Episcopal church, he arrived in Shanghai as a missionary sent by that denomination in 1859. After two years, he moved to Peking, where he took part in the Mandarin translation of the New Testament. From then on, he devoted himself to Chinese Bible translation until his death in 1906.

While they worked on the translation of the New Testament, the Peking Committee generally agreed that Schereschewsky's time would

---

32. This was the translation of the Russian Orthodox Church published in 1864. For details on Gury's translation see Zetzsche, *Bible in China*, 133–36; quoted on page 149.

33. Wherry, "Historical Summary," 56.

be better used if it were devoted solely to translating the Old Testament. Schereschewsky was willing to accept the task. He knew Hebrew better than any other language as he was a native-born Jew and had received a good Jewish education. He had the confidence to see himself as more fit for the work than anyone else. He responded enthusiastically to the challenge and regarded it as his special call that he could make a particular contribution, with the help of God, to the missionary cause in China. As for his Chinese ability, Martin estimated that "no man of that day equaled him in idiomatic command of the spoken Mandarin."

Schereschewsky's remarkable linguistic abilities enabled him to base his translation on the Hebrew text, the Greek Septuagint, the Latin Vulgate, and some other translations. The first edition of Genesis was published with private funds given in 1866, followed by a further grant from the ABS in 1872. He finished work on the first draft of the Old Testament in 1873; it was published at the end of the following year. Schereschewsky's Old Testament was noted at once for its fidelity to the original as well as for its clear style. Martin commented, "[I]t stands by itself and is not likely to be superseded." In his version, Schereschewsky used the term *Tianzhu* for God. For publication, he permitted his version to be printed with other terms for God, however.[34]

In 1878, Schereschewsky's Old Testament was published along with the Peking Version New Testament through a combined effort by the American Bible Society and the British and Foreign Bible Society. This version, *Shengjing Quanshu* (Complete Bible), was widely used for many years, especially in northern China.

J. C. Gibson in his review of the various colloquial versions, commented on both the New Testament and Old Testament: "Its Mandarin style and general faithfulness have been highly praised . . . I believe this praise is well deserved. It is probably . . . the most valuable vernacular version we possess."[35]

Griffith John's Mandarin New Testament Version

Although the Peking Version of the New Testament was generally regarded as good, there were many people who thought that it only represented the Mandarin of northern China and not that of central China. Griffith

34. For Martin's quotations, see *Recorder* (1899), 288.
35. Gibson, "Review," 65.

John (1831–1912) of the LMS had gone to Shanghai in 1855 and moved to Hankou in 1861, where he resided until he returned to Britain in 1907. In 1887, the British and Foreign Bible Society and the National Bible Society of Scotland (NBSS) approached John. They jointly asked him to undertake the preparation of a new Mandarin colloquial version in hopes that it might become the authorized version for China. The two societies would share the responsibility and the cost of publication. John disagreed with the societies' proposal that they should invite fifteen delegates from Northern, Eastern, and Central China to revise his work, however, because he considered the scheme infeasible due to the large costs of time and labor involved. John felt that he could work better alone.

John carried on with his plan to base his Mandarin translation on his own Easy *Wenli* New Testament, which had been published in 1885. Both the Nanking and the Peking Versions were the stylistic models for his translation, as he himself declared. He finished his Mandarin New Testament in 1889, and the NBSS published it that same year.

In his research, Zetzsche found that John, as a Bible translator, "was admired by some—mostly British—and strongly criticized by others—mostly American."[36]

Easy Wenli Versions

More Chinese understood Mandarin than any other spoken dialect, but not all Chinese did. Not until 1913 was Mandarin, after a long debate, officially defined as the Chinese national language. So, in nineteenth century Mandarin translations did not find favor in the South—the non-Mandarin speaking areas. The missionaries also realized that both *Wenli* and Mandarin versions were in a style too high for the majority of readers. They attempted, therefore, to find another form of language that would fall between classical Chinese and Mandarin. A style that Schereschewsky described in his paper for the 1890 general conference as "a *Wenli* version in the modern style; in a style which, whilst not unacceptable to scholars, could be read and understood by all who are not illiterate; a style which should employ words in their primary sense and call a spade a spade; which should not strive after classicalities, and that should avoid ready-made phrases and expressions culled from poetical and rhetorical compositions; in short, a

---

36. Zetzsche, *Bible in China*, 163.

style employed by the Chinese themselves in their graver works and more serious transactions."[37]

The missionaries called this lower classical style "Easy *Wenli*" and believed it should be a satisfactory style for a universal Bible. Griffith John of the London Missionary Society shared the same opinion, and he was the first person to put it into practice.

Easy Wenli New Testament Translated by Griffith John

Griffith John of Hankou made the first attempt to produce a version of the New Testament in Easy *Wenli*. He was primarily an evangelistic missionary. During the process of his work, he soon realized that the existing translations of the Bible in *Wenli* were too difficult for ordinary people to understand, while the Mandarin versions were too local. He therefore set out to make his own translation in Easy *Wenli*, beginning the work in 1883 with the Gospel of Mark.

In his article "Leading Rules for Translation," John listed seven points as his principles of translation:

1. Aim at making the version an exact image of the original.

2. Use those words, and only those words, which shall clearly express all the meaning of the original.

3. In so far as it is possible, use those words which best correspond with those of the original.

4. Where a translation *ad verbum* would result in an obscuration or a perversion of the author's meaning, abandon a *literal* version, and translate *ad sensum*.

5. In doubtful passages, a version *ad sensum* is to be preferred to a *literal* translation.

6. Where particular words are wanting in Chinese, have recourse to circumlocution, if by so doing the sense can be made clear.

7. In all cases consult the genius of the language in which the version is made and let its characteristic qualities rule as far as faithfulness to the truth, and exactness of interpretation, will permit.[38]

37. *Records (1890)*, 42.
38. *Recorder* (1885), 381.

The #4 and #5 non-literal principles of translation drew criticism, and his translation was criticized for being a partial paraphrase. Some Chinese writers have compared John's translation principles to Nida's theory of "dynamic equivalence." Zetzsche disagrees and thinks that comparison "must be seen as overstated."[39]

Regarding the textual basis of his translation, John declared that he translated from the Greek, consulting the English versions and the commentaries, and he also freely used other existing versions, such as the Peking Version, the Delegates' version, and the translation by Bridgman/ Culbertson. At first, John's idea was to translate only the Four Gospels. This work led him to undertake the translation of the whole New Testament, however, which was published in 1885. It became a base text for his Mandarin New Testament of 1889.

This translation was not considered perfect, of course, but it was recognized as marking another substantial advance in Bible translation.

Easy Wenli New Testament Translated by Burdon and Blodget

The American Blodget and the Englishman Burdon, two of the Peking Version translators, started work on an Easy *Wenli* translation of the New Testament in 1884. It was completed in 1888 and published in 1889. All previous *Wenli* versions were used and their major source was not the Greek text of the New Testament but the Peking Version.

This version did not have wide circulation, although it met with some approval among missionaries in the south of China where Mandarin was not common. It did not have much influence on the future course of Bible translation and has simply disappeared from sight.

Easy Wenli Old Testament and New Testament by Schereschewsky

Schereschewsky was made a Bishop of Shanghai diocese when he returned to Shanghai from the United States in 1875. There he established St. John's College in 1879, which became one of the foremost Christian institutions in China.

While in Shanghai, Schereschewsky also became aware that the Mandarin version had not found acceptance in the south. The non-Mandarin

---

39. See Xu, *Jing yu Yijing*, 135; Zhao, *Yijing Suyuan*, 23; Zetzsche, *Bible in China*, 167.

speaking environment convinced him that there ought to be a Chinese Bible translation in another style of Chinese: lower classical. For several years he was not able to start an Easy *Wenli* translation because he was stricken with paralysis in 1881, "which deprived him of the use of his limbs and of his speech, but which left his intellectual powers unimpaired."[40]

Schereschewsky had to leave China in 1882, traveling to Europe and America in search of a cure, but this was of no avail. Retaining his undaunted spirit, he continued with the revision and translation of the Chinese Bible. He first finished the revision of his Mandarin Old Testament as well as that of the Peking Version in 1888, and then he commenced work on an Old Testament translation into Easy *Wenli*. His original plan was not to translate the New Testament, because there were already two versions in the Easy *Wenli*, one by John and the other a joint version produced by Burdon/Blodget. He noticed that the style he had adopted was higher than either of these versions, however. For the sake of uniformity, he decided to proceed with his own translation of the New Testament after all.

Due to his paralysis, Schereschewsky could only type the Chinese characters in Roman letters using one finger. Using this method, he insisted on revising the Mandarin version and printing out a complete translation of the Bible in Easy *Wenli*. He had to do all the work himself, as no one would pay for the Chinese helper for whom he had applied. Until he was able to return to China, neither his own missionary society nor the ABS had enough confidence in his abilities to support him. Nonetheless, he finished the first draft of his translation of the Easy *Wenli* Bible in 1894. He returned to Shanghai in 1895 and remained there for two years, supervising the transcription of his work into Chinese characters. He later removed to Japan, where the ABS printed his work in 1902 (see Figure 3). This work is often humorously described as "the One-Finger Edition."[41]

Schereschewsky's translation into Easy *Wenli* was based on his Mandarin translation, as well as on the original Hebrew and Greek. The style of his Easy *Wenli* version, to quote Martin, "is simple enough to be understood of the people, yet sufficiently polished to meet the taste of the most fastidious of China's literati."[42]

---

40. Garnier, *Chinese Versions*, 41.

41. Some historians like Broomhall (*Bible in China*, 83) and Xu Mushi (*Jing Yu Yijing*, 135) refer to the "two-finger Edition," a description which Muller (*Apostle of China*, 251) regards as incorrect. He cites several sources that prove that Schereschewsky only used one finger instead of two.

42. *Recorder* (1899), 288.

The Schereschewsky's Easy *Wenli* version was highly praised. He continues to be one of the most fascinating figures in the history of Chinese Bible translation, named by his fellow missionaries "The Prince of Bible translators" and "one of the world's greatest Bible translators." He earned this high admiration mainly through his uncommon abilities and astonishing achievements. Zetzsche writes:

> Another fact that may have influenced the high estimation of Schereschewsky's work was a sunstroke in 1881 that completely paralyzed him for the rest of his life; nonetheless, he continued with the translation and revision of the Chinese Bible. He spent 32 years of his life solely on Bible translation, more than anyone else in the course of Chinese Bible translation. This perseverance in the face of great hardship gave his fellow missionaries and later historians the highest respect for his work.[43]

Summary

The honor of giving China an entire Bible goes to the Protestants, who considered Bible reading equivalent to preaching and evangelizing in importance. The translation of the Bible into Chinese was a major concern for Protestant missions from the very beginning of their work for China. They began translating in the early days of the nineteenth century in Serampore, India, even before the missionaries had entered China itself. The complete version of the Scriptures known as Marshman/Lassar's appeared in 1822. This version was the foundation of a later Baptist translation. Between the non-Baptist and the Baptist churches in nineteenth century China, a difference in Bible translations of the term used for "baptism" (namely, *jin* and *xi*) marked the most apparent division. This general rivalry continued to exist throughout the history of Chinese Bible translation. The fact remains that it is not merely a matter of translating the original meaning of the word, but of interpretation and doctrine, which has made any solution of the problem impossible up to the present day.

Morrison/Milne's version appeared in 1823, one year later than Marshman/ Lassar's. Most historians consider this version the true groundwork of Chinese Bible translation. Such an evaluation is due to the fact that Morrison is held in high estimation and will ever be remembered as the

---

43. Zetzsche, *Bible in China*, 153–54.

first Protestant missionary who lived in China; besides, his version was the first one actually done in China.

The Protestant translation is indebted to Catholic effort because Marshman and Morrison based their work, to a certain degree, on the Catholic translation by Basset.

The early translations were considered too literal to be suitable for the growing mission work. Medhurst/Gützlaff's new version emerged to meet later needs. Based upon non-literal translation principles, it was translated into readable Chinese. The terminology of this version greatly influenced later translations. Medhurst, as the leading translator, continued to be active in later important translation projects, such as those of the Delegates' version and the Nanking Version.

The translation of the Delegates' version was the most significant event in the early history of Protestant missionary Bible translation in China. The most obvious and influential result of its work was the division of Protestant missions over the question of terms, translation principles, and style. The Term Question that had troubled the Jesuits in the seventeenth and eighteenth centuries continued to disturb the Protestants in the nineteenth and twentieth centuries. The Jesuits' controversy over terms lasted for almost a century, as did that of the Protestants. Unlike the Jesuits, the Protestants could not rely on a single authority to end the controversy by choosing a solution. As a result, Protestant translations continue to use both terms, *Shen* or *Shangdi,* as the equivalent Chinese translation for "God."

Goddard's version reflected the Baptist efforts in Bible translation. This version, more than other translations, relied on Chinese participation. As a result, it succeeded in obtaining an easy and agreeable flow of polished Chinese. It was little known or used outside Baptist circles, however.

Mandarin versions appeared with the opening of both the interior and the north of China. The missionaries embraced Mandarin as providing a better linguistic avenue for their mission work than they had found in classical Chinese. The Peking Version was the counterpart to the Nanking Version. Unlike the Delegates' committee, the translation committee of the Peking Version formed itself, and it was the very first committee of both an international and interdenominational nature to remain together until the work was completed. It produced the most successful Bible version up to that point, which was used in the Mandarin-speaking areas of China.

Mandarin translations did not find acceptance in the south, however. It ultimately became clear to missionaries in China that a universal version had to be neither *Wenli* nor Mandarin but in another style of Chinese: lower classical—Easy *Wenli*. This style of Chinese seemed to be perfectly suited for a universal version: It was acceptable to all Chinese, even the literati, and understandable for most, even those without a high education or from the non-Mandarin speaking areas.

The help of a Chinese scholar of high repute made the version unique. Chinese assistants were mostly neglected in missionaries' statements about translation work, but the good stylistic features of the Delegates' version as well as of the Peking Version attest to the significant role the Chinese played.

All Chinese Bible versions produced by missionary translators thus far fall into three classes: *Wenli*, Mandarin, and Easy *Wenli*, which demonstrates the effort made to give China an acceptable version.[44] The missionaries first tried the classical Chinese, *Wenli* style, which the literati accepted, but later found that, as with Latin translations, the educated read this version but the partially educated or illiterate neither read nor understood it. Mandarin was intelligible to ordinary people, but it also had its limitations at that time. As a result, missionary translators became convinced that Easy *Wenli* would be the most appropriate style, being neither too classical nor too colloquial, for a union version. At this stage, no one had anticipated that the Easy *Wenli* Version would be the first of the three styles outlined above to be eliminated. This subject is dealt with in the next chapter

Figure 3: Schereschewsky with His Two Assistants
Lian Yinghuang (left), Chinese Secretary, and Bun, Japanese Copyist in Tokyo, 1902.

44. Many writers give account of the efforts of missionary translators in the wrong stages as: *Wenli*, Easy *Wenli* and Mandarin.

3

The Union Version Project

The 1890 General Conference: A Milestone in the History of Chinese Bible Translation

THE SECOND GENERAL CONFERENCE of Protestant Missionaries in China was held in Shanghai from May 7–20, 1890.[1] Bible translation, which had provoked so much discussion and division in the past, was the first subject to be discussed. From the conference records, we learn that William Muirhead (1822–1900) of Shanghai and John Wherry of Peking presented their papers on "Historical Summary of the Different Versions, With Their Terminology, and the Feasibility of Securing a Single Standard Version in *Wenli*, With a Corresponding Version in Mandarin Colloquial." They both gave a brief historical account from the Nestorians to their own time. A paper on "Translation of the Scriptures into Chinese" by Samuel I. J. Schereschewsky was presented in his absence, in which he appealed for the desirability of a *Wenli* version in a lower classical style. These presentations were followed by an intense discussion.

Two committees were appointed to prepare reports for the conference: one, with twenty-four members, "on the Feasibility of a United *Wenli* Version of the Scriptures," and another, with twelve members, "on the Feasibility of a United Mandarin Version of the Scriptures." After several

---

1. The General Conference was held in China three times: in 1877, in 1890, and in 1907. These conferences provided forums for the Western missionaries to meet, discuss, and coordinate matters related to missionary policy.

days of full discussion in the committees, the vast majority came to see the need for a union version in Chinese. On the ninth day of the conference, two reports suggesting a "translation of the Bible into simple but chaste *Wenli*" and an "improved version of the Old and New Testaments in Mandarin" were presented to the conference and were unanimously accepted. A supplementary report proposing a "translation of the whole Bible in the higher classic style" was presented on the following day and was accepted to the same degree.[2]

By the 1880s there were more than forty versions in use, including translations in local dialects. The debates and divisions surrounding Bible translations were increased by the rival translations which were being issued by a variety of translators. Although there was a general desire among all missionaries for a uniform, standard version, only in 1890 did they realize that its time had arrived. When the Conference unanimously adopted these reports and decided to have "one Bible in three versions"—*Wenli*, Easy *Wenli*, and Mandarin, the whole audience rose and sang the Doxology.

Reports of Committees

It was recommended in the reports that the conference should elect an executive committee for each of the translations, and that these committees should then choose translators. The executive committees were to work according to plans consisting of eight articles.

The first three articles were different due to each committee's particular tasks:

Article one was about selecting members of the translation committee. Two *Wenli* versions committees were to be formed of not fewer than five competent translators each, and no less than seven men for the Mandarin committee. The Mandarin committee was to be known as the Committee on Mandarin Revision, not "Translation." This was because the pre-existing Peking Version had been produced with great care and labor, and its popularity was great. The executive committee's suggestion that there should be a revision instead of a new translation reveals the Peking Version's excellence and success.

Article two provided for the quality of translators. They had to be competent scholars who would represent different denominations and

2. *Records 1890*, 587.

nationalities. Only the Easy *Wenli* committee had three translators nominated by the conference.

Article three was concerned with the basic version. For Easy *Wenli*, no existing version, or even partial versions, was to be made the basis of the new version. For *Wenli*, they were to base their translation of the Old Testament on the Medhurst/Stronach translation and the Bridgman/Culbertson translation. The New Testament was to be based on the Delegates' version, and the Bridgman/Culbertson Version as well as Goddard's version were to be employed wherever available. For both testaments, all other existing material was to be used at the discretion of the translators. For Mandarin revision, three versions were recommended for the New Testament: the Peking Version, Griffith John's version, and the Nanking Version. For the Old Testament, they were to use the Schereschewsky translation. All questions concerning translation were to rest with the translators, not with the executive committees, which was the principle applying to all three committees.

Articles 4–8 were identical for each committee:

4) That the text which underlies the revised English versions of the Old and New Testaments be made the basis, with the privilege of any deviations in accordance with the Authorized Version.

5) That in order to secure one Bible in three versions, the Executive Committee is instructed to enjoin upon the translators [or revisers], that in settling upon the text and in all questions of interpretation, they act in conjunction with the Committee on Mandarin [or Easy or Wenli] and higher *Wenli* [or Mandarin or Easy *Wenli*] revision [or translation], and for these purposes they constitute one Committee.

6) That this Executive Committee shall continue to act and to superintend the work until its completion. If any of the first Committee of translators shall cease to act before the completion of the work, the Executive Committee shall, if they think best, select others in their places.

7) That in the case of the absence from China, or other disability of any member of the Executive Committee, he has the right to name his proxy or successor, but that if he fails to exercise this right it shall revert to the Committee.

8) That the Executive Committee ask, in the name of this Conference, the concurrence and financial help of the Bible Societies of Great Britain

and America in carrying forward this work; and that when completed it be the common property of the societies which have given their patronage to the work, each having the right to publish such editions as it may choose, and with such terms for God, Spirit and baptize, as many be called for, and also to add explanatory readings, page, chapter and sectional headings, maps and such other accessories as it may deem expedient.[3]

Executive Committees for Three Projects

Three executive committees were elected on May 19, the day before the conference ended. They were elected by ballot in order to give the participants the best opportunity to express their unbiased wishes. The executive committees for the *Wenli* and Easy *Wenli* versions were formed of twelve men: five British, five American, and two German. Three British and one German had responsibilities in both committees. The Mandarin version committee consisted of ten men: five British, four American, and one German. The ballot results were surprisingly unanticipated, as these ten people happened to represent ten different mission societies.[4]

The three committees involved twenty-five missionaries who were from fifteen mission societies, six American, six British and three German. The Briton T. Bryson was the only one who was a member of all three committees.

The amended resolution of "one Bible in three versions" was regarded as the great achievement of the conference. The conference record reads:

> The most distinguishing feature of the Conference was the spirit of harmony that prevailed. This spirit not only characterized the discussions but was essentially exhibited in the unanimity with which various important and delicate practical measures were acted upon. Conspicuous amongst these was the subject of Bible translation and revision. It was known beforehand that this subject, which had been the source of so much discussion and division in the past, would come up for consideration . . . Many felt very skeptical as to the possibility of reaching any practical result, and few felt sanguine of success. When the large representative committees appointed to consider this subject, brought in unanimous

3. Ibid., xliii.
4. See Three Executive Committees in Appendix 2

reports, proposing practical schemes for realizing the end desired, there was a general feeling of surprise; and when twenty-four hours later, the Conference unanimously adopted these reports, the high-water mark of unanimity and of enthusiasm was reached. This achievement was no doubt the *great* work of the Conference, the attainment of which alone is worth far more than all the Conference cost.[5]

That the conference would smoothly reach such a satisfactory result so quickly far exceeded the general expectation.

Union Versions: The New Testament Translation

When all the three executive committees had elected their own translation and revision committees, they met together in Shanghai, from November 18–23, 1891. The purpose of the meeting was to arrange for the work of translation and revision of the Scriptures and to define the principles of translation. Based on former experience in Chinese Bible translation, principles of translation were fully discussed. The three groups launched their work according to eighteen rules adopted in the meeting.

The three committees also adopted the same system of working procedures: The text of the New Testament was divided into several parts, then assigned to each translator. Each one translated his own portion on a specifically prepared sheet with parallel blank columns, and sent it around to the others, who then could add their suggestions in their assigned columns.[6] Having received the emendations of all, the original translator was to make out his second proposal written on the same sheet. The last column was for the final rendering determined by the whole committee, which would meet for that purpose.

The work of each of the three committees will be examined in turn.

Easy Wenli Translators and their Translation

According to the 1890 conference resolution, the Easy *Wenli* translation committee was to consist of at least five competent translators. The three translators recommended by the conference were: H. Blodget, G. John,

---

5. *Records 1890*, xi.

6. The traditional Chinese was written from top to bottom, from right column to left.

and J. S. Burdon. The other two elected were the German missionary, Ernst Faber (1839–99), of the General Evangelical Protestant Missionary Society, who had been in China since 1865, and the American missionary, Rosewell Hobart Graves (1833–1912), of the American Southern Baptist Mission, who had worked in Canton since 1855. John and Faber both declined to serve on the committee for their own reasons, however.[7] The committee finally consisted of two Britishers: J. C. Gibson (Chairman) and J. S. Burdon; two Americans: H. Blodget and R. H. Graves; and one German: Gottlieb I. Genähr (1856–1937), of the Rhenish Mission Society, who had resided in Dongwan (Guangdong) since 1890. The following table includes their mission societies and mission stations.

Easy *Wenli* translators and their stations

Nation	Translator	Mission Society	Station
Britain	J. C. Gibson (1849–1919)	English Presbyterian Mission (EPM)	Shantou
	J. S. Burdon (1827–1907)	Church Missionary Society (CMS)	Hong Kong
America	H. Blodget (1825–1903)	American Board of Commissioners for Foreign Missions (ABCFM)	Peking
	R. H. Graves (1833–1912)	American Southern Baptist Mission (ASBM)	Guang-zhou
Germany	G. I. Genähr (1856–1937)	Rhenish Missionary Society (RMS)	Dongwan

It took about five years for the initial translations and suggestions to be completed. During that period, Blodget returned to America and retired from both the Easy *Wenli* and Mandarin committees in 1894. John Wright Davis of the American Southern Presbyterian Mission, who had been in Suzhou since 1873, filled the vacancy. The first meeting of the committee was held in Hong Kong in the summer of 1896. From then on, they met once every year, which indicates that the translation process went smoothly. Different parts of the New Testament were dealt with at each meeting:

1896/7–8: Matthew and Mark

1897/7–8: Luke, John, and the book of Acts

1898/7–8: Romans and 1 Corinthians

7. Detail see Zetzsche, *Bible in China*, 206–208, 209–12.

1899/1–2: Second Corinthians through Ephesians and Hebrews

1899/7–8: James through Revelation

1900/1–2: Philippians through Philemon

Six meetings took place in five years, either in Hong Kong or Shantou, Guangdong. All members of the committee lived in Southern China, which made their gathering easier and enabled the work to be completed as soon as possible. When the Easy *Wenli* New Testament was published in 1902, the *Wenli* committee had not yet had its first meeting.

Wenli Translators and Their Translation

The *Wenli* Committee as first constituted by the Executive Committee consisted of J. Chalmers (Chairman), J. Edkins, J. Wherry, D. Z. Sheffield, and Martin Schaub (1850–1900). The following shows their mission societies and mission stations.

Wenli translators and their stations

Nationality	Translator	Mission	Station
British	J. Chalmers (1825–99)	LMS	Hong Kong
	J. Edkins (1823–1905)	CMS	Shanghai
American	J. Wherry (1837–1918)	American Presbyterian Mission (APM)	Peking
	D. Z. Sheffield (1841–1913)	ABCFM	Peking
German/ Swiss	Martin Schaub (1850–1900)	Basel Mission	Hong Kong

After the 1891 meeting in Shanghai, the work seemed to have started off well. In 1892, some parts of the New Testament were completed by individual translators. From that time on, however, progress was slow. No full committee was able to meet. This was partly because of the immense distances between the translators. It was also due to the furloughs of Chalmers, Schaub, Sheffield, and Wherry at different periods between 1895–1902, and the death of three members.[8]

Sheffield became the chairman of the committee after the death of Chalmers in 1899. In 1901, Edkins, Sheffield and Wherry met in Peking. The work proceeded slowly. After three months, they had only produced

8. Chalmers died in 1899, Schaub in 1900, and Edkins in 1905.

a tentative translation of Matthew. In 1903, successors for Chalmers and Schaub were chosen: T. W. Pearce (1855–1938) of the London Mission Society, in Canton since 1879; and L. Lloyd (1850–1931) of the Church Missionary Society, in Fuzhou since 1876. When Edkins died in 1905, no successor was elected to take his position and the vacancy remained.

The first meeting of the full committee was held in 1905 in Beidaihe, attended by the four remaining translators, working in great harmony. The four Gospels, Acts, and Romans were translated and published in the same year. The rest of the New Testament was translated in the following year. Thus, the completed *Wenli* New Testament Union Version was published just before the 1907 General Conference.

The Mandarin Revisers and Their Revision

The Mandarin Revision Committee consisted of seven men, five American and two British, as prescribed by the 1890 Conference. The following table shows their missions and stations.

Mandarin Revisers and their Stations

Nation-aliity	Revisers	Mission	Station
American	C. M. Mateer (1836–1908)	APM	Dengzhou
	J. L. Nevius (1829–93)	APM	Shandong
	H. Blodget (1825–1903)	ABCFM	Peking
	C. Goodrich (1835–1925)	ABCFM	Tongzhou
	J. R. Hykes (1852–1921)	Methodist Episcopal Church	Jiujiang
British	T. Bramfitt (1850–1923)	Wesleyan Methodist Missionary Society	Hankou
	G. S. Owen (1847–1914)	LMS	Peking

The individual preliminary revision, as there were seven members to circulate the work, took a number of years before the first meeting was called in 1898. Mateer, the chairman of the committee, gave the reason in his report to the 1907 General Conference as follows:

> The work went on very slowly, owing largely to the fact that none of the translators were free from other engagements and obligations, literary, educational, or otherwise. During these years it is doubtful whether as much as half of the time of any translators was

given to this work. In the meantime, changes were taking place in the constitution of the Committee, which interfered seriously with the progress of the work.[9]

Mateer went on to give an account of the changes caused by deaths and retirements of translators.

The first meeting was not held until 1898 and took place in Mateer's home in Dengzhou (now Penglai), Shandong. After over two months of meeting together, the only result was the translation of the book of Acts, which was far from what they had expected. They had hoped to revise up to one-half of the New Testament. A wide difference of opinion as to the style of Mandarin to be used, and the differences in the Chinese dialects of the translators, caused a large amount of discussion and consumed a great deal of time. Goodrich described almost every verse they discussed as a battle.

Despite its rough start, the committee was able to meet once a year, each time focusing on different parts of the New Testament:

1898: Acts

1899: Mark and John

1901: Matthew and Luke

1902: Romans through Philippians

1903: Colossians, 1–2 Thessalonians, and Hebrews

1904: 1–2 Timothy through Revelation

1905: Revision of the Four Gospels

1906: Final meeting, held in Zhifu (now Yantai); completion of New Testament

The committee of translators originally consisted of seven men, but as time went on, many changes in personnel took place on account of death, retirement, illness, and other causes,[10] so that, when the New Testament was ready for publication in October 1906, there were only four members: C. Mateer, C. Goodrich, F. W. Baller and Spencer Lewis (1854–1939) of the Methodist Episcopal Church (see Fig. 4). They had been on the committee from its beginning, except Lewis, who joined in the committee in 1904.

9. *Records 1907*, 278.

10. Nevius died in 1893; Blodget resigned in 1894, Bramfitt in 1897, and Hykes in 1898.

The Mandarin Union New Testament went through many revisions and was in circulation for several years before the Old Testament was completed.

Figure 4: Mandarin Union Version (NT) translators with their Chinese assistants

Union Versions: Old Testament Translation

The Resolution of the 1907 Conference

The third General Missionary Conference in China was held in Shanghai from the 25th of April to the 8th of May 1907. Reports were given by the committees on Easy *Wenli*, *Wenli*, and Mandarin Versions on the 4th of May. The question arose as to whether it was necessary or desirable to have both *Wenli* and Easy *Wenli* versions of the Old Testament.

A great deal had happened in the seventeen years since the resolution was made to prepare one Bible in three versions. The very language had changed. *Wenli* and Easy *Wenli* were tending towards a common ground. The Conference therefore decided that there should be only one *Wenli* version instead of two.

Other decisions about further work on the Old Testament translations were also made:

- That two executive committees of seven men each, one for *Wenli* and one for Mandarin, should be elected by the conference to supervise the work of producing one Union Bible in Chinese in two versions— *Wenli* and Mandarin.

- That each Executive Committee should select a translation committee of five qualified missionaries to translate the Old Testament into *Wenli* and Mandarin.

- That appeals should be made to the various mission societies to give more support in relieving the selected translators from other duties in order to better secure the work of translation.

- That the three Bible societies working in China should be requested to provide full financial support for this work; each society should appoint an agent as an *ex officio* member of each executive committee, and the societies should print the three issued union versions of the New Testament for three years before any changes were made to them.

The Re-selection of Committees

Two executive committees were selected by the conference to make adjustments for further Old Testament work. They were similar in many ways:

- The size of both committees was reduced to seven.

- Both committees contained five American and three British missionaries.

- No German missionaries were now considered for the new committees.

- Six out of seven were new to this union project, all except their chairmen.

The chairman of the *Wenli* committee was the American missionary A. P. Parker of American Southern Methodist Episcopal Mission, who once took part in the Easy *Wenli* translation as the successor to Blodget. The chairman of the Mandarin committee was the British missionary Bryson of the London Mission Society, who had served on all of three New Testament executive committees.

The election of *Wenli* and Mandarin translation committees was different from that of the Executive Committee. Of the five men in each committee, four were members of their New Testament committee; only one was new to the group.

The Wenli Old Testament Translators and their Work

The *Wenli* Old Testament committee consisted of Sheffield (chairman), Wherry, Lloyd, Genähr, and P. J. Maclagan (1865–1958), the new member. Maclagan, who also served on the executive committee, was a missionary of the English Presbyterian Mission in Shantou.

When the first committee meeting was held in 1908, it was without Genähr, who had resigned at the end of 1907. T. W. Pearce was elected to take his position. Sheffield resigned in Oct. 1912 because of ill health. He eventually died in Beidaihe on July 1, 1913. The German, Nagel, was elected to take his place. Wherry became the chairman after Sheffield. Maclagan left in 1912 for his furlough and was unable to continue translation work due to his election as secretary of the Foreign Missions Committee of the English Presbyterian Mission in 1914. The vacancy he created remained. After 1912, four remaining translators carried on the work to its completion: Wherry, Lloyd, Nagel, and Pearce.

Figure 5: *Wenli* **Union Version translators with their Chinese assistants**
The Western translators are: (front row, from left to right) J. Wherry, T. W. Pearce,
(back row) L. Lloyd and A. Nagel. The names of the Chinese are unknown.

The Proceedings of the Wenli Old Testament Work

The work on the Old Testament was carried out in a manner similar to that of the New Testament translation. Each translator had an assigned portion to translate on the prepared sheets and these were circulated among the other members of the committee for suggestions. After the original translators had finished their second revisions, the whole committee met together to determine the final rendering. The initial individual work took almost two years. The first committee meeting was held in April 1909. By the second meeting in 1912, their membership had stabilized, and they worked together with unprecedented harmony and success. Wherever different translations needed agreement, they discussed them amicably. Pearce recorded, "We realized more than ever before the sacred sanctions of friendship and fellowship, the outcome of joint endeavor."[11] Zetzsche comments: "No other phase of any translation committee in the process of the Union Version translations had ever reached such a degree of agreement and effectiveness."[12] Five times they met either at Tongzhou or Fuzhou to deal with different parts of the Old Testament:

1909: Job, 1 Samuel 1–14: Tongzhou

1912: Proverbs: Tongzhou

1913: The five books of the Pentateuch: Fuzhou

1914: Twelve books from Joshua to Esther, a few Psalms: Fuzhou

1915: The remaining 20 books of the Old Testament: Fuzhou

Different parts of the Old Testament were dealt with at each meeting, but before the completion of the whole Old Testament, there were no tentative translations published. In 1919, the first edition of the *Wenli* Union Version was published, which consisted of the 1907 *Wenli* New Testament and the *Wenli* Union Old Testament.

The Mandarin Old Testament Translators and Their Work

It took about twelve years for the Mandarin Old Testament committee to fulfill its task. The committee membership experienced a number of changes over the years. At first, it consisted of: Mateer, Goodrich, Baller, Lewis,

11. *London Missionary Society Report* 1916, 104.

12. Zetzsche, *Bible in China,* 302.

and C. W. Allan (1870–1958), the new member. Allan was a missionary of Wesleyan Methodist Missionary Society in Hanyang. Mateer was again elected chairman of the Mandarin Translation Committee. This group of translators had sad and unpleasant experiences in the first two meetings at Zhifu. In the summer of 1908, Mateer called the first meeting of the translators, but he had to leave the meeting early because of illness and eventually died on his way home to Dengzhou. A. Sydenstricker (1852–1931) of the American Southern Presbyterian Mission from Zhejiang was elected in his place. The second meeting was held from June until October 1909. On July 26, Sydenstricker withdrew from the meeting because of disagreements with others about the principles of translation, and then submitted his resignation a month before the meeting was ended in October.

James Walter Lowrie (1856–1930) of the American Presbyterian Mission joined the committee as the successor of Sydenstricker. Lowrie, a member of the executive committee, had come to China in 1883 and was working in Baoding. In 1911, he resigned and proposed as his successor Edwin E. Aiken (1859–1951) of the American Board of Commissioners for Foreign Missions, who had been in Tianjin and Peking since 1885.

With the support of the Bible societies, all the translators were settled in Peking in 1913, which made it possible to work speedily through the whole year. They started committee work in April 1913. A few weeks later, Allan resigned because of ill health. No successor for Allan was elected. Four translators, similar to those of the *Wenli* Old Testament committee, did the remaining translation. They were Goodrich, Baller, Lewis, and Aiken. Goodrich, the only member who had been with the committee from its beginning, was elected chairman of the committee in place of Mateer.

Figure 6: Mandarin Union Version (OT) translators with their Chinese assistants (from left to right) Lee Chihli, Goodrich, Yen, Lewis, Allan, Wang, Aiken, Baller, Liu Dacheng

The Proceeding of the Mandarin Old Testament Work

1908/6–9: Genesis and Psalms 1–34

1909/6–10: Psalms 35–150, revised Psalms 1–34 and New Testament

1910/6–9: Job and Exodus

1913/4–6: Leviticus and Numbers

1913/9–1914/1: Deuteronomy, revised Genesis and Exodus

1914: Joshua, Proverbs through Isaiah

1915: Jeremiah through Hosea

1916: Judges through 1 Kings, Ezra, Nehemiah, Esther and Joel through Malachi

1917: 2 Kings, 1–2 Chronicles

Unlike the *Wenli* translation, parts of the Mandarin work were published as they were completed. The Psalms were published in 1910, Job was published in 1911, and the Pentateuch was published in 1914. The completed Mandarin Union Version appeared in 1919.

This version was well accepted and soon superseded the various existing versions. It became a veritable uniform and standard version, known as *Guanhua Heheben Shengjing*. Eber is right in stating:

> When the Union Old Testament was published it was greatly indebted to Schereschewsky's vernacular, 1899 revised version. Since that translation was rendered directly from the Hebrew, today's Chinese Union Old Testament still reflects the traditional Hebrew Masoretic text.[13]

Chinese Assistants

Every missionary translator had a Chinese assistant as his personal Chinese teacher and copyist while he translated the Bible into Chinese. The Chinese participated in the preparation of the draft translations and corrections that were made before the meetings. They then accompanied the missionaries to the committee meetings. They might join in the discussion but did not have the right to vote in final decisions until the late union translation project.

However, their names were seldom mentioned in the missionaries' reports. For instance, Bridgman did recognize the Chinese assistants' contribution to the Delegates' version but failed to mention their names in his letter to the American Bible Society.[14] Some of them were known only by their surnames. Although there are some copies of photographs taken while they were working together, which were kept in ABS Archives or recorded in *The Chinese Recorder*, it is hard to tell who is who without names given.[15] Thus, it happens that the painting of Robert Morrison and his Chinese assistants has been frequently adopted in books and articles regarding the history of Protestantism in China; yet, it is sad that some writers inaccurately identified the Chinese in the painting as Liang Fa.[16]

13. Eber, *Jewish Bishop*, 153.
14. See "Style of Language" in Ch. 2.
15. See Figure 5
16. Such as Luo Weihong, *Zhongguo Jidujiao*, 2.

Such a mistake illustrates the fact that Chinese coworkers and their crucial role in the missionary translation process have been neglected for too long.

Fortunately, this issue has increasingly attracted the attention of Chinese and foreign scholars. Recent works by Eber, Zetzsche, Strandenaes, and Su Jing have contributed greatly to the identification of the names of many of the Chinese coworkers of Protestant missionary translators. Many of these coworkers come alive from archive materials and documents where they have been dusty for years. Eber has successfully traced the names of several Chinese scholars who assisted Schereschewsky for the last eleven years of his life. Zetzsche has not only made many Chinese literati, tutors, and scribes known to us, but also argues convincingly that the Chinese who worked with Western missionaries were not merely helpers but that they played a crucial role in the process of Chinese Bible translation. Strandenaes, in his monograph, has fully explored the anonymous nineteenth century Chinese Bible translators who worked during the first hundred years of translation work. Su Jing has made a study of Morrison and his circle and has been enabled, by access to archives and first-hand material, to supplement valuable information on Morrison's assistants.[17]

The present study has benefited from the researches of scholars mentioned above in producing a list of identified Chinese coworkers, including both those known by name and those unnamed with suggestions for further study and identification.[18]

The Chinese Coworkers in the UV Project

The important role the Chinese played in many translation processes was increasingly valued, especially in the Mandarin Union translation. In the preface of the 1907 New Testament, there were special words of thanks to Chinese assistants: "The faithful help of Chinese assistants is acknowledged; one teacher was connected with the work since its inception, while another served for twelve years." The first one referred to Zhang Xixin, who was Goodrich's assistant, and the second one was Zou Liwen, who was assistant to Mateer and died in 1903. The preface was written both in English and in Chinese, and their names appeared in the Chinese preface only. Mateer's other assistant was Wang Yuande, also known under his *zi*

---

17. Eber, *Jewish Bishop*, 1999; Zetzsche, *Bible in China*,1999; Strandenaes, "Anonymous Bible Translators," 2004; Su Jing, *Zhongguo, kaimen*, 2005.

18. See Appendix 4.

(style) Xuanchen, who worked with Mateer from 1903 to 1908. After the death of Mateer, Wang Yuande went to a seminary to develop his knowledge of theology and later made his own translation of the New Testament, which was published in 1933. Lewis's assistant was Li Chunfan, who served unobtrusively but very helpfully, and died in 1938. Baller summed up the increasing contribution of the Chinese assistants in the Mandarin Old Testament translation: "No rendering was adopted, in regard to the Chinese of it, without their agreement." His assistant was Liu Dacheng, who died in 1918. In his obituary in *China's Millions*, Liu was highly esteemed:

> For sixteen years he had been associated with Mr. F. W. Baller in the revision of the Mandarin Bible . . . and had rendered most valuable service. He was a quiet, unassuming man, who lived a consistent life, and has left behind a record of faithful, conscientious labor. The Chinese revised version will owe a good many of its felicitous phrases to him, as also a general improvement both in style and expression in not a few passages.[19]

Goodrich, in his letter to Bondfield of June 18, 1918, praised their Chinese teachers' work as invaluable. When he was the chairman of the Old Testament translation committee, the Chinese assistants had the right to vote in decisions regarding the final text. The excellence of the UV reflects the decisive influence of these Chinese coworkers.

The Role of Chinese Coworkers

The Chinese who were involved in Western missionaries' Bible translation are referred to various as "teachers," "assistants," "helpers," "secretaries," "scribes," "writers," "amanuenses," "counterparts," "coworkers," "literati," "scholars," "Chinese tutors," "linguistic consultants," and "translators." From these designations, it is possible to ascertain the role of the native literati in the translation project. Strandenaes aptly concludes:

> They were part of translation teams, and they assisted individual translators as well as groups of translators in preparing readable—sometimes even elegant—Chinese translations into literary and spoken Chinese. Their knowledge of the receptor language was needed, and so was the classical Chinese education and apprenticeship that many of them brought to the translation effort. Except for the fact that they were not theologically trained and had

19. Baller, "The Revised Mandarin Bible," 55.

81

not studied the original languages of the Bible, and therefore could not translate *from* the originals, they were indeed translators who ably rendered the biblical texts *into* the receptor language, with which they were familiar. As such, these Chinese literati deserve to be called Bible translators and consultants.[20]

These Chinese coworkers obviously participated in every aspect of the translation process. It is true that nineteenth-century Bible translation was the project of Western missionaries. They were the policy decision makers who funded the translation project and employed the Chinese literati, so they had dominant status. The Chinese literati were in a subordinate position. However, in the translation process, the Chinese contributed in many ways to the successful completion of the work and shared with the foreigners the burden of the work, especially in the UV project, even though the missionaries received most of the honor.

The Challenging Task of Identification

Unless the names of Chinese coworkers are recorded in Chinese, it is difficult to determine their original Chinese characters. Firstly, this is because it is not known whether the missionaries' transliterations refer to local dialects, such as Cantonese, or Mandarin as the basis of pronunciation. For example, there are four suggestions given for the name of Morrison's teacher: Yun Kwanming, Yuan Guangming, Yin Kunming, Yun Guanming. Secondly, transliterations are not consistent among missionaries and scholars. For example, Zhou Liwen, Mateer's assistant, is referred to by Goodrich as Tsou although Mateer refers to him as Tso; Choo Dih-lang (Zhu Delang), the assistant to Medhurst, is referred to by Zetzsche as Zhu Dilang, whereas Strandenaes refers to him as Ju Dilang. Thirdly, there are differences between Western and Chinese scholars in decoding the missionaries' transliterations. For example, Kō-Mow-Ho, the Chinese teacher to Morrison, is identified by Strandenaes as Mr. Gao, while Su Jing identifies him as Ge Maohe.[21] Finally, Chinese is not an inflected language; it has a vast number of homonyms which are distinguished from one another only by tones, of which there are four in Mandarin. Thus, even a surname could be written

20. Strandenaes, "Anonymous Bible Translators," 145–46; original emphasis.

21. Su Jing, *Zhongguo, kaimen*, 37, 51; Strandenaes, "Anonymous Bible Translators," 128. I am very grateful to Dr. Strandenaes for his clear reference, which enables me to find the Chinese characters and to offer accurate pinyin.

in different characters. For example, Li, Wang, Yan, and Liu, surnames of four Chinese coworkers appearing in the 1913 photograph with Western translators: each of them has its different characters, and they are all extremely common surnames in China. Much further work on identification is needed.

Since more and more attention is being paid to this subject and many Chinese co-workers have now been identified, greater efforts must still be made to uncover every possibility of giving the picture as a whole. When the names of Western missionary translators are remembered in connection with their particular Chinese translation of the Bible, so also should be their Chinese coworkers.

Figure 7: *Wenli* Union Version, 1919 and Figure 8: Mandarin Union Version, 1919

Summary

"One Bible in three versions" was the decision made in the 1890 Protestant Missionary General Conference as a response to the common desire for a standard and uniform Bible for China. By 1907, when the General Conference met again, three Union New Testament translations, Easy *Wenli*, *Wenli*, and Mandarin appeared. As the language had changed over the years, the time came for there to be one *Wenli* instead of two. The further task of union translation set by the conference was for both *Wenli* Old Testament and Mandarin Old Testament editions. These were completed in 1915 and 1917, respectively. In 1919, both the Union *Wenli* and Mandarin versions of the whole Bible issued from the printing press.

The Union Version project took twenty-nine years to be completed, from 1890 to 1919. Thirty-seven Western missionaries served on executive committees. Twenty-three missionaries involved in translation. How many Chinese had a share in this union project remains unknown. Obviously, they played an indispensable role in the translation process.

Wherry and Goodrich, chairmen of the *Wenli* and Mandarin translation committees, were the only two to see the whole translation through from its beginning to its completion.

The process of changing language style from *Wenli* (the classical language for the literati), to Mandarin (the colloquial language for ordinary people), and then to Easy *Wenli* (the lower classical style, which was acceptable and understandable by all), demonstrates the attempts Western missionaries made to give China an acceptable version.

Easy *Wenli* was once considered the most appropriate style for a union version. Translation into this style ended unexpectedly after the production of only the New Testament. No further work was considered necessary. The term "Mandarin" was replaced in 1909 with "*Guoyu*," and was defined in 1913 as the Chinese national language, which was to be used in modern Chinese literature. With this official decision, classical Chinese declined and was viewed by a new generation as archaic and unfit for modern times. The last edition of the *Wenli* Union Version was printed in 1934. Copies are found in Bible societies' records and in their collections of old Bibles. It is the Mandarin Union Version, later known as the *Heheben* (Union Version), which has been accepted by the Chinese Church all over the world as the standard version of the Bible up to the present day.

The Union Version is the last and the greatest Chinese translation of the Scriptures where the work of translation was dominated by Western missionaries. It marks the pinnacle of Protestant missionary Bible translation in China and provides a satisfactory end to the history of Western missionary Bible translation for Chinese.

Part II

The Evolution of the Mandarin Union Version

4

Translations

THE MANDARIN UNION VERSION resulted from decisions made by the Protestant Missionary Conferences held in Shanghai in 1890 and 1907. At the 1890 Conference, it was decided to initiate work on three union versions of the Chinese Bible. The translation of the New Testament part of all three versions was completed before the Centenary Conference in 1907 and it was decided at the Conference to settle for only one *Wenli* version instead of the two originally planned. This decision made it clear that only two Union Versions need to be completed, namely, the *Wenli* Union Version and the MUV, which were both published in 1919. Of these two, the MUV became the more popular and more widely distributed and finally it became a common version used by Chinese Christians worldwide.

In the first twenty years, nothing in the MUV changed, except for its Chinese name. *Guoyu* Union Version replaced "Mandarin Union Version" in 1939. This version later became known as the Chinese Union Version. However, since it is now the only union version in use this work will refer to it as the Union Version (UV) for consistency.

This chapter consists of three sections: 1) the principles of translation; 2) comparison of the UV with the Peking Version by examining Mark 1–3; and 3) translation of the key theological word—God. These are considered in turn.

The Principles of Translation

When translating the Bible, the translators obviously followed certain principles in their work, whether or not they consciously recognized this. It took about three decades to complete the UV, and it was the result of a group effort. What kind of translation principles did they adopt? How did they practice these principles? It is a matter worthy of exploration. This section first introduces certain relevant historical documents related to the UV, then attempts to analyze and give examples when necessary.

There are two facts we should bear in mind: First, foreigners dominated the translation of the UV. From the beginning of the nineteenth century, Western missionaries, mainly British and American, led every field of mission activity including Bible translation, in China.

As Mandarin is a daily life language, it had no definite form at that time; therefore, reliance on native speakers was essential. Western missionaries continued to play the primary role in Bible translation work, however. Translation is always laborious, but it is even more difficult for translators to render a text into a receptor language that is not native to them. These were the challenges that the UV translators faced.

Second, Mandarin had a particular problem that made it more difficult to handle than *Wenli*. Here is one extract from the committee's report, which expressed the difficulty well:

> It [Mandarin] is in constant danger of falling into undignified colloquialisms and unintelligible localisms, or else of mounting into the cloudland of *Wenli*. Its vocabulary is limited, and its construction lacks suppleness, whereas *Wenli* has a vocabulary co-extensive with the Imperial dictionary [*Kangxi Zidian*], and its style, as used by foreigners, is as supple as a rubber ball.[1]

No set norm existed for Mandarin, so it had a style of language subject to individual judgment. Mateer, Chairman of the New Testament translation committee, advocated a Mandarin formed after the spoken language, employing only widely used terms rather than classical terms. This would enable not only the reader but also the listener to understand. Goodrich, Chairman of the Old Testament translation committee after Mateer passed away, promoted a Mandarin that had to be colloquial yet high enough to be elegant. It was to be a written language rather than a spoken language in written form. Baller's ideal was a dignified Mandarin; i.e., the colloquial

---

1. *Records 1907*, 282.

style should not be too low. Competing concepts of Mandarin caused immense difficulties during the actual translation work. The various dialectal forms—Northern, Central, and Southern—in use at the time caused an additional problem. The translators had picked up Mandarin with a local accent and usage, which varied widely depending on where they lived. For instance, Mateer was a fine speaker of the Shandong dialect, and Owen was a rare speaker of Pekingese. Aiken served in Tianjin and Goodrich in Tongzhou. The differences between them often caused a long discussion to settle even one word. Goodrich once portrayed the committee's work in a lengthy description, providing a good impression of the difficulties and the most important points that the translators discussed and considered:

> We are trying to settle the text of the Book of Acts. How simple it looks in English! But almost every verse means a battle. It is not easy to understand each other with our quintuple sets of pronunciation and tones, but we all understand English. A verse is read, and the debate begins, sometimes as follows:
> "The Style is too low, just what the coolies on the street use." "But we want a style that even the coolies can understand. The trouble with our Bibles is that they have been translated for the learned, and not for the common people. . .." "This phrase is quite impossible in our section; it isn't what the Greek says. We are translating the original language of the Bible, and it is our duty to give the meaning correctly, and without a paraphrase." "But I maintain this phrase gives the correct sense. We are not here to render the same Greek word always by the same Chinese character. I hold that if Luke [author of Acts] had been writing in Chinese, he would have used this phrase." "And I am sure he would have never written it. I wish the members of the Committee to note carefully just what the Greek word means. It never has the sense which we are asked to give it, while the translation I have given renders the word perfectly." "That would do very well if we were writing in the classical style, but we are making a Mandarin version of the Scriptures, brethren, to be understood by everybody, when read out from the pulpit." "Yes, we are making a Mandarin version, but we must render the original into a style that is chaste and crisp, or our version will be laughed at." "I want to say right here, that if I had known we were to translate the Bible into a classical style, I would never have allowed my name to be on the Committee. I have very important work waiting for me, that I ought to be doing at this moment." "I beg, brethren, that you will speak in Chinese. We are carrying on our debate in English, and here are five native

brethren, sitting by quite ignorant of our remarks, who might help us to the proper rendering, if we spoke in Chinese." We all agree, and presently are talking again in the language in which we were born.[2]

Goodrich's very honest description above points out the major problem, which was the lack of a standard form of Mandarin and consequent differences in perception of what written Mandarin should be like. It was apparent that they had to spend a great deal of time to agree on the translation of a single word. As the translators themselves said: "Any one of the translators working alone would have completed the work long since."[3] They ultimately learned how to work together to produce an acceptable version, however. That this version remains the most popular one at the present time witnesses to the fact that the translators' endeavors were not in vain.

The UV translators adopted eighteen principles of translation at a meeting held in Shanghai on November 21, 1891. These rules drew from former experiences of team translation, namely the Delegates' version. A comparison reveals that the first eight of UV's principles were similar to those of the Delegates. The eighteen principles read as follows:

1. Passages expressed in the same terms and in the same or similar connection in the original, translate in a uniform manner.

2. Translate Greek and Hebrew words occurring in different places and used in the same sense by the same Chinese words.

3. When practicable, use the nearest Chinese words to express weights and measures, terms in natural history, botany, etc., putting in the margin, when necessary, their actual value if ascertainable. In other cases, transliterate the original words.

4. Allow the interchange of noun and pronoun when conducive to clearness.

5. Where, according to Chinese idiom, pronouns would not be repeated, use them only when required for special emphasis or to prevent ambiguity.

---

2. Goodrich, "The Experience," 378–79.
3. *Records 1907*, 283.

6. In passages in which by a Hebrew idiom different person of the pronoun occur to denote the same person or persons, the use of one person be allowed throughout when necessary to prevent obscurity.

7. In the *Wenli* versions exclude all signs of the plural in pronouns which are not necessary to prevent ambiguity, unless good Chinese taste requires them.

8. Render euphemisms in the original by corresponding euphemisms in Chinese and use euphemisms in other cases when desirable.

9. Retain metaphors and comparisons so far as possible.

10. When, in the division of our work amongst the translators, books are divided, take special pains to make the separate parts uniform in style and expression.

11. Make a special effort to render literally words and phrases which have a theological or ethical importance, and which are, or may be, used by any school for proof or support of doctrines; putting explanations in the margin, if necessary.

12. As bearableness is essential to an acceptable version, allow more freedom of expression and arrangement of clauses, so as to secure perspicuity, measures and idiom in portions that have no special theological significance.

13. In translating the poetical books of the Old Testament, preserve the form of the Hebrew parallel as far as practicable.

14. When any passage in the original is ambiguous, adopt, as a rule, that rendering which seems best to suit the context.

15. When two or more interpretations seem quite or nearly equally good, give one in the text and the other, or others, in the margin.

16. Write the genealogical table at the beginning of St. Matthew's Gospel three characters lower than the following text, to show that it is an introduction.

17. Punctuate by using the ordinary Chinese dot [`] for comma and semicolon, a small circle [∘] for period and a large circle [O] to divide paragraphs.

18. While general uniformity of style is desirable in the whole Bible, do not press this so strenuously as to obliterate the individuality of the original writers.[4]

The next section explores the nature of these principles of translation, with examples given as needed.

Nature of the Eighteen Principles of Translation

Principles (1) concordance, (2) consistency, (8) rendering "euphemism by euphemism," and (9) retaining "metaphors and comparisons" all attempted to protect the formal correspondence between the translation and the original text when rendering Greek and Hebrew.

Principles (4), (5), (6), and (7), all dealing with pronouns, restricted the translators when they integrated idiomatic Chinese phrases. Principle (4) allowed the interchange of noun and pronoun for clarity; (5) avoided repeating pronouns when contrary to Chinese idiom, except when special emphasis was needed to prevent ambiguity; (6) to prevent obscurity, used one pronoun throughout when the Hebrew idiom employed different pronouns to denote the same person. (7) Was a special principle for *Wenli*; it excluded plural pronouns, unless good Chinese taste required them.

Principle (10) secured the harmony of a union version.

Principle (11) made a special effort to render literally words and phrases with a theological or ethical importance, (14) rendered ambiguous passages according to the context, and (15) gave two or more interpretations when both seemed equally good, one in the text and others in the margin. For example, I Samuel 2:17 "for they treated the offerings of the Lord with contempt" precedes an alternative translation in brackets in smaller characters: "or translated: for they caused the people distaste for offering to the Lord." These rules were intended to secure the character of a union version, avoiding former splits like that of the Delegates' committee. The fact that the translators were preparing union versions for a wide group of denominations compelled them to take precautions in order to ensure that the translation would be theologically acceptable to the various churches.

---

4. The original was in *Chinese Recorder 1892*, 26–27. Quoted in Zetzsche, *Bible in China*, 225–26.

Principle (12) states that there should be freedom of expression and freedom of arranging clauses "in portions that have no special theological significance" in order to "secure perspicuity, neatness and idiom." This provision assisted the translators in achieving idiomatic Chinese.

Two specific restrictions in form: (13) when translating the poetical books of the Old Testament, to preserve the form of the Hebrew parallel; (16) to write the genealogical table at the beginning of Matthew, using three characters lower, to show that it is an introduction.

Principle (17) dealt with consistency in punctuation. The translators used three punctuation marks: the solid sharp dot [ˋ] for both comma and semicolon, a small circle [∘] for the period and a large circle [O] to divide paragraphs. Only the Mandarin version followed this rule. *Wenli* versions used only two punctuation marks, the ordinary Chinese dot and large circle.

Principle (3): aim to "use the nearest obtainable Chinese words to express weights and measures, terms in natural history, botany, etc. In other cases, transliterate the original words. As we read:

Weights	*mina*	for mina in 1 Kgs 10:17
	bijia	for beka in Exod 38:26
Money	*dalike*	for daric in 1 Chr 29:7
	shekele	for shekel in Gen 23:15
Measure	*hemeier*	for homer in Lev 27:16
	luoge	for log in Lev 14:10

For linear measures, the traditional Chinese measurement corresponds to the Hebrew original, employed as:

- *Zhou* (elbow) for cubit in Gen 6:15

- *Yizhangkuan* (a palm wide) for handbreadth in Exod 25:25

- *Hukou* (part of the hand between the thumb and the index finger) for span in Exod 28:16

The New Testament employs the traditional Chinese time measure system for the traditional Roman system, such as:[5]

- *Sichu*   for "the third hour," that is 9am in Matt 20:3 in Acts 2:15

---

5. Ancient Chinese used the 12 Earthly Branches (*Zi, Chou, Yin, Mao, Chen, Si, Wu, Wei, Shen, You, Xu* and *Hai*) to designate hours.

- *Wuzheng*   for "the sixth hour," that is 12pm in Matt 20:5
- *Weishi*   for "the seventh hour," that is 1pm in John 4:52
- *Shenchu*   for "the ninth hour," that is 3pm in Matt 20:5
- *Shenzheng* for "the tenth hour," that is 4pm in John 1:39
- *Youchu*   for "the eleventh hour," that is 5pm in Matt 20:6

Case Study

How did the UV practice these principles of translation? The following case study demonstrates their uses.

Pronouns

Four of the eighteen principles were specifically about the use of pronouns, indicating the importance attached to their correct use, which should be according to principle (4), "the interchange of noun and pronoun when conducive to clearness." In Ruth 1:18 we find the following example:

וַתֵּרֶא כִּי־מִתְאַמֶּצֶת הִיא לָלֶכֶת אִתָּהּ וַתֶּחְדַּל לְדַבֵּר אֵלֶיהָ׃

Here, a Chinese literal translation would leave the reader in a state of complete bewilderment, because Chinese personal pronouns use only one character "*ta*" (she, the 3rd person, feminine, pronouns), for all cases, unlike English, which has two words "she" for the Subjective Case and "her" for the Objective Case. There are five personal pronouns in verse 18: "She (*ta*) saw that she (*ta*) was determined to go with her (*ta*), so she (*ta*) stopped speaking to her (*ta*)."

Instead of using *ta* for all five pronouns, the UV interchanges personal pronouns and the proper nouns, "Naomi" and "Ruth," to avoid confusion. The translation reads, "Naomi saw that Ruth was determined to follow her, so she did not persuade her anymore."

Retain metaphors

In Amos 4:6 "I gave you cleanness of teeth in all your cities," the translation retains the original figure of speech, "cleanness of teeth." A reader who is not familiar with the figurative use of "cleanness of teeth" to represent "famine—nothing to eat" may not understand that it refers here to a punishment from God. The translators were not prepared to adapt this phrase to a more functional equivalence.

Poetical Form

To preserve the form of the Hebrew parallel in translating: the poetical form of the Old Testament can be seen in Genesis 1:27; 4:23–24; Psalms, Proverbs, Song of Solomon and Lamentations, etc. The 1919 version only printed Psalms in the poetical form, however. It was not until the 1980s, when the Bible was printed in two horizontal columns, that poetical translation was arranged and printed in poetical form. This principle was implemented in the Chinese Union Version revision 2010.

Explanation of Proper Names

Proper names in the Bible are not translated but transliterated. Hebrew proper names usually have meanings which play a significant role in the biblical narrative, however. When transliterated into Chinese, these names become meaningless.

A few examples will suffice to illustrate the problem.

Gen 16:11 "You shall call him Ishmael, for the Lord has given heed to your affliction." The name, Ishmael, is transliterated as *Yishimali*, largely a meaningless name to a Chinese reader. Any Hebrew reader would readily recognize that the name Ishmael implies "God hears." In addition, the text turns on a pun: "for the Lord has given heed to your affliction." The transliteration does not make that clear to the Chinese reader. In this case, an explanatory note is added to the name in the bracket: *Ishmael* (That is "God hears"). Other examples can be seen in the names of the twelve sons of Jacob in Genesis 29:31–30:24. *Reuben* (That is "have a son"); *Simeon* (That is "hear"); *Levi* (That is "join"); *Judah* (That is "praise"), etc..

Similar examples are also found in names of places, such as: Gen. 28:19 *Bethel* (That is "House of God").

There are seventy-two proper names for which explanatory notes are given in the UV.[6] In this way, the translation is adequate, and the meaning is

---

6. For details on the process of publishing annotated Scriptures without violating the Bible Societies' prohibition against versions with notes and comments, see Strandenaes, "Principles," 97–98.

clear when read silently. However, its meaning is lost when it is read aloud, because the explanatory notes in brackets are not, of course, intended to be read aloud. Among seventy-two proper names, only two have explanatory notes that appeared within the text. They are Acts 1:19 "*Yagedama*, that is, Field of Blood." and Hebrews 7:2 "king of *Salem*, that is, King of Peace."

Chinese characters are ideographs, with no capitals. Underlining is employed to indicate proper names. Double underlining is used for places and single for persons. This extra principle is found in the preface of the 1907 New Testament. It is a useful system, especially when a proper name, like that of Israel or Tarshish, is used for both a person and a place. The proper name with double underlining would help readers to understand that the text refers to a place but not to a person. Nowadays, only a few translations, such as Chinese Standard Bible, consistently adopt this method. Most of the versions and revisions after the UV 1919 use only a single underscore to follow the modern standard punctuation.

Punctuation

Principle 17 states that three punctuation marks are to be used: the solid sharp dot [ˋ] for both comma and semicolon, a small circle [○] for the period, and a large circle [O] to divide paragraphs. This system was seen as being too confining for the purpose of indicating the same variations within the Mandarin version as those that are possible in the English system with its comma, full stop, semicolon, colon, etc. For this reason, the UV employed three new punctuation marks. First, a solid full stop [.] denoted semicolons and colons as in English punctuation. This mark is now no longer used in the modern punctuation system, however. Second, a double quotation mark denoted a quotation. At that time, the semicolon had not been adopted. Finally, three light dots under each character to indicate the word is not found in the original Hebrew or Greek but was added by the translators for clarity. This feature has the same function as the italics used in the English Bible. To help understand this unusual mark, some examples are given as below: In the Gospel of John 3:16 we read literally, "God loved humanity, even gave his only Son (to them)." The object "to them" was added according to Chinese usage, and under each character of "to them," there were three light dots. Another example can be found in Genesis 3:6, which reads "the woman saw the tree was good for food." It would be very odd to think that "the tree" could be "good for food" in

Chinese. So, the phrase "the fruit of" was added to make it reasonable and acceptable, because it is implied in the context, according to the translators' understanding. Therefore, under each character of "the fruit of" three light dots were added, which aimed to make the original meaning clearer. A revised explanation of new punctuation marks is given in the preface of the 1907 Mandarin New Testament.

Notes of Formal Correspondence

When translators freely adopted a word, which seemed best to suit the context, they gave a note on the original meaning in brackets. This note does not indicate alternative readings but gives the functional equivalent of words rendered in formal correspondence with the original text. For example, Genesis 29:15 "Because you are my kinsman" was translated into Chinese as *ni suishi wode gurou* (though you are my bone and my flesh), because the functional equivalent translation *my bone and my flesh* would have been too far from a formal correspondence translation. Therefore, they added a note indicating that "The original means my brother." Another example is found in the Gospel of John 19:12. Pilate tried to release Jesus, but the Jews cried out, "If you release this man, you are no friend of the emperor." "Friend" was translated into the Chinese as *zhongchen* (loyal officer). A note was added to indicate that "The original means friend." A further example is in Genesis 46:4 "Joseph's own hand shall close your eyes." was translated into the Chinese as *Yuese bi geini songzhong* (Joseph shall arrange for your funeral.) followed by a note in brackets: "The original text was Joseph's own hand shall close your eyes." In the UV, there are 379 notes of this type.

Alternative Renderings

The translators gave explanatory notes of alternative renderings when there are different interpretations based either on ambiguities in the original language or alternative means of expression in the receptor language. For example, Song of Songs 2:12 "The time of singing has come, and the voice of turtledove is heard in our land." The clause "the time of singing" is followed by an alternative rendering put in brackets, "alternative translation: the time of pruning the vine." Genesis 28:13 "The Lord stood above it" is followed by a note in brackets, "alternative translation: stood beside him."

Proverbs 23:33 "Your eyes will see strange things" is followed by a note, "alternative translation: the whore." All these notes are in smaller characters, indicating they are not to be read aloud. In the UV, there are 376 alternative rendering notes.

A Comparison of the Union Version with the Peking Version: Mark 1–3

Why the Peking Version?

Among various Chinese versions, the Peking Version (PV) is the most appropriate one to compare with the UV. There are five reasons for this choice:

First, it has a shared passion. The PV was the result of a combined effort by a group of outstanding missionaries who all equally understood the urgency of a Mandarin version in a literary style.

Second, it was translated in a spirit of unity. The translation committee which formed itself in Peking was the very first of an international and interdenominational nature to continue working together until it completed the translation.

Third, it was widely accepted. The PV was the most successful version up to that point and was used in the Mandarin-speaking areas of China.

Fourth, it was influential. Lees and Wherry even compare the PV to the *Authorized Version* in England or the Luther Bible in Germany.[7]

Fifth, it was the primary reference for the UV even though several Chinese versions existed. On the sheets prepared for the first draft translation of the UV, one column was pre-filled with the text of the PV. This is evidence that the UV translators used the PV as a model.

Probing Mark 1–3

Vocabulary

In Mark 1–3, the UV employed *Shengling* for "Holy Spirit," whereas the PV adopted *Shengshen* for "Holy Ghost." Other terminological changes included *wenshi* (men of letters) for "scribes," instead of *dushuren* (book reader); *xiegui* (evil demon) in the PV was replaced with *wugui* (foul demon) in the UV for "unclean spirit." *Jisizhang* (chief priest) was replaced with *dajisi*

7. Lees, "Letter to a Friend," 180; Wherry, "Historical Summary," 56.

(great priest) for "high priest"; *huan tanfengbing de ren* (paralytic) was replaced with *tanzi* for "the paralytic."

A comparison with the PV shows that the translators of the UV introduced new dissyllabic combinations. Their intention was to enrich the style and make it more expressive of the original's varied thought.[8] According to Mateer, the UV introduced over a thousand new dissyllabic combinations.

As a consequence of this move, Yao Xiyi, a historian of Chinese Christianity, stated with admiration that "the [C]UV played a pivotal role in providing and shaping the theological vocabulary of the Chinese Protestant Church." He wrote: "It did not take long for the UV's translation of such key biblical terms as "faith," "sin," "salvation," and "grace" to become the standard "language of faith," used by church leaders, theologians, and evangelists as well as the average churchgoer on a daily basis."[9]

Proper Nouns

The PV transliterated the proper name "David" as *dapi* but the UV replaced this translation with *dawei*. For "Judas Iscariot," the UV replaced *yise jialue youda* with *jialueren youda*. However, the PV transliterated the proper name "Abiathar" as *Ya-bi-ya-ta* which is better than the UV's *Ya-bi-ya-ta*. The pronunciation is the same, but the Chinese characters are different. Whereas the PV used a common noun for *ta*, the UV adopted the character for the third person masculine pronoun for *ta* (he), which should not be used as a person's name. In the UV, *ta* (he) was used as a part of many proper names. Readers might have been misled to think *tama* (Tamar), in Genesis 38:6, was a man because it used the masculine personal pronoun *ta*. The recent edition revised it to *ta* (she) the feminine personal pronoun to indicate that Tamar is a female. However, the key point of this issue is that a personal pronoun should not be used to in a transliteration of a proper name. A future revision should consider making a change. In this case, the PV's transliteration was more acceptable than that of the UV.

---

8. See the preface of the 1907 New Testament.

9. Yao, https://www.chinasource.org/resource-library/articles/a-century-later-still -dominant.

Aspects of Style

The UV translators attempted to lower the style of the PV in its use of terms. *Qushen* (bend over) from the PV in of Mark 1:7 became the colloquial *wanyao* (bow). See also *jingqi* for *jingyi* (amazed) and *ganchu* for *zhuchu* (cast out). To accord with Chinese common usage, the UV used *mingsheng* instead of *shengming* (fame); and *zhai* replaced *qia* (pluck).

There are several other cases where the UV avoided the PV's more literary translation. In Mark 3:16, the PV's translation "Jesus gave the name Peter to him" is not as colloquial and smooth as the UV's "Jesus named him Peter."

The UV translated Mark 2:19 "Jesus said to them," with *Yesu dui tamen shuo*. The PV did not translate the object "to them" in introducing the reported speech, because it is implied in the context, and thus considered adding "to them" stylistically inferior.

The UV employs interrogative words consistently: *ne* in interrogative sentences, for example, in 2:7–8 *Chule shangdi, shui neng shezui ne* (Who can forgive sins but God only?) while the PV is inconsistent in their use.

Fidelity to the Original

In many instances the UV shows greater fidelity to the original in comparison to the PV. For example, the UV uses *shenshang* (on his body) instead of *toushang* (on his head) for Mark 1:10 "on him" and "show your body to the priest" instead of "ask the priest to examine your body" for Mark 1:43 "show yourself to the priest." In Mark 2, the UV has *dishang* (on earth) instead of *shishang* (in the world) and *liekai* (split) instead of *kai* (open) for "torn up." The UV translates the imperative verb with the emphasis *kanna* whereas the PV omits the emphatic particle. In Mark 1:10, the PV reads, "he came up out of the water" while the UV reads, "Just as he came up out of the water." Here "just as" is a precise translation.

Paraphrastic Translation

The PV was criticized for using too many paraphrases instead of direct translations. For example, the PV translated Mark 2:5 "Jesus saw their faith," by rendering "their faith" as "their trust in him." The UV rendered Mark 2:17 as "I have come to call not the righteous but sinners;" whereas the PV translated it, "I come, not to call the righteous to repent but to call the sinners to repent." The paraphrase "to repent" was added to explain the purpose of calling. This is also true for Mark 3:5 "He stretched it out, and his hand was restored." The PV reads "That man stretched it out, and his hand was restored like the other hand." Here "like the other hand" is an extra paraphrase. Another example is in Mark 3:15, where the PV reads "and granted them authority to cure diseases and to cast out demons." Here the phrase "to cure diseases" is an extra element which the UV avoided in rendering this verse as "and granted them authority to cast out demons."

Pronouns

One of the striking differences between the PV and the UV is the use of pronouns. The translators of the UV tried to limit the use of pronouns according to Chinese stylistic requirements, regardless of the Greek text. In Mark 1:2, 22, 31, 36; 3:5, 31, the PV placed a pronoun where the Greek text has one, but the UV did not. Pronouns have often been replaced by nouns to avoid distortion of meaning and to make the relationship between sentence constituents clearer. The most obvious example is in 1:13, which the UV translated as "He was in the wilderness forty days," instead of using the pronoun in the PV: "He lived there for forty days." Another example exchanges nouns for pronouns, such as "Simon" for *ta* in 1:16; again, "Jesus" is repeated for *ta* in 1:12 and 1:40.

Syntactical and Grammatical Features

In Mark 1:36 "Simon and his companions hunted for him (Jesus)," we have a good example of the different techniques between the two groups of translators. The PV rendered the verse as "Simon and his companions came to trace Jesus . . . ," whereas the UV translated it as "Simon and [his] companions went to trace him." The adverb *lai* (come to) in the PV implies that the disciples came over to search for Jesus, whereas the *qu* (go to) of the UV implies the correct meaning: that they went from where they were to search for Jesus. Here the UV translators' broader experience with the correct use of Mandarin becomes evident. The PV translators were translating literally in this case, but not according to Chinese usage.

The syntactical changes also aimed at a better Chinese style rather than absolute fidelity to Greek syntax. The PV translated Mark 1:7 "The one who has more power than I is coming after me," whereas the UV rendered it as "The one who is coming after me has more power than I." The sentence is modeled according to Chinese speech patterns and syntax, separating the syntactical topic "the one who is coming after me" with a comma. Similarly, the PV translated 1:23 "there was in their synagogue a man with an unclean spirit," while the UV rendered it as "in their synagogue, there was a man with an unclean spirit." The adverbial clause is marked off by a comma to avoid a long compound sentence. The opposite example is found in 2:23, which the PV translated "One Sabbath, he was going through the grain fields," separating the adverbial clause with a comma. The UV's translation goes against the Chinese speech pattern and syntax, with two adverbial clauses between the subject and verb.

Punctuation

The two versions used different punctuation systems. Mark 1:2–4 is a good example for showing the differences.

The PV translators employed only two marks: a Chinese sharp point dot (ˋ) to denote slight pauses and a large circle (O) to divide paragraphs.

Besides these two marks, the UV employed also a quotation mark, a small circle (∘) for period, a solid full stop (.) to denote colons and semicolons as in English punctuation and a dotted line added under terms that were not in the original text.

The above comparison shows that based on the production of other previous translations, the UV translators were able to present a more desirable and more excellent edition. Comparison with the PV demonstrates that the UV improved on vocabulary, style, and punctuation, correctly using interrogative words, and changing inaccurate or extra paraphrastic translation. On the other hand, the PV retains a superior translation in some areas, which the UV did not surpass.

Translation of the Key Theological Word: God

Protestant missionaries in the nineteenth century who had set themselves the task of translating the Bible into Chinese encountered a major problem in developing a religious terminology. Chinese had no equivalents for such terms as "angel," "Holy Spirit," "kingdom of God," "repentance," "faith," "grace," "reconciliation," or "baptism." They had to find a suitable vocabulary for several phrases, but no term was more vexing than the one for "God." Not only were they concerned with literary style, but also with how to render Hebrew *Elohim* and Greek *Theos* into Chinese. The Chinese recognized or worshipped numerous major and minor deities or spirits and there was a prevalence of different pantheons. These factors meant that choosing the best term for "God" involved finding one that would indicate these deities' difference from God. This provoked heated and endless controversies among Western missionaries, a controversy that came to be known as the Term Question.

The Protestants found it difficult to agree as to which term had a sufficiently theistic significance to be taken over by the Christian Church. Various characters were proposed for "God," but by the time the discussion narrowed down to *Shen* and *Shangdi*, the debate had called forth a flood of articles and pamphlets, none of which led to unanimity.

The spokesmen of the two parties in the argument during the translation of the Delegates' version, Boone (pro-*Shen*) and Medhurst (pro-*Shangdi*), published their respective views in *The Chinese Repository* of 1848 and 1850. The Delegates' version was completed but controversies continued. When the Peking Version was on in process of translation, controversy again arose from the mid-1860s to the 1870s with a series of articles in *The Chinese Recorder*. It also resurfaced with renewed ardor when the Union Bible translation was in progress during the 1890s. The three waves of debates are considered in turn.

The First Wave of Debates: Shangdi vs Shen (1843–52)

The controversy began in August 1843 when missionaries from different missionary societies held a meeting in Hong Kong. The purposes of this meeting were to reach an agreement on a revised version of the Bible and to seek approval for a new translation from both the British and American Bible Societies. The crucial issue of how to translate "God" was not resolved. The delegates for the Bible translation eventually met again in Shanghai in 1847. During the general committee's first meeting in July, the delegates came to the translation of Gospel of Matthew 1:23 where "God" had to be rendered into Chinese. In the earlier four-man version, the translators, including Bridgman, had decided on *Shangdi* instead of *Shen*, the term used in the Morrison/Milne and Marshman/Lassar translations. Bridgman now again proposed *Shen* for "God," which led to a further discussion lasting several days. Walter Lowrie, the youngest of the six delegates, gives us the best insight in a letter to his brother, dated July 23, 1847. This letter introduces us to some of the problems concerning the best Chinese term for "God":

> After we had got together, all went on well for a week, when we were stopped by a question which has excited no little talk and writing for some time, "What is the proper word for God in Chinese?" Morrison and Milne have adopted the word Shen, which, according to the best judgment I can form, means God or Divinity in general. Mr. Medhurst for many years used the same term, and even so late as this present year, 1847, has published a dictionary in which he says: "The Chinese themselves, for God, and invisible beings in general, use Shen." But some twelve years ago or more, he began to use Shang Ti [Shangdi], Supreme Ruler, for the true God, and Shen for [a] false god. Mr. Gutzlaff also did the same; and these two being the best and most experienced Chinese scholars, had of course, great weight. And most of the missionaries were carried away by their example.
>
> For some years past, however, there has been a good deal said on the subject, and a strong disposition manifested to return to the old way. Shang Ti is objected to, first, as being the distinctive title of the national deity of China, and hence something like the Jupiter of Rome; and second, it is not a generic term, and cannot be used in such passages as "Chemosh thy God and Jehovah our God," "If Jehovah be God," etc., "The unknown God, Him declare I unto you," etc. In fact, there are many verses where the point and emphasis rest on the use of the generic word all through, as in John x. 35, 36, I Cor. viii. 6, etc. Hence of late many of the missionaries wish to return to the old word, and a good deal has been written in the Chinese Repository, and a great deal said on the subject.
>
> Dr. Medhurst, however, has taken up the cudgels in earnest, and printed a book of nearly three hundred pages, in which he maintains that *Shen* never means god, much less the supreme God. This, by the way, is in opposition to three dictionaries of his own, published in the last ten years. And he further maintains that *Ti*, which properly means ruler, is the generic term for God in Chinese; and that *Shang Ti*, High or Supreme Ruler, is the proper word to translate *Elohim* and *Theos*, when they refer to the true God. So the case stood when the convention met.
>
> We went on with the revision very well, till we came to Matthew 1. 23, where the word *Theos* occurs. Dr. Bridgman then proposed that we use the word *Shen*. Bishop Boone seconded

this; and it was well known that my views coincided with theirs. Dr. Medhurst and Mr. Stronach took decided ground for *Shang Ti*: and so we have now been discussing this question for three weeks, Medhurst and Boone being the chief speakers. The latter is a supreme debater, and having a very quick and logical mind, pressed Dr. Medhurst so closely that he declared that he must have all down in black and white. We agreed to this, and Bishop Boone and myself worked hard for a week, and wrote out an argument for *Shen*, covering twenty-six folio pages. Mr. Medhurst, who had spent five months in writing his book, and scarcely allowed us ten days to answer it, took our answer so seriously, that he said he must have some weeks to prepare a reply. So, he and Mr. Stronach are engaged on this. I greatly fear that the result of all will be, that each side will hold its own view, and Dr. Medhurst and Mr. Stronach will secede. It [In] that case there will be two versions or none.

A large majority of the missionaries in China, I believe, are for *Shen;* most of our missionaries are strongly for it, though one or two hesitate a little; all the Baptists; all the Episcopalians, both English and American; most of the American Board missionaries, and several even of the London Missionary Society. This of itself is a strong proof for *Shen*, for it shows that even the acknowledged scholarship of Medhurst and Gutzlaff is not able to command assent for *Shang Ti*. But I did not mean to write so much on this.[10]

We learn from this letter the core of a subject which divided the missionary body, and the debate by no means reached an end in the first meeting. The argument continued in writing and appeared in The *Chinese Repository*. In the following decades these arguments led to the greatest controversy among Protestant missionaries in China.

We cannot explore the controversy without mentioning Medhurst, Boone and Legge; they were representative figures in the Term Question.

Pro-Shangdi: The Argument of Medhurst

Influenced by his predecessors who used *Shen* for God, Medhurst first believed such was its meaning. Through continued study he found the opinion of his predecessors inaccurate and was compelled to change his mind. As he wrote:

---

10. Broomhall, *Bible in China*, 65–67.

> With regard to *Shin* [*Shen*], I may observe briefly, but as the result of long experience and careful and extensive examination of native documents, that it (when standing alone, without any adjunct) *never* conveys the idea of unity, or supremacy, or infinite excellence.

In order to support himself and to convince his opponents, Medhurst took the Catholics as an example:

> The Catholics, who have had wider and longer experience of China than we have, and who, in their day, knew more of Chinese literature and ideas then we can expect to know for the next century, are in this respect capable of affording us a lesson. They, on their first arrival in the country, adopted the word *Shin* for God, and they in their translation of part of the New Testament employed that word; this was more than a century ago; but they have been compelled to give it up, and have adopted instead *Tien Chu* [*Tianzhu*], as indicative of that unity and supremacy which *Shin* never could give.[11]

Medhurst believed that *Shen* means the gods or the beings of the invisible world, and not the living and true God. Distinguishing "God" from "gods" requires two different terms because in Chinese ideographs, there are no capitals, and no indications of singular or plural except as shown in context. The more research he did, the more strongly he advocated that *Shangdi* would be a better term to denote the true God. Eber describes Medhurst's exploration as follows:

> During his decades in China, Medhurst acquired an extensive knowledge of the Chinese Classics, Song dynasty commentaries, and works which dealt with popular folk religion. In pursuit of the proper term for God and aided by his Chinese co-worker, he embarked on an extensive research project.
> To define *Shangdi* [the two syllables are two separate words in Chinese] Medhurst first consulted the venerable and authoritative *Kangxi Dictionary* from which he concluded that *shang* having the meaning of efficaciousness and supreme—and *di* (deity)—being immaterial, incorporeal and pre-existent before Heaven and Earth—does indeed denote a "High God." He systematically combed not only the Confucian Classics, including the *Great Learning* (*Daxue*) and the *Mencius* (*Mengzi*), but also works dealing with popular religion, such as *Scripture of the Three Wonderful*

---

11. Medhurst, "Remarks in favor," 35–36.

Officials (Sanguan miaojing), or the *Comprehensive Mirror of Holy Immortals* (Shenxian tongjian). In the latter, consisting of popular fictional biographies of immortals, myths and similar materials, *Shangdi* is variously referred to as a great deity (*dadi*), August heavenly high lord (*Huangtian Shangdi*), or Lord of heaven high lord (*Tianzhu shangdi*). As far as Medhurst was concerned, this re-affirmed that *Shangdi* is perceived as having had no origin, and not being produced, but as the source of creation since *di* produced and endowed all things with form.

An admirably thorough investigator, Medhurst did not rest content with establishing *Shangdi* as the proper term for God. He went on to show why *Shen* was not an appropriate term. Toward this end, he searched an early eighteenth-century phrase diction-ary, the *Beiwen [Peiwen] yunfu*, copying out and translating each mention of *Shen*. This task led him to conclude that "no ingenuity can extract the idea of God from this class of quotations."[12]

Eber comments that Medhurst was not far off the mark. The fact is that *shen* means spirit and deity. Two or three illustrations must suffice for supporting Eber's comment. *Shen* was coupled by both literate and illiterate Chinese with malevolent spirits (*gui*) as well as with ancestral spirits. For instance, *shen chu gui mo* (lit. come like spirits and go like ghosts—appear and disappear mysteriously); *zhuang shen nong gui* (lit. play gods feign ghosts—mystify), *niu gui she shen* (lit. ox ghosts and serpent gods—base elements). According to Medhurst, *Shen* is not a proper name; it is a com-mon noun and it may have either singular or plural number. Thus, it lacks the 'uniqueness' essential to Christian thought about God.

Pro-Shen: The Argument of Boone

Boone held that *Shen* was the only true translation for "God," even though it had never had this meaning historically because of the absence of a Chi-nese monotheistic faith. As polytheists, Chinese cannot know the True God. Boone forcefully argued that not *Shangdi*, but *Shen* was the proper term. As *Elohim* is a generic term not a proper name for the True God, Boone suggested that *Shen*, a generic term, should be used to translate *Elo-him* into Chinese.

Boone's disagreement with Medhurst was mainly that *Shangdi* as a proper name rather than a generic term could not be considered for "God."

12. Eber, *Jewish Bishop*, 210–11.

S. Wells Williams (1812–1884), a linguist and Sinologist of the American Board of Commissioners for Foreign Missions, supported Boone and believed *Shen* would avoid confusing people with *Huangtian Shangdi* (August Heavenly) and *Yuhuang Dadi* (August Jade Emperor). Although he was aware that *Shen* had pantheistic implications and singular and plural usages, he held out more hope for *Shen*, believing that as the knowledge of the Scripture increased, it would be understood in a more limited sense. His idea is approved by the fact that the *Shen* edition now enjoys a high popularity in Chinese Christian communities.

Boone also quarreled with other participants in the controversy, especially with James Legge, who went to great lengths to refute Boone's views in 1852.

The Argument between Boone and Legge

Equipped with advanced intellectual abilities in linguistics and the Chinese language, Legge was invited to participate in the 1843 meeting, where the decision for the Delegates' version was made, and therefore he could hardly escape from chains of hot rebuttals over the Term Question. The central argument of Legge's position on the Term Question was that *Shangdi* as the most compatible term in Chinese for the concept of the Christian God.

Like Medhurst, Legge's first choice was to use the term *Shen*, which traced its source from Morrison. After thoughtful study and reflection, he reconsidered that *Shangdi* would be a better word, however. As he wrote: "When I returned to China in 1848, I speedily resumed the consideration of the subject, and was led after a few months to give up all thoughts of *Shin* [*Shen*]. This was the result of my seeing that God was not a generic, but a relative term. It has, however, only been by slow degrees, that I have arrived at my present conviction that *Shang Te* [*Shangdi*] and *Shang Te* alone, is the word which the Chinese language affords us to translate the original words for God, in every instance of their occurrence."[13]

The more he became involved in the rebuttals, the clearer and firmer Legge's position became. Legge, with his excellent expertise in Chinese texts, presented a strong argument against Boone. Unlike Medhurst, who had a similar idea but turned to texts of popular religion for confirmation, Legge's search led him not only to the classics and their commentaries but also to observances of dynastic rituals, the *Collected Ming Statutes* (*Daming*

13. Wong, *James Legge*, 104.

huidian). Legge argued that, in 1538, the Jiaqing emperor of the Ming dynasty decided to alter the manner of addressing *Shangdi*. At a solemn ceremony, the emperor notified the celestial and terrestrial spirits (*shen*) of sun, moon, clouds, hills and so on that *Huangtian Shangdi* (August Heavenly *Shangdi*) was henceforth to be used instead of *Haotian Shangdi* (Vast Heavenly *Shangdi*). This event, according to Legge, proves conclusively that the spirits thus notified were considered subordinate to *Shangdi*, who is unitary, singular, and one only, because not some but all of the spirits were notified. Six days later, when the new address was finalized, they offered prayer, called songs (*yue*), which Legge described as not unlike the Psalms. The opening song or prayer associated *Shangdi* with creation: "In the beginning, there were formless mists (*hunmeng*); the five elements (*wu xing*) did not revolve; sun and moon had no light; there was no form (*rong*) or sound. The exalted one (*shen huang*) emerged and began to divide the turbid (*zhuo*) from the pure (*qing*), establishing heaven, earth and man, giving birth to all things and to life."[14]

Legge's discovery of the remarkable series of songs in the *Collected Ming Statutes,* which assigned creation to *Shangdi*— "the exalted one," was important, but it failed to convince the missionary community. Schereschewsky, for instance, firmly rejected *Shangdi* as Creator, declaring the term to be "positively wrong." Eber very well analyzed Term Question while studying the life and times of Schereschewsky. From her research, we learn more about Schereschewsky's opinion on *Shangdi*. He believed, "*Shangdi* is not a designation; it is the proper name of a certain being, or beings, in Chinese mythology." He came directly to the point: "The more I have examined native authorities as to the meaning of this term, the more I am convinced that to render God by *Shangti* [*Shangdi*], is simply to play into the hands of materialism or gross idolatry, to obscure, if not wholly to obliterate the cardinal doctrine of Revelation; namely the existence of an absolute personal living God, independent of and above nature."[15] Schereschewsky suggested *Tianzhu* for God. The reason was it had not been used in an idolatrous sense so that the Chinese would not refer the term to any of their gods.

Eber also noticed another major point of contention between Boone and Legge: the difference between the Tetragrammaton (YHWH) and *Elohim* or God of the Old Testament. As she wrote:

14. Legge, *Notions of the Chinese,* 25–28.
15. Eber, *Jewish Bishop,* 222.

Boone had argued that *Elohim* must be an absolute term, whereas Legge maintained that the Tetragrammaton was an absolute term. Even if both "denote the same Being," the Tetragrammaton is absolute, and *Elohim* is relative. As Yehovah, wrote Legge, He is "as He is in Himself." As God, He is in relation to other beings. Legge also rejected transliterating the Tetragrammaton, as Schereschewsky was to do a decade later, stating that the Chinese would understand it as a proper name and would therefore consider it another god. Instead, he was in favor of reproducing the meaning of the Tetragrammaton, proposing "self-existent" (*ziyouzhe*) and, when in combination with *Elohim*, "self-existent *Shangdi*" (*ziyou zhi Shangdi*).[16]

Boone was so careful in constructing his arguments that he set out five propositions to invalidate the above arguments:

a) The Chinese do know a being, who is truly and properly God; or in other words, the highest being known to them is not a false god, but is the very Being whom we call God, whose name is therefore the proper word by which to render *Elohim* and *Theos* in all cases; or,

b) Admitting that the Chinese do not know the true God, contend that we would use a relative, not an absolute term or generic term to render *Elohim* and *Theos*, because these words are relative, and not absolute terms; or,

c) Admitting that the highest being known to the Chinese is not truly and properly God, yet affirm that his name or title, and not the generic name of the Chinese gods, should be used to render *Elohim* and *Theos* in all cases; or,

d) Admitting the facts to be as stated in Prop. b) affirm that, we should render *Elohim* and *Theos* only when these words are used *propriè*, by the name or title of this highest Being, i.e. *Shangti* [*Shangdi*]; and when used *impropriè*, they should be rendered by *Shin* [*Shen*], or *Shin-ming* [*Shenming*], or lastly,

e) Admitting that under the above-mentioned circumstances, the generic name of the Chinese gods should be used, if such can be found, deny that *Shin [Shen]* is the generic name, and affirm in the contrary, that as the Chinese have neither a name for any being who is truly and properly God, nor any generic name of their gods, and the words

16. Ibid., 218.

Elohim and *Theos* must be rendered by a generic term we have no resource but that of transferring the original word.[17]

Legge articulated his ideas to rebut Boone's argument within the structure that Boone suggested. The details of Legge's ideas are as follows:

> Against his first proposition—I maintain that the Chinese do know the true God, and have a word in their language answering to our word God, to the Hebrew *Elohim* and to the Greek *Theos*.
>
> Against his second proposition—maintain that no "general or generic name" can be used to render *Elohim*, *Theos*, or God, because these are all relative terms. Though I should fail, therefore, in establishing, beyond the possibility of contradiction, the former thesis, it will still be necessary to seek for a relative term in Chinese, to render *Elohim* and *Theos*. We cannot use for that purpose the generic *Shin* [*Shen*] and it may be that the name or title of the highest being known by the Chinese will answer sufficiently well.
>
> Against Dr. Boone's third proposition—I mentioned that *Shin* [*Shen*] does not answer even to our words a god, gods but is the generic name in Chinese corresponding to our word spirit, to the Hebrew *ruach*, and to the Greek *pneuma*, and that it ought therefore to be employed to render those terms and those alone.[18]

In 1852, Legge presented a clearer and stronger statement of his position that he maintained as his answer to all questions regarding the proper rendering of "God."

The Second Wave of Debates: Shangdi/Shen vs Tianzhu (1863–75)

A second phase of the Term Question began in the 1860s when the Peking committee launched their translation effort. The translators proposed to use *Tianzhu*, the Roman Catholic term for God, which added further fuel to the Term Question.

By then, two of the major participants of the controversy, Medhurst and Boone, had already passed away, while Legge was fully engaged in other endeavors. The participants were now mostly younger missionaries, although the debates on *Shangdi* and *Shen* had not changed. The Peking translation committee comprised five outstanding missionaries who had been working in China for some time. They had acquired an excellent

17. Boone, "Defence of an Essay," 347–48.

18. Legge, *Notions of the Chinese,* 2.

command of Chinese and were fully aware of the major positions on the Term Question. Besides believing *Tianzhu* was a better term than *Shen* or *Shangdi*, one of their motives for proposing this term was that they did not want to be allied with either the *Shangdi* or *Shen* party. They hoped using *Tianzhu* would promote harmony among the missionaries.

Having decided to use *Tianzhu*, the translators by no means ignored the ongoing controversy. They based their argument on the assumption that the Chinese were pantheists. According to them, *Shangdi* had been used in a pantheistic sense for a long time, making it impossible to equate this term with *Elohim* in the Old Testament or *Theos* in the New Testament. Using *Shangdi* would obscure the meaning of an absolute personal living God. They also did not support *Shen*. As Schereschewsky pointed out, the main difficulties with *Shen* were its multiple meanings in Chinese: It can be plural for gods; it can designate goddesses; it may be an adjective, such as "divine." They advocated the use of *Tianzhu* because it had not been used in an idolatrous sense, and the Chinese knew that the term did not refer to any of their gods. *Tianzhu* was not an indigenous Chinese term, but the two characters in it were so familiar to the Chinese that when linked together they formed a name that indicated with unmistakable clarity both the universality and the personality of God as perceived in Christian faith.

Early in 1852, Legge penned his strong opposition to the use of the Catholic term *Tianzhu* (Lord of Heaven), however. *Tian*, he argued, relegates God to heaven when He is, in fact, the Lord of the universe. *Zhu* represents the idea of "lord" but not of "ruler," and as *Tianzhu* is merely a synonym for *Shangdi*, it would be better to use the latter. Because it was closely associated with Roman Catholics, missionaries more than once expressed their concern that the Chinese believers might mistake Protestants for Catholics. Many individuals recognized the merits of the term *Tianzhu*, but its connection with the Roman Catholic Church precluded it from being acceptable for general use as the Divine Name.

The Peking committee hoped to harmonize missionaries' divergence by using *Tianzhu* and did not make a major effort to persuade missionaries elsewhere that *Tianzhu* was preferable. This could have been for three reasons: 1) their desire to promote harmony; 2) the lack of capable men to articulate their arguments; 3) the hope that the translation itself would have sufficient weight to win support.[19]

19. Eber, *Jewish Bishop*, 224.

Unfortunately, contrary to the committee's wishes, their translation—the Peking Version—was published in 1872 with at least five different editions using *Tianzhu, Shangdi, Shen, Zhenshen,* or *Shangzhu.* Public discussion reached its height about the middle of the nineteenth century, then gradually subsided.

The Third Wave of Debates: The Compromise Terms (1890–1907)

The Term Question once more gathered momentum when missionaries launched the Union Versions project in 1890 with a sincere desire to find some kind of compromise. At the general conference in 1890, where the missionaries decided to undertake the Union Versions translation, they stated that each of the Bible Societies would be allowed to publish editions with its respective preferred terms for God, narrowed down again to *Shangdi/Shen,* with multiple translations also allowed for "spirit" and "baptize." In 1904, they made a proposal for "Compromise Terms," which would translate "God" with *Shangdi* and "Spirit" with *Shengling.* In the name of the Bible Societies, the participants sent out a letter to all mission stations with a questionnaire about their willingness to use Bibles with the Compromise Terms. In reply, a large majority voted to substitute the terms *Shangdi* and *Shengling* for the terms already in use. After thus obtaining the missionaries' consent, the Bible Societies permitted their agents to issue Scriptures with the Compromise Terms.[20]

This last great effort toward a solution for the Term Question put an end to the conflict, but it did not define the terms as the Societies had intended. The failure to agree on terms would continue as a source of division within the Protestant churches. Later, when the demand for *Shen* editions increased considerably, the Bible Societies published them also. Even today both *Shangdi* and *Shen* editions are published for people to choose according to their preference.

Reception of the Terms

The three waves of debate reveal that the Term Question was neither merely a linguistic problem nor a theological matter. It brought up issues related

20. Letter from Hykes to American Bible Society of Nov. 22, 1907 in *ABS Report 1908,* 181.

to the notion of God, the nature and content of Chinese religion, and missionary strategy in China. It also raised a conflict that divided British and American missionaries.

Huang Pinsan (1823–90), a Southern Baptist and prolific writer on biblical subjects, brought forward his point of view as a Chinese believer in *Global Magazine* in 1877. He deemed that the West had the concept of one Lord and only one word to designate him, but in Chinese, one can refer to God as either *Shen* or *Shangdi*. This simple inclusive perspective was not widely shared; heated controversy along national lines overwhelmed it. It is interesting to see that the two terms continued to be used, however, due to the missionary Bible translation projects' reaching no consensus.

The unresolved controversy finally faded into the background as the UV appeared in 1919, rendering the divine names in Chinese as follows:

The Divine names in Chinese

Romanized Hebrew, Greek	English	Romanized Chinese Pinyin
Elohim, *Theos*	God	*Shangdi/Shen*
YHWH	LORD, GOD/Yahweh	*Yehehua*
Adonai YHWH	Lord GOD	*Zhu Yehehua*
YHWH Elohim	LORD God	*Yehehua Shangdi/Shen*
Adonai/*Kurios*	Lord	*Zhu*

Besides using *Shangdi* or *Shen* for *Elohim* and *Theos*, the UV adopted the Chinese character *Zhu*, meaning master or lord, for *Adonai* without any dissent. English-language Bibles use all capitals "LORD" and "GOD" are used for the Tetragrammaton YHWH, and also to distinguish *Adonai* (Lord). Although Legge had argued against transliterating YHWH, the UV employed the Chinese character *Yehehua* for the Tetragrammaton, which actually transliterated the English Jehovah rather than the Hebrew YHWH. This did not raise much debate among missionaries in China. As Archie Lee, a professor at the Chinese University of Hong Kong, points out: "The transliteration of the Hebrew proper name for God in the Tetragrammaton YHWH, as *Yehehua*, has largely been agreed upon without taking consideration of Hebrew piety and the practice of not pronouncing it. The name has been used by Chinese Christians without difficulties."[21]

---

21. Lee, "God's Asian Names," http://sbl-site.org/Article.aspx?ArticleID=456.

This was the situation by the time the UV was published. When Chinese people came to make their own translations of the Bible, the native translators considered reproducing the meaning of YHWH. This is apparent from comparing the different forms of address used in four Chinese versions: the UV, Today's Chinese Version (TCV), *Lü Zhenzhong's* version (LZV), and the New Chinese Version (NCV), showed as following in table:

Rendering Divine Names in Different Versions

	Elohim/ Theos	YHWH	YHWH Elohim	Adonai YHWH	Adonai/ Kurios
KJV	God	LORD	LORD God	Lord GOD	Lord
UV	*Shangdi/ Shen*	*Yehehua*	*Yehehua Shangdi/ Shen*	*Zhu Yehehua*	*Zhu*
TCV	*Shangdi*	*Zhu/ Shangzhu*	*Zhu Shangdi*	*Zhigao de Shangzhu*	*Zhu*
LZV	*Shangdi*	*Yonghengzhu*	*Yonghengzhu Shangdi*	*Zhu Yonghengzhu*	*Zhu*
NCV	*Shangdi/ Shen*	*Yehehua*	*Yehehua Shangdi/ Shen*	*Zhu Yehehua*	*Zhu*

The above comparison demonstrates that the NCV inherited the divine names from the UV, while the TCV and the LZV adopted *Shangdi* only. Both the TCV and the LZV rejected transliteration of YHWH/ Yahweh and used different expressions. The TCV adopted *Zhu/Shangzhu*, meaning High or Supreme Lord; and the LZV created *Yonghengzhu*, meaning Eternal Lord.

Reasons for Reception

The majority of those reading the Chinese Bible are in mainland China, where the leadership of the atheistic Communist Party has launched several liberation, revolution, and political movements. What of the conception of God was retained? During the Cultural Revolution, which turned out to be quite anti-cultural and not much of a revolution either, Chinese Christians suffered severely. So-called rebels regarded their cherished Bibles as nothing but poisonous weeds that must be uprooted. They criticized Christianity as a foreign religion and an imperialist cultural invasion. *Shangdi* had a strong foreign image, which was associated more with "Western imperialism" than with Chinese culture, while *Shen* was mostly associated with "ignorant and backward" ideas or "feudal superstition." My own experience of living in mainland China confirms this assertion. These attacks have forced the Chinese people to rethink and re-examine what they believe when they use the terms *Shangdi* or *Shen*. The Chinese churches have been growing rapidly since the Cultural Revolution, which reveals that knowledge of the true God has taken root, and that the terms are merely a sign. The knowledge of God that has come to the Chinese through the Bible and their experience of the living God give new meaning to whichever name they use. Both *Shangdi* and *Shen* are appropriate terms, which are Christianized and indicate the one true God. Archie Lee aptly concluded:

> In some cases, the impact of naming the biblical God in an Asian language results in the gradual Christianizing of the name, causing it to lose its original religious content. The proper name *Shangdi* in Chinese Classics and popular religions and the generic name *Shen*, referring to deity in general, are now mostly monopolized by Christians to refer to the biblical God.[22]

The catechism entitled *Questions and Answers on Important Doctrines of Christian Faith*, compiled and published by the Chinese Christian Council, has been widely distributed in mainland China since it first appeared in 1983. It has, to a large extent, contributed to the acceptance of both terms *Shangdi* and *Shen*. The catechism consists of one hundred sections in seven chapters. It is designed to be a fresh catechism following the dissolution of denominations according to the policy of mutual respect, based on the principle of seeking agreement and reserving differences. Thus, the catechism used alternative vocabularies side by side for certain terms, such as Sprinkling (or Immersion) for "Baptism," and Holy Communion (or The Breaking of Bread) for "Eucharist." However, the catechism used *Shangdi* or *Shen* interchangeably instead of giving alternative terms for "God," and the two terms appeared with almost equal frequency. According to the author of the catechism, Wang Weifan, a professor at Nanjing Theological Seminary, *Shen* represented the concept of Divine Immanence and *Shangdi* stood for Transcendence. However, at times he simply made his choice based on the rhythm of the expression. For example, he chose the monosyllabic term *Shen*, not the dissyllabic term *Shangdi*, in the expression *Duyi*

22. Ibid., 5.

zhen Shen (the one, true God) in order to fit into the Chinese four-worded phrase pattern.[23]

Why are there two editions of the Chinese Bible, one using *Shen* and one using *Shangdi*? The CCC's catechism answers: "It is simply a matter of difference in translation. In the original text of the Bible *Shen* and *Shangdi* have the same meaning."[24]

At the churches in various localities, enquirers' classes have used the catechism, where it serves as basic material for enabling new Christians to learn key doctrines of faith. It also serves as a work of reference for Bible study, both for groups and for individuals. Its influence is evident from the wide extent of its distribution.

Generally speaking, more conservative Chinese Christians favor *Shen*. The reasons given are as follows:

- Influence of the Little Flock.[25] The Little Flock, the largest Chinese Christian group among Protestant churches in China, was the only one that remained active and increased in numbers throughout the Cultural Revolution. This Christian group favors *Shen*.

- The *Shen* edition leaves a blank space before the Chinese character *Shen* implying reverence and denoting the difference from false gods. It may also have had a more practical consideration: the same plates as those used for printing the *Shangdi* edition could in that way also be used for the *Shen* edition, or the other way around. The term *Shangdi* needed space for two characters, which could be exchanged on the plates. However, Chinese believers have appreciated this because it coincides with Chinese culture, which leaves a space before an honorable subject to imply respect.

- *Shangdi* is used as a tag to express surprise or strong emotion, such as "O my God!" This practice of taking the Divine Name in vain never implicates the term *Shen*.

- The *shen* character can be combined with another part of a word, to form compounds, such as *shenji* (miracle,) *shensheng* (holiness,)

23. Interview with Wang in New York, in Oct. 22, 2006.

24. *Questions and Answers*, 4.

25. Little Flock is the nickname of an indigenous Chinese Christian group founded by Watchman Nee in the 1920s that called itself the "Christian Assembly" or the "Meeting Place." This title is popular and well known around the Western world, and it is a convenient means of identification. I use it here without intending any derogatory sense.

shenxue (theology,) *shenxueyuan* (seminary), etc. In these cases, *Shangdi* cannot replace *Shen*.

Evidence of Reception

As time passed, the difference between *Shangdi* and *Shen* increasingly faded into the background. To some degree, both terms are accepted and used according to the situation. In his speech on "Womanhood, Motherhood, and Deity," given to students at Nanjing Theological Seminary in 1986, Bishop K. H. Ting (Ding Guangxun), the principal of the seminary, selectively used *Shen* to refer to God instead of *Shangdi*, which he usually uses as an Anglican bishop. He explained his reasoning as follows:

> You may have noticed that I have not used the word *Shangdi* in my speech today but only the word *Shen* instead. Our God is the one who has many names. Each name reflects one of God's attributes. However, human language has certain limitations. *Shangdi* is a good term of address, yet it has a strong male connotation. To some people, this term is associated with the image of a fearsome emperor or powerful official who imposes his will on others. So, I will refrain from using this term in today's address.[26]

While giving this speech concerning womanhood, Bishop Ting carefully chose to use *Shen* instead of *Shangdi*, which he believes has a strong male connotation. Notably, this paragraph was omitted in his two collections in English: *Love Never Ends* (2000) and *God is Love* (2004). These two collections represent Ting's theological thinking. Both were published within five years of each other at the time when Ting was advocating his idea of "theological reconstruction," which shows Ting's willingness to be understood by the western world. The omitted paragraph about *Shangdi/ Shen* and God's image addresses the Term Question, which had plagued the Western Protestant missionaries in China for almost a century during the 1800s and 1900s. Ting omitted this paragraph from the English version, perhaps because he did not want to revive any term question troubles with his definition of *Shangdi*, which might draw people's attention away from the controversial idea of "theological reconstruction" that he advocated. It could be seen that he was trying to prevent any possible obstacles in order to gain more understanding and support from the outside world.

26. Ding, "Nuxing, Muxing," 232. Translated by the author.

Yuan Zhiming and Feng Bingcheng became senior intellectuals in the 1990s after expatriating to the United States. They are among the most prominent Chinese intellectuals abroad who have converted to Christ. Yuan, producer of the documentary film *The Cross: Jesus in China*, which appeared in 2003, and *Missionaries* in 2016, believes that the revelation of God did come to China in ancient history. *Tao, Tian,* and *Shangdi* are religious terms that Chinese ancestors used to refer to the Creator of the universe.[27] Nevertheless, *Shangdi* is not the only term Yuan uses. He adopts *Shen* as well, alternating it freely with *Shangdi*. Feng (pen-name Li Cheng), the author of *Song of a Wanderer: Beckoned by Eternity*, is a graduate of Beijing University and the Chinese Academy of Sciences and a former atheist. He earned his PhD from Michigan State University in the United States and has excellent credentials as a medical researcher. (Before trusting in Christ, he examined Christianity from a logical and scientific perspective. In 1992, he was baptized.) Despite being an advocate for atheism and individualism throughout his life, he was completely transformed by God's great love. He well understands how and what mainland Chinese scholars think, and he wrote this book to help answer the challenging questions of scholars who are searching for the truth. Yuan and Feng were baptized in 1991 and 1992, respectively, and have since become active and popular evangelists among the Chinese in North America and elsewhere. It is natural that they use both *Shangdi* and *Shen* when they refer to God in their sermons and works, which have a great impact on students and scholars in and outside of China.[28]

Obviously, the two terms no longer trouble the new generation of Christians who have grown accustomed to them. The result of my survey confirms this hypothesis. A Questionnaire on Chinese Bible Versions was used to investigate the opinions of Chinese Bible readers about the UV and their willingness to use *Shangdi/Shen* editions.[29] 36 percent of respondents preferred the *Shen* edition, but only 10 percent preferred the *Shangdi.* However, 54 percent of respondents claimed that it did not matter; they accepted both terms.

Even more relevant to my investigation is a popular song of "Canaan Hymns," written by a woman from the countryside with a grass-roots house

27. Yuan, *Shenzhou Chanhuilu,* xi.

28. See Yuan, *Dialogues on Christian Faith* 1997; Feng, *Youzi Yin* (Song of a Wanderer) 1996.

29. See appendix 5.

church background, the composer quite unselfconsciously uses *Shen* and *Shangdi* interchangeably. I will quote the lyrics of the song:

> O Lord! I praise you,
> because you've chosen me
> In the vast sea of people,
> it was you who found me.
>
> . . .
>
> O our almighty *Shen*!
> Our almighty *Shangdi*!
> It is you who raise us from the dust.

The composer's use of *Shen* and *Shangdi* interchangeably represents an increasingly common view that *Shen* and *Shangdi* are both one of the many forms of addressing God. These three reliable representatives—a leader of the official church, overseas converted intellectuals, and a lay person from a house church—demonstrate that Chinese Christians accept a plurality of names. Archie Lee sees this matter from a post-colonial framework:

> This [plurality of names] has not been accepted by the missionaries because of a limited ideology. The mission field did not allow the divine to be presented in multiple names. Given the elimination of the notion of the mission field, the plurality of religious traditions in Asia, and the multiplicity of translated divine names, the option is once again open.[30]

Since two terms are still in use, some consider the Term Question unresolved. However, there has been a shift from choosing either *Shen* or *Shangdi* to adopting both *Shen* and *Shangdi*. From the above examples, it is possible to draw the conclusion that the Term Question no longer persists among Protestants: *Shen* and *Shangdi* are Christianized names that both represent the true, living God. That they are used side by side shows that the term for God is no longer a point of conflict. For new generations, choosing the preferred Bible edition will depend more on their custom and preference rather than on the meaning of terms used that perplexed Western missionaries for so many years.

---

30. Lee, "God's Asian Names," http://sbl-site.org/Article.aspx?ArticleID=456.

Summary

The eighteen principles adopted by the UV translation project reflect the experience that missionaries had gained from almost a century of Protestant Bible translation in China. From this study, it is possible to draw the conclusion that the UV continued in the missionary tradition with a new emphasis on fidelity and readability. The translators also introduced some extra principles of marks and punctuation to make the text comprehensible.

Comparing the UV with the Peking Version shows that the UV successfully employed colloquial terms and Chinese common usage to lower the style of the PV. Close textual analysis of the first three chapters of Mark in the PV and the UV confirms that the UV translators presented an improved edition, though the PV had superior translations in certain aspects, such as proper nouns and syntactical features.

Among the 18 principles of translation, principles (3), (5), (7), and (8) might be an indirect reflection of the Chinese coworkers' presence and function.

Goodrich's description of the UV committee's work directly confirms involvement of the Chinese— "five native brethren"—who contributed to the proper rendering of more idiomatic Chinese versions.

One can safely conclude, therefore, that in spite of not being formal members of the committee, Chinese coworkers in reality had great influence on the committee work and on the final result. The fact that the UV achieved such a good literary standard, and as a result enjoyed widespread acceptance for almost a century, must be attributed in no small part to the active participation of the Chinese coworkers.

Deciding which Chinese term most suitably expressed "God," being called "Term Question," vexed Protestant missionaries throughout their Chinese Bible translation efforts. Every attempt to produce a conclusive result through collaboration ended by launching heated debates. Missionaries expressed their different opinions on this or that term in writing and wrote many letters to the press expressing strong convictions and deep feelings. The controversies continued for many decades without reaching any agreement. Eventually, with the passage of time, the controversies subsided.

Terms for "God" formerly regarded by one party or the other as unsatisfactory or wrong are still in use. Nonetheless, Christianity has not failed to take root in China, nor is it apparent that the quality of faith or character suffered thereby! The controversy forced the participants to examine their own beliefs while trying to understand the beliefs of the Chinese. Two camps made remarkable presentations, and some advocates, such as Medhurst, Boone and Legge changed their positions, but they failed to reach unanimity. While foreign missionaries were incapable of solving the Term Question, Chinese Bible readers and interpreters have resolved the problem of the name for God in their own way. The Chinese Christian Council's Catechism summed up the complex controversy of *Shangdi* vs. *Shen* simply as a matter of difference in translation. Most Chinese Bible readers are aware of the different *Shangdi* and *Shen* editions, but the two terms no longer perplex them. Although the greater number of Chinese Christians favor *Shen*, as my survey shows, both terms are increasingly accepted and used interchangeably.

5

Revisions

Early Efforts at Revising the Union Version

Efforts at revising the Union Version started early in the twentieth century. They may be called the Yanjing project as they were made by the professors of Yanjing University in Beijing led by their President John L. Stuart (1867–1962) and Liu Tingfang (1891–1947), Dean of the School of Religion of Yanjing University. Liu accepted Stuart's invitation and joined him at Yanjing in 1920 after ten years study in the United States. He, being also the main editor and translator of *Hymns of Universal Praise*, the most popular Chinese hymnal of the period, noticed that the language of the UV was often "unnaturally strained" and that changes in construction would better bring out the meaning. He believed that such a necessary revision "must be done by Chinese scholars."[1] There was no tangible action as a result, however. Liu left for the US in 1926 and his position was taken by Li Rongfang (1887–1965), the Old Testament professor. Li was considered to be an expert in Hebrew and Stuart also called him the "Chinese authority of Old Testament."[2] Another prominent professor at Yanjing University, Zhou Zuoren (1885–1967), one of the authorities and zealous advocates of the New Culture Movement, also supported a further revision of the UV. In 1926 a talented revision committee was formed, which, in addition to the

---

1. Kramers, "Some Thoughts," 157 n. 4.
2. Xu, *Jiaohui Daxue*, 124 n. 3.

above-mentioned Yanjing professors, included three capable men, Cheng Jingyi (1881–1939), Wei Zhuomin (1888–1976) and T. N. Wong, as well as two translators of the UV, Lewis and Aiken. Unfortunately, their work did not yield any significant results.

In 1939, the UV's name changed from *Guanhua Heheyiben* (Mandarin Union Version) to *Guoyu Heheyiben* (National Language Union Version) to reflect the new common term for Mandarin Chinese. This was the only change introduced to the UV in the first half of the century.

Opinions and Suggestions for Revision

Gu Dunrou

Some Chinese criticized the Union Version because foreigners had translated it rather than Chinese. Gu Dunrou, former President of Donghai University in Taizhong, Taiwan, was one of the sharpest critics. Gu was active as a Bible translator. He translated Philemon and the Beatitudes with Frank Price in 1958, and Psalm 90 and parts of Psalm 19 with Carl J. Schroeder in 1964. While working on a concordance for the UV, published in 1961, Gu had the opportunity to read the translation carefully. He detected many mistakes in it and recommended a number of revisions. In 1965, his article "Review of the Bible translation of the Mandarin Version" listed fifty-six shortcomings of the translation under three classifications (1) errors in the choice of words; (2) weaknesses in grammar and style; and (3) mistakes in translation.[3] These points are discussed in turn. The first classification included:

a) For terms that had become obsolete in modern Chinese, for example, Gu pointed out that *guizhou* for "noble-man" in Luke 19:12 should be replaced by a modern and popular term *guizu*. Another example was in Daniel 3:2 "the satraps, the deputies, and the governors, the judges, the treasurers, the counsellors, the sheriffs," these titles, which were translated into official titles in the Qing dynasty, were no longer in use and should be replaced by modern usage for the new generation.

---

3. This article was written in Chinese and collected in *Collection of Articles on Chinese Bible Translations*, edited by Jia Baoluo (Kramers), 1965. See Gu, "Shengjing Guoyu Ben," 110–34.

b) For terms that had changed meaning, for example, in Mark 7:3 "tradition" was rendered into *yichuan*, which now meant "heredity" as used in biology. Gu suggested *chuantong* as the term to replace *yichuan* for "tradition." In Philippians 2:1, *jiaotong* for "fellowship" was now used for "traffic;" a more contemporary term for "fellowship" could be *tuanqi*. The important word "fellowship," which appears four times in the first chapter of 1 John and at least seventeen times in the whole Bible, was translated as *xiang jiao*, which conveys the idea of "mutual relations" but does not have the precise meaning of fellowship.

c) Terms that were too colloquial included *Da mafeng* for "leprosy" in Matthew 8:2. Instead, *mafengbing* is now used. The word *yanzhong* for "approve" in 1 Thessalonians 2:4 was an expression only used in the Shandong colloquial dialect.

d) Transliterations that could cause misunderstandings included *youahdie* for "Euodia" in Philippians 4:2, which is an often-quoted example for such a transliteration. Another example was *hamule* for "Hamul" in Numbers 26:21. Characters giving the meaning of these transliterations could cause confusion in gender. Gu even suggested shortening proper names that were of seven syllables or more in length to suit Chinese custom and for readability, for instance, *jilisidu* for "Christ" in the early transliteration, is now shortened to *jidu*.

In the second category, weaknesses in grammar and style, Gu expressed two points:

First was the inharmonious mixture of classical Chinese and Mandarin, as in Proverbs 28:21 "To show partiality is not good." In the Chinese version, *kan ren qingmian, naiwei buhao,* the word *naiwei* is in literary or classical style, but the phrase *buhao* is strictly colloquial. To use *naiwei buhao* as a continuous, single expression sounds extremely amusing to native Chinese speakers. Nahum 1:9 asks "What do you plot against the Lord?" The Chinese version has the literary rendering of *she he mo* (what do you plot) within a colloquial interrogative sentence; this does not read smoothly.

Secondly, Gu also pointed out unclear or stylistically uncouth phrases. The UV translates the phrase "not in me" in Job 28:14 "The deep says, 'It is not in me,'" into Chinese as *bu zai wo zhong*. While *bu zai* is acceptable in Chinese, *wo zhong* is not at all natural. Gu correctly criticized this as simply not good Chinese.

In the third category, only a few instances were listed, as in cases where the original meaning of a phrase that was too difficult to translate had been changed, simplified, wrongly understood, or not clearly analyzed. For example, the UV translates the phrase "all the kings of Arabia" in 1 Kings 10:15 as "all the kings of the miscellaneous tribes." Another example is found in Galatians 3:1 "before whose eyes Jesus Christ was publicly portrayed as crucified." The translators rendered the short phrase "publicly portrayed" into Chinese as *huo hua* (lit. lively drawing) but this was an expression without any clear meaning.

Gu urged quick action to correct these errors that shouldn't appear, specially, in "the page of Holy Writ." He wrote, "These translation problems in the present Chinese Version (the Union Version) are by no means exhaustive. They do, however, represent some of the basic difficulties, matters which must be dealt with, and if possible, without delay, if the Scripture are to speak effectively to the Chinese-speaking community."[4] It was only in 2010, however, thirty-four of his fifty-six suggestions were considered and adopted by the Revised Chinese Union Version of 2010.

Wang Mingdao

Wang Mingdao (1900–91) was a well-known Chinese evangelist and founder of Peking Tabernacle Church, which was an independent Chinese church. He established a Christian magazine called *Spiritual Food Quarterly*. During 1936 to 1939, he published a series of articles in his quarterly magazine, suggesting revisions of the UV from a theological point of view. For instance, in I Corinthians 15:57 "But thanks be to God, who gives us the victory through our Lord Jesus Christ." The UV reads, "thanks be to God, who enables us to triumph through our Lord Jesus Christ." Wang criticized the translation because the word "victory" in the original Greek is a noun, but in Chinese it translates as a verb *desheng* (to triumph), which changes the meaning to be that we ourselves should fight and win the battle through Jesus Christ. He suggested the alternative translation *cigei women shengli* (to grant us the victory).[5]

Wang listed fifty verses in the New Testament where the expression *cong si li fuhuo* should be replaced by *cong siren li fuhua* for "rise from the

4. Gu, "Notes on the Chinese Version," 165.

5. Wang, "Xinyue Hanwen," 61.

dead." This suggestion was adopted by the New Testament revised version of 2006.

Liu Yiling

Liu Yiling (1901–94), an expert in Bible translation into Chinese, was another early critic. He loved the UV and considered it almost perfect, praising the UV as "the most beautiful classic literature in Mandarin."[6] Nevertheless, Liu was aware that the Chinese language had changed immensely since the publication of the UV, making revision necessary. In his article "A Suggestion for Revising the Chinese Bible," he gave fifty-eight deficiencies of translation that needed revision, particularly in the fields of terminology, grammar, punctuation, and new words. The following are some examples.

The terminology field included words that have different meanings in modern usage, e.g., the UV translated Isaiah 58:8 "and your healing shall spring up speedily" into *ni suode de yizhi yao susu faming*. The word *faming* for "spring up" had changed its meaning to "invent." Another example is *shouduan* for "handiwork" in Psalms 19:1. Modern Chinese used *shouduan* for "trick," which is derogatory. Obviously, it would not be a proper way to express "the firmament proclaims His handiwork." This group also included words that are no longer in use, such as: *zhizi* for "measure" in Ezekiel 4:11; *fanggao* for "the courts" in Acts 19:38; and *tongshi* for "interpreter" in Genesis 42:23; the latter should be replaced by the modern term *fanyi*.

Grammar examples included adding the particles *ba, ne, na* etc., to the end of phrases or sentences according to modern usage. It also included adding an adjective or adverb to make sentences clearer.

Liu's suggestions were based on his knowledge of Chinese grammar alone, however, since he knew neither Hebrew nor Greek, as he himself declared.[7] He also proposed the use of *ta* (he) with the "god" radical for God, and *ta* (she) with the female radical for a female third person pronoun, instead of using a male third person pronoun for all third person pronouns.

Liu's main concern was that a revision had to be strictly limited in order to keep the "UV style." He even suggested that Hong Kong would be a proper place for revising the UV as it would be easier for communicating with scholars from all over the world. He emphasized that the revision committee should be composed of skilled men from different denominations

---

6. Liu, "Gaiyi Zhongwen," 95.

7. Ibid., 98

and different disciplines: biblical scholars, well-known authors and translators from church circles, experts of Hebrew and Greek, and scholars of Chinese grammar.[8]

A great majority in the Chinese church viewed the UV as *the* authorized version, so criticizing the UV meant criticizing the Chinese Bible.[9]Liu later became one of the most zealous defenders of the UV when it was criticized in a series of articles by the translators of the *New Chinese Version*. *Yijing Luncong* is the collection of debates about the two Chinese Bibles, edited by Liu in 1979.

Li Rui

Li Rui was an industrialist of Shanghai. For many years he studied Hebrew and Greek. In his old age, he made an attempt to translate the Bible but appeared unsuccessful. Li proposed the revision of the UV particularly in the field of proper names. He listed more than three hundred names to be revised according to:

1) Hebrew meaning;

2) Consistency between the Old and New Testaments; and

3) Hebrew masculine or feminine endings.

However, the revision proposals in the 1950s and 1960s were never put into practice. In order to stimulate interest and concern for Chinese Bible translation, Robert P. Kramers collected all these articles on revising the UV into a book, entitled *Shengjing Hanyi lunwenji* (Chinese Bible translation), published in 1965. But revision of the UV was not really launched until the 1980s.

Various Revision Attempts

Revision Efforts by the United Bible Societies

The Chinese church recognized the need to revise and modernize the UV. In 1962, Eugene A. Nida, executive secretary for translation of the American Bible Society and translation research coordinator of the United Bible

8. Ibid., 108.

9. Liu, ed., *Yijing Luncong*, 96.

Society (UBS), visited Hong Kong and Taiwan. When he proposed the idea of a revision, the community expressed much hesitation, however. Nida met with church leaders to consider a dual approach, consisting of first a moderate revision, followed by a more general revision. Zetzsche aptly stated: "The consensus was that revisers should undertake the work outside Mainland China, since at that time there would be neither interest for such a project within China nor cooperation with churches outside of China."[10] In 1965, Christian leaders decided to produce a limited revision, with an emphasis on stylistic modification. They laid down basic principles and procedures, appointed revisers, and set up a plan for a review committee and a consultative committee. The work was scheduled to take five to six years, with as little publicity as possible so as not to arouse undue alarm.

The revision failed to take place as scheduled, however, mainly because the UBS and the Taiwan Bible Society began to focus their attention and invest their resources in a new translation based on Nida's translation theory of 'dynamic equivalence' (later 'functional equivalence'). The final product was named *Xiandai zhongwen yiben* "Today's Chinese Version" (TCV). After its publication in 1979, many promoted the TCV as the new Chinese Bible and the successor of the UV.[11]

In 1983, the respective Bible societies and church leaders got together again, holding conferences in Hong Kong, Taiwan, and Singapore to discuss the necessity of a UV revision. These discussions reached the consensus that they desired a revision that maintained the style of the UV and with changes as minor as possible. They would nevertheless continue to distribute the old edition of the UV after the publication of the revised edition. At a meeting held in Taiwan in August 1984, churches and UBS representatives discussed and defined thirteen principles for revision. They dealt with matters such as punctuation marks, names of persons, names of places, Chinese characters, terms with new meanings, pronouns, particles at the end of phrases, official titles, awkward expressions and sentence structures, section divisions, base texts, familiar terms, time, currency, and measures, see the list below for details:

1. Punctuation: Use the punctuation marks employed by everyday authors.

10. Zetzsche, *Bible in China*, 347.

11. Xiao Min, *Shangdi de Ai*, 1981

2. Names of Persons: Revise a small number of personal names that are crude or easily misunderstood. List old and new names in a comparative table in the appendix.

3. Names of Places: Alter biblical geographical names according to current usage. List old and new names in a comparative table in the appendix.

4. Chinese Characters: As much as possible alter characters that are difficult to read, or of a locally restricted use, to characters that an average reader can understand and are commonly used in modern Chinese.

5. Words: Some words in the Union Version were appropriate and well-defined at the time, but after having gone through many changes, may have acquired a different meaning. To avoid confusing the reader, change these into words that everyone can understand.

6. Pronouns: Distinguish the third person pronouns *ta* according to gender. Use the masculine pronoun *ta* if applied to "God," "Jesus," and "Holy Spirit," and use the neuter pronoun *ta* if applied to demons, animals, or things.

7. Particles at the End of Phrases: Revise particles like *ya* or *a* according to the natural trend of standard pronunciation.

8. Official Titles: If a title must be revised, use another ancient official title that is fairly well known, but add an annotation to make the range and office of administration clear to the reader. For instance, use *zongdu* "viceroy" instead of *fangbo* "governor."

9. Words and Sentences: If expressions are awkward for readers, revise them without harming the original style to make them understood or smoother when read aloud. These include: 1) words that are difficult to interpret; 2) words that belong to the classical or semi-classical language (change these to colloquial words under the condition that this does not influence the meaning); 3) some sentences with unclear meanings; 4) sentences that are grammatically incomplete, especially those without a subject.

10. Division of Sections: Do not change chapters and paragraphs, but for the sake of clarity do something about the division of sections; at the same time consider revising those headings that do not conform to the contents of the biblical text.

11. Biblical Text: For the revision of the New Testament, use the third edition of the Greek text of the UBS; for the Old Testament, use the Hebrew text of the UBS. In case there is a discrepancy between the text of the UV and the original texts, do not revise sentences of great familiarity, but add an annotation to explain that other manuscripts have a different reading.

12. Familiar Terms: Do not alter them; in cases of unclearness, add an annotation or explain them in a list of short annotations.

13. Time, Currency, and Measurements: Render according to the old version, but list the metric system or a table with today's exchange rates in the appendix and add explanations.[12]

After deciding on these principles, a revision committee was formed and started its work in Taiwan in 1985. The manuscript was to go through a review committee and a consultative committee. In 1986, a trial revised edition of Matthew was published and sent out for criticism.

At the same time as the revision work of the UV, the UBS undertook another UV revision project on a smaller scale in the mid-1980s and accomplished it with the publication of the New Punctuation UV in 1988. Despite its title, however, this revision did not only include punctuation, but also some other changes. The new edition's preface listed the changes:

- Replace the punctuation used in 1919 UV with common punctuation.
- Poetic passages of the original texts were arranged in poetic form.
- Some characters that were no longer in current usage were replaced with a different form of the same character. Used interrogative pronouns (*na*, 哪) rather than (*na*, 那) in questions.
- The names of persons that were written differently in current common use were emended;
- Geographical names were changed to modern usage;
- References were made to parallel passages under the headings of sections;
- The different characters used for the appropriate gender of the third person pronoun *ta* distinguished between the masculine gender *ta* 他

12. Liang, "Guoyu Heheben," 26. Translated by Zetsche.

and the feminine gender *ta* 她, as well as the neuter pronoun *ta* 牠 for animals, and yet another neuter pronoun *ta* 它 for things;

- The genitive particle *de* was added between related geographical names;

- Terms that occurred in both the Old and New Testaments were rendered consistently.[13]

None of these revisional changes included any major stylistic or terminological alterations to the biblical text, as its preface carefully stated that the text of 1919 UV they adopted had not been modified, so it could hardly arouse protests. This UV with new punctuation immediately won popularity, and it has supplanted the one with old punctuation. However, the introduction of new punctuation certainly can result in a different conveyance of meaning. In particular, the use of punctuation is often too heavy, and therefore points to the need for further revision.

Revision Efforts in Mainland China

Before the churches resumed their normal life in the vast land of China, Bishop Ding Guangxun, the former chair of the China Christian Council and the Three-Self Patriotic Movement (TSPM), gathered a group of his colleagues, including Wang Shenyin, Chen Zemin, Luo Zhenfang, Mo Ruxi, and other Protestant scholars, to revise the UV New Testament and Psalms in the summer of 1979. The work was taken up immediately, but it was uncertain when it would produce results. At the Third National Chinese Christian Conference in 1980, Ding said:

> Over the last decades, there have been developments in our Chinese language and written characters. Ancient biblical manuscripts have also been newly discovered. Therefore, it is necessary to carry out revisions of the Chinese translation of the Bible in order that it better expresses the original meaning. This, however, is a solemn, holy work and it must be carried out with care. It is impossible to estimate now when a new translation can be published and supplied for members' trial use. In any event, it will be a number of years hence.[14]

---

13. Preface of the New Punctuation UV, 1988. Translated by the author.
14. Ting, *Love Never Ends*, 66.

Besides the introduction of a new punctuation system and the use of simplified characters, it also included changes in terminology. Zetzsche summed up these changes in three categories:

- The first included the exchange of terms which were wrongly used, like the ancient term *qianliang* (land taxes) for "pay, wages" in Luke 3:14 with *liangxiang,* an ancient term for "soldier's pay."

- The second category included those terms which were not suitable or did not give the accurate meaning, like *youxing* for "to go about, to walk around" (John 7:1) which today predominantly means "demonstrate, march."

- The third category included those terms or phrases which wrongly translated the original. *Ta qibupiexia zhe jiushijiuzhi, wang shanli qu-zhao* . . . —"would he not leave the ninety-nine (sheep) and go into the mountains to search . . ."—of the Union Version in Matt. 18:12 was translated (and still is in the revised 1986 edition) according to the traditional interpretation of the *Authorized Version, English Revised Version,* or *American Standard Version.* According to modern interpretation, this phrase would have to be translated as *ta qibupiexia zhe jiushijiuzhi zaishanshang, quzhao* . . . — "would he not leave the ninety-nine (sheep) on the mountain and go and search. . ."[15]

However, the revised sections, which eventually included the Gospels, Acts, the Pauline Epistles, and the Psalms, were never published. According to Wang Weifan, this revision work could not be pursued due to the great activity that began in the Protestant church throughout the country, including the reopening of Nanjing Seminary in the beginning of the 1980s, because the main revisers were professors of Nanjing Seminary.[16]

When the churches reopened in 1980, it was found that the number of Christians had not declined during the ten-year calamity; on the contrary they had greatly increased. Reprinting the Bible became an urgent task, as some churches could not find a copy of the Chinese Bible for the pastor to take into the pulpit for Sunday services. So, the first Bible reprinted was not the revised UV but the photo-offset of the UV from the old 1919 edition with traditional complex characters in vertical lines. As church leaders had other preoccupations and more urgent matters to attend to, they had

---

15. Zetzsche, *Bible in China*, 357–58.
16. Wang, "Shengjing Yiben," 71.

neither time nor energy to consider revising the UV. Besides, a strong conservative voice from congregations had been against the idea of revising the UV, and this paralyzed the trial revision which began in 1979. The national Committee of the CCC/TSPM decided, instead of revising the UV, to establish a printing press to print the existing Bible in order to meet the great demand. With the help of UBS, the Amity Printing Press, a joint-venture, was set up in 1987 with the priority of printing the Bible. In 1988, after only one year, 505,291 copies of the UV were delivered from the printing press. In the first five years, the total printing reached 5,510,000 copies, including 240,000 Bibles in various minority nationality languages, such as Korean, Miao, Lisu, Yi, Jingbo, Wawa, and Lahu.[17]

In order to gain acceptance from the new generations, the CCC changed the layout of the Bible from vertical lines with complex characters to horizontal lines with simplified characters. The first New Testament and Psalms, with simplified characters in a horizontally printed version, appeared in 1986. It was the result of two years of hard work, as Shen Cheng'en, secretary of the revision committee, said:

> In April of that year [1984], with the support of the Shanghai churches, a group of twenty retirees, Christians of long standing, with experience in publishing or in language teaching, were gathered from among the churches in Shanghai to assist in this holy task. They had to be retired to ensure that they had the time to give to the task. They had to be Christians of long standing to ensure that they had the necessary familiarity with the Bible. It was also necessary that they have experience in publishing or in language teaching; the reason for this is self-evident. The task for these brothers and sisters was to copy out by hand the entire Bible and in the process mark out the verses (the old edition was divided into chapters but not verses), change traditional characters to simplified, and modernize the punctuation. In order to have a version printed in a horizontal format, they naturally had to do this in their copy.[18]

At the same time, some moderate revisions were included. The new edition's preface explains carefully the editorial changes:

---

17. Ibid., 71.

18. Shen, "Tantan Hengpaiben," 18. Translated by J. Wickeri.

- Modern punctuation was adopted according to the Mainland punctuation system (there were some differences from the 1988 UBS revision, such as quotation mark usage);

- The different characters used for the appropriate gender of the third person pronoun *ta* (he) were used for the masculine gender (including the persons of the Trinity) and *ta* (she, character with female radical) for the feminine gender, as well as the neuter pronoun *ta* (it, with animal radical) for animals and yet another neuter pronoun (it for things). (The latter was also different from the 1984 UBS revision where the same neuter pronoun was adopted for animals and things.)

- Characters for geographical names were changed according to current usage;

- Change was made to the particle *de*: another *de*, if applied to verbs, and *di* if applied to adverbs;

- The ending character of question sentences was changed from *me* to *ma*;

- Awkward wording was revised according to the Dictionary of Modern Chinese.

For certain traditional Christian terms, no alteration was made, however, such as *bobing* for "breaking bread," which was retained. All these revisions were accepted, except that *shifeng* (wait upon) was rejected as a substitute for *shifeng* (serve, ministry). Although the latter cannot be found in the Dictionary of Modern Chinese, it was believed to have a richer meaning than the former.

The whole Bible in the same format was issued by the Amity Printing Press in 1989 and was well received. By 1998, there were hundreds of letters sent to the CCC offering friendly suggestions on proofreading and punctuation, which greatly improved the quality of the printing.

In 1992, ten commissions were formed under the CCC/TSPM. One of them is the Commission of Bible Publication. Its main concern was reprinting the Bible to meet the great demand. Eighteen years after the establishment of the Amity Printing Press, the 40-millionth Bible, including in many different languages for other countries, was printed at the end of 2005. It took the Press nine years to reach its first 10 million Bibles but only three years to complete its fourth 10 million copies, (now the number has reached more than 75 million), due to escalating demand for Bibles in China and overseas.

The Commission of Bible Publication has served the Chinese churches in mainland China since the early days of its reopened after the Cultural Revolution. As its name implies, revision of the Bible was not in its plans. The Commission has goals in seven fields:

1. to make annual plans for Bible publication

2. to arrange and coordinate Bible distribution

3. to edit and correct errors of printing

4. to publish the Bible in existing ethnic languages, such as Korean, Yi, and Miao

5. to publish various Bible reference tools including the Bible with a commentary

6. to promote Bible translation in modern Chinese

7. to take part in international exchanges for Bible publication

The Commission made great achievements in the first five fields. The original four Bible distribution centers located in the big cities have grown to seventy, distributed throughout the country. Although their proposal for setting up a UV revision committee was not accepted, the effort they made to produce a more user-friendly Union Version bore fruit in 1998. The product was named *Shengjing: Jianshiben* (Holy Bible: concise commentary version), comprising the following new features:

- abstract and outline of each book,

- simplified characters in two columns, with a horizontal layout,

- poetic passages of the original texts printed in an arrangement of lines displaying the characteristic form of poetry,

- modern usage of the genitive particle *de*,

- characters for geographical names changed according to current usage,

- certain simplified characters were revised according to *The Chart of Simplified Characters* reissued by National Literary Committee in 10 October, 1986.

These revisions were mostly of an editorial nature. At the invitation of the UBS, the CCC/TSPM decided to participate in its UV revision project by reviewing the drafts. The UBS even more valued their participation. After all, the majority of Bible readers live in mainland China.

Recent Results of Revision

Revision Effort in Taiwan

From 1996 to 2005, there was an ongoing effort to revise the UV, led by Wang Zhengzhong in Taiwan. This revision project emphasized the original text. Based on the eight principles used for revising the King James Version, they laid down three elementary principles: 1) do not add or subtract from any original text meaning; 2) identify proper names with the original characters along with Chinese transliteration, to retain consistency; 3) do not affect the fluency of the original sentence while modifying a sentence or a word.[19] There were more than three thousand revisions throughout the whole Bible. This was the first production of a UV revision according to the Hebrew and Greek texts. It is named The Holy Bible: Chinese Union Version (Standard Edition). It appeared in March 2005. Without Bible Society support, it remains a question as to how widely this revised Standard Edition can be circulated.

The Latest Result of United Bible Societies

Since 1983, the UBS have held a number of Chinese Union Version revision seminars in Hong Kong, Singapore, and other Asian countries to discuss with church leaders the details of the project. Most Chinese church leaders have unanimously agreed with the need to revise the existing edition, but the revision project did not really get off the ground until 1984. The chief reviser was I-Jin Loh, with Zhou Lianhua as the editor; both were the translators of the TCV.

From its inception in 2000, this project was supervised and financed entirely by the Hong Kong Bible Society (HKBS), but it is understood that once published, the revised UV will be promoted and distributed by the CCC/TSPM in China and by Bible societies in other places. To ensure the revision is accepted by Chinese churches in Mainland China and overseas,

19. Wang, *Shengjing Hehe Yiben*, 74.

HKBS invited Chinese pastors and ministers from varying denominational backgrounds and from all over the world to participate in the project. According to news reports, there was a total of 149 church leaders acting as consultants of the revision project in Hong Kong.

After 22 years, the revision project finally produced its first fruit: The New Testament of the Revised Chinese Union Version. The dedication service was held on April 24, 2006 in Hong Kong. During the service, copies of the Revised New Testament were given to representatives of churches, adults, and young people, symbolizing that the revised edition is suitable for everyone to read.[20]

There was a plan to see the Old Testament completed and published by 2007, to coincide with the bicentenary of Robert Morrison's arrival in China. Unfortunately, it was impossible to fulfill. The new goal set for publication was 2010. The goal was finally achieved, the fruit of 27 years labor, and now known as CUV2010.

Summary

When the UV was first published in 1919, the missionaries involved in the translation acknowledged that their work would play only a temporary role before another Bible translation produced by native Chinese speakers could replace it. The Chinese Church has developed a conservative momentum of its own over the decades, however. The UV immediately gained acceptance by the Chinese Church after its publication. Not only was it accepted, it was also embraced as an authorized, canonical book, not to be replaced or altered. In the 1950s and 1960s, individuals offered several revision proposals. They were never carried out, however. Despite the ongoing evolution of the Chinese language over the years, when the idea of revision was proposed in 1962, the reaction was much hesitation. Nevertheless, the need for a better and more readable text was clearly felt.

Various revision efforts have been made since the 1980s. Moderate revisions appeared from time to time, most of which being of an editorial nature. Recent results included two revisions of the UV; one is the Chinese Union Version (Standard Edition), which was published in Taiwan in 2005; the other is the Revised Chinese Union Version New Testament, published in Hong Kong in 2006. The complete revision of the UV took almost a much time as the original translation, and finally appeared in 2010.

20. See http://www.Gospelherald.com.

Part III

Probing the Authority of the Union Version and Its Challenges

6

Unique Significance

FOR A CENTURY, THE Union Version (UV) has enjoyed a solid position in the hearts of Chinese Protestants worldwide. It has become the one version that meets every need in a Chinese Christian's life. Whether it is for congregational worship, training church leaders, group Bible study, or individual devotions, the UV has gained the status of the most acceptable version. This is an astonishing phenomenon.

Since the 1920s, the church in mainland China has stressed the need to be indigenous: self-governing, self-supporting, and self-propagating. It has sought to free itself from foreign mission affiliations, which were viewed as imperialist, and all foreign missionaries were required to leave China. Not a single missionary or mission society could be found in China in the early 1950s. Western missionaries disappeared, but the Bible translation that they had labored to create remained. The Three Self Patriotic Movement (TSPM) leadership did not seem to realize that the UV stood as a witness to the missionaries' contribution to the Chinese church. The urge to carry out the principles of the TSPM did not shake the authority of the UV.

During the Cultural Revolution (1967–77), Bibles were burned, and churches were closed. When churches reopened after the Cultural Revolution, one of the most urgent tasks of the China Christian Council (CCC) and the TSPM was to provide Bibles to the people. Although there were already translations produced purely by native Chinese, the CCC and the TSPM leaders did not pursue self-translation, but rather simply embraced the UV, and thousands of copies were printed to meet the tremendous needs. Despite its close relationship with Western missionaries, not only has the UV not been banned, but it has enjoyed being the most popular version in China for a century.

Also noteworthy is the fact that the UV was produced during an era when the nation experienced a change in language. While literature had traditionally been written in classical Chinese, the vernacular language of the masses now became a literary vehicle. From the late 1970s to the beginning of 1990s, translation teams published a number of versions in modern Chinese. These include: The Chinese Living Bible (1979), Today's Chinese Version (1979), and The New Chinese Bible (1992). Yet none of these versions has been as widely circulated or been as accepted by Chinese Christians worldwide as the UV.

Why did the UV quickly supersede the other versions that existed before it and why has it so far not been supplanted by the various versions coming after it? What is the uniqueness which gives it such a firm position in the hearts of Chinese Christians? The phenomenon of the authority of the UV deserves further careful study.

1919, a Demarcation Line in the History of Chinese Bible Translation

Scholars who study the history of Chinese Bible translation, whether foreigners or Chinese, have different ways of dividing the process and periods. Some organize according to significant periods, others according to translators, translations, or translation stages. Whatever way they choose, they all take 1919, the year when the UV appeared, as a crucial date.

1. Division by significant periods.

   From the Beginnings to 1890

   From 1890 to 1919

2. Division by translation stages

   Early Translation Stage: Tang Dynasty–1807

   Developing Translation Stage: 1807–1854

   Bible Popularization Stage: 1854–1919

   Indigenous Chinese Translation Stage: 1919–Present

3. Division by the development of translation

   Elementary Translation Era: Tang Dynasty–1807

Mature Translation Era: 1807–1850

Common/Union Era: 1850–1919

Translation by Chinese Era: 1919–Present

4. Division by translators

The Nestorian: 7th Century

The Roman Catholic: 13th and 16th Century Onward

The Protestant Missionaries: 1807–1919

The Protestant Chinese: 1920–[1]

It was just as Murray said in his review of the completed UV, "the year 1919 will remain memorable in the history of the Chinese church as marking the completion of that great task." Evidently, the UV is generally acknowledged as an important landmark in the history of Chinese Bible translation. Gu Dunrou, a Bible translator, regarded the emergence of the UV as an "epoch-making event"; Xu Mushi, one of translators of the TCV, praises the UV as a "brilliant star," and Zetzsche, a German expert on Chinese Bible Translation, judges that it is the culmination of Protestant missionary Bible translation in China.[2]

The Missionaries' Enduring Desire

There were two distinguishing features during the period of Protestant missionary Bible translation (1807–1919). One was the considerable quantity of Bible translations and the other was that Bible translation became a dominant issue in missionary meetings. Many heated debates on the theory of translation, language style, theological terms, and other questions arose among the missionaries.

Did missionaries and churches eagerly desire a uniform, standard version at this time? Three historical events may cast light on this question.

First, a circular addressed to the Protestant Missions in China sent out by the Methodist Episcopal Mission in 1864 expressed the general expectation:

---

1. For the list see 1. Zetzsche, *Bible in China*, 1999; 2. Zhuang, *Jidujiao Shengjing*, 2000; 3. Li, "Zhongwen Sheng jing," 1978; 4. See Introduction.

2. The quotes in this paragraph: Murray, "New Mandarin Bible," 439; Gu, "Shengjing Guoyuben," 110; Xu, *Jing yu Yijing*, 142; Zetzsche, *Bible in China*, 1999.

We are happy to believe that all the Protestant missionaries labor-
ing among the Chinese are united in opinion as to the propriety
and importance of having one uniform and standard version of
the Sacred Scriptures in the general language of China. The evils
resulting from circulating, in the same language, different versions
of the Word of God, are so great and manifold that no Christian
mind can reflect upon the subject without profound sorrow. You,
doubtless, have deplored the apparent antagonism which has existed for years between the great representative Bible Societies of
Europe and America, and also between the different Protestant
Missions in China on this subject . . . We are not insensible to the
difficulties in the way of the proposed enterprise . . . But we cannot
believe that the present conflicting views of Protestant Missionaries are to become stereotyped and indicate for all coming time the
normal state of the Christian Church in China.[3]

As early as the mid-nineteenth century, missionaries desired to have
one standard version. However, due to the differing opinions among missionaries and their mission societies, it was twenty-five years before it could
become reality. An 1888 record stated: "there is a general desire for a Union
version, but the impression prevails that the time for it has not yet come."[4]

Secondly, the momentous decision to adopt as the union version
project— "One Bible in three Versions"—was made at the 1890 Missionary Conference. The emotional reaction of the delegates was remarkable,
revealing their great desire for a unified version. When they unanimously
adopted the reports of the three Union Version committees, the whole
company rose as one man and sang the Doxology. Dr. Wright, editorial
secretary of British and Foreign Bible Society, recalled the enthusiastic moment and said: "I saw tears of joy in the eyes of strong men, and my heart
was too full to permit my lips to sing."[5] It was through such an emotional
response that missionary delegates showed their desire for a union version.

Thirdly, when the UV was completed and published in 1919, the mission of translating the Bible into Chinese was fulfilled by this satisfactory
translation. However, any translation for which the main responsibility lay
with foreigners was considered to have a preliminary character. A general
hope was expressed that the next revision or re-translation of the Bible
would be the work of Chinese Christian scholars. H. B. Rattenbury of the

3. Broomhall, *Bible in China*, 87–88.

4. Ibid., 88.

5. *Records 1890*, 518.

Wesleyan Methodist Mission Society expressed this sentiment in his review of the UV:

> On the whole my feeling is that this is the last and the greatest translation of the Scriptures where the burden of the work ultimately rests on foreigners, but that the final Chinese version will be very different, especially in the New Testament . . . The final Chinese version will never come until we have *Chinese* scholars, deeply versed in the original tongues, masters also of Mandarin, translating into their own native tongue. It is for the church to prepare her Hebrew and Greek scholars.[6]

This indicates that the UV was, within the missionaries' ability, the translation that most satisfied their desires. This satisfaction brought a temporary end to the largest Bible translation project in the history of the Chinese Protestant church. The quotation above shows that missionaries realized that a translation made by non-native translators had its limitations and inadequacies. Thus, they presented the UV, the best translation they could effort, to the Chinese church. At the same time, they also passed the baton of Chinese Bible translation to the Chinese Church in great expectation of seeing the final Chinese version made by native translators into their vernacular.

The Need of the Chinese Church

The period between the Protestants' first entry into China (1807) to the emergence of the UV (1919) was the "planting stage" of evangelism by Western missionaries in China. How did the Chinese church grow? Why was Bible translation so assiduously pursued at this stage? Was the UV the result of a need of the Chinese church? To answer these questions, we may receive some inspiration from the works of Zhao Tian'en, who analyzes the development of the Chinese church by dividing it into nine periods.[7] We will focus on the first five periods:

1. The preparation stage for mission in China (1807–42). In the early nineteenth century, European and American Protestant churches had a vision for missions and launched their overseas mission ministry. However, under the closed-door policy of the Qing dynasty, foreigners

6. *Recorder 1919*, 442–43.
7. Zhao, "Cong Huaren Jiaohui," 345–46.

were not allowed to travel or to spread the gospel in China. They had to make preparations in Hong Kong and Macao for future mission to China. The first Protestant missionary to China, Robert Morrison of the London Missionary Society, arrived in 1807. He had originally secured his presence in Guangzhou as a translator for the East India Company. In this way, he was able to work on Bible translation.

2. The beginning of the China mission in treaty ports (1842-60). When the first Opium War concluded with the Treaty of Nanking, foreigners were allowed to establish churches for evangelism in five treaty ports: Shanghai, Ningbo, Fuzhou, Xiamen (Amoy), and Guangzhou (Canton). However, missionaries were forbidden to go any further into the inland of China. Therefore, the only people for them to evangelize were their house servants or the poor in the streets. Only a few people were won to Christ during this period.

3. The pioneer stage of mission to the interior of China (1860-90). The Tianjin Treaty (1858) and the Peking Treaty (1860), signed after the wars between China and Great Britain (1858), gave Western missionaries a great priority and opportunity. More treaty ports were opened, and missionaries were allowed to evangelize Chinese, to spread the gospel all over China, and were protected by Chinese government. After 1861, missionaries went to China in large numbers to begin their ministry in many fields: educational, medical, social, and literary. However, this stage was also the height of anti-Christian agitation stirred up by Chinese officials and intellectuals (1860-74). During this period, there were many local conflicts involving missionaries, and numerous missionaries were killed. The church in China had to face great pressure and Christian ministry was restricted.

4. The stage of mission development all over China (1890-1911). During this period, the socio-political situation changed greatly as a result of the Sino-Japanese War (1894-95), Boxer Uprising (1900), Nationalist Revolution (1911), and collapse of the Qing Dynasty (1911). Chinese officials and intellectuals lost faith in Confucian culture and politics and became interested in Western civilization. In general, the attitude of Chinese people toward Christianity started to change; cultural and political resistance to the gospel was reduced. Western missionaries, Chinese assistant preachers and pastors, and church

members increased in number. This was the first important period for the growth of the church in China.

5. The heyday of China mission (1911-1919). During the period from the establishment of the Republic of China to the May Fourth Movement, despite problems created by warlords, Christianity was accorded legal status and Christians became legal citizens rather than "believers of a foreign religion" protected by Western missionaries. The new educated class expressed a keen interest in Christian teaching. Many new churches were opened, and China witnessed its most rapid growth of Protestant Christianity to date. Well-known foreign evangelists were invited to hold national crusades, and Chinese church leaders initiated several great movements for evangelism, such as the Chinese Home Missionary Society (1918) and the China for Christ Movement (1919). In this period, successful church growth was obvious. From 1910 to 1920, the number of missionaries increased from 5,144 to 6,204; the number of believers increased from 167,075 to 366,524; the number of seekers increased from 71,500 to 313,254. That was the highest record ever since Christianity first arrived in China.

From the above, we learn that throughout this whole planting stage the process of China mission development was slow in the first three stages (1807–1890). Due to enormous political and cultural resistance to Christian ministries the number of believers increased very little and various Chinese Bible translations were produced. It was only in the fourth and fifth stages (1890–1919), that Christians began to enjoy any freedom of evangelism. During this period, in the United States and Great Britain, the student gospel movement arose on university campuses, which led to the Student Volunteer Movement for Foreign Mission. Many came to China and greatly influenced the development of the Chinese church. These well-educated missionaries raised the educational level of the mission schools in China. Many mission high schools and colleges were established at this time; they introduced to the Chinese Church the method of training in Western seminaries and Bible schools, which helped the Chinese greatly in training ministers and disciples. The Western culture and ideology they brought with them not only made a contribution to the development of the Chinese Church, but also to the modernization of China, and won the admiration of Chinese scholar-officials and the respect of Chinese society for Christianity. Thus, the church grew rapidly. With the increase of foreign and local ministers, the number of believers and seekers multiplied. A Chinese Bible was greatly needed.

"Let the people read the Bible in their own language." This was the vision of Protestant missionaries, and Bible translation was a practical action for fulfilling this vision. However, as missionaries from different countries and backgrounds went into different parts of China, they produced different translations of the Bible. According to Spillett's catalogue, by the 1880s, there were at least eleven versions in use, excluding twenty-five translations in local dialects, either in Chinese character or in roman script.[8] The growing church could not benefit from such a multitude and variety of Bible translations. The proliferation of versions caused increasing confusion, which gradually led to a strong desire for a standard, uniform translation. So, it was regarded as a remarkable achievement when the 1890 General Conference reached an agreement to produce the Union Version—one Bible in three versions—to replace all other versions.

Coincidently, this period, from 1890 to 1919, was the formative period of the UV. The union version project was launched in 1890 and the UV appeared in 1919. The arrival of the UV met the great needs of the Chinese Church at that time and was well received. Despite much criticism, the UV remains popular and has served the Chinese Christians at every time of need.

The Role of the Union Version in the New Culture Movement

Soon after the Nationalist Revolution of 1911, the New Culture Movement began, which was marked by freedom of expression and an attitude of criticism. All schools of classical culture were under severe re-examination. All old patterns of thought and custom were relentlessly criticized. Even Confucian ideology and practice came under strong attack and were regarded as products of traditional feudalism, seen as incompatible with a democratic society and unfit for the demands of the modern world.

The New Culture Movement was led by a new type of Chinese intellectual: those who were educated in the colleges and universities operated by Christian missionaries in China, or those who received academic degrees abroad and returned to their homeland. These Chinese intellectuals were well educated in the spirit of Western modernity and also possessed

8. Spillett, *Catalogue of Scriptures*, 1975.

strong backgrounds in Chinese culture. Above all, they were patriots who found themselves facing the important question of how to build a new and modern China out of the political and social disorder that warlords had brought to the nation. For them, the only hope of modernizing China was to introduce "Mr. Sai" (Science) and "Mr. De" (Democracy) to the nation. The return of these Chinese intellectuals from overseas and the introduction of Western ideas through literature contributed to a process of cultural confrontation and assimilation.

One of the greatest achievements of the New Culture Movement was to replace the classical literary style with Mandarin, the written vernacular. Mandarin was no longer to be called *guanhua* (official language), but *baihua* (plain language), clearly showing the aim of the reformers to create one common language for all of China. The *baihua* movement really marked the beginning of a new development in the field of language. Obviously, it was the reason why the Mandarin Union Version, and not the *Wenli* Union Version, became the more popular.

It is highly significant that the term *baihua* soon had to make way for the term *guoyu* (national language), as it was, after a long debate, officially defined as the Chinese national language in 1913. This change in terminology indicated that the literary renaissance, begun by a handful of intellectuals in Peking, had gained the official sanction of Republican leaders. *Guoyu* became the vehicle of newly-born Chinese nationalism, and it began to be promoted by official means.[9]

Two years later, the New Culture Movement was followed by the May Fourth Movement, begun in Peking under the inspiration of some intellectuals from Peking University. While it soon became a demonstration of widely felt national feeling among the urban working class, the May Fourth Movement was also an intellectual and cultural revolution in the name of science and democracy. It repudiated the old China and sought to replace it with a new, modern China able to stand on her own. The movement was directed against feudalism and the reigning Confucian orthodoxy. While its emphasis was based on the influx of new Western ideas, its primary goal was to erase the humiliation of China by imperialism and strive for national power and prosperity.

---

9. The term *guoyu* is still used in Hong Kong, Taiwan, and among the overseas Chinese, whereas Mainland China uses today's official term *putonghua* (common language) which was coined in 1956 by the Chinese government. *Putonghua* replaced *guoyu* to respect national minorities.

A comparison of dates reveals some interesting facts about the UV: The Nationalist Revolution took place in 1911; what is called the "Literary Renaissance"—the New Culture Movement—began in 1917; and the May Fourth Movement began in 1919. The decision to produce the UV was made in 1890; a first draft of the New Testament appeared in 1907; and the complete Bible, with a revised New Testament, was published in 1919. Comparing these dates immediately shows the great significance of the UV, in that it appeared at precisely the right time. Not only was the publication of the UV in tune with the general spirit of the time, but this version could also play a role in contributing to the formation of the new literary language. The UV was recognized by many as a model for *baihua*. In fact, the Gospels were apparently even used in some governmental schools as a model for standard *baihua*, a fact which has been noted by many scholars.

As we can see, the movements that took place in the field of linguistics were an outward sign of a spiritual crisis that was rocking the whole of traditional Chinese society. Western notions had been influential in bringing about a revolutionary tension in the old empire, hastening the day of the 1911 Chinese Revolution. Christianity, brought through the efforts of Western missionaries, was very much seen as part of this Western impact. Moreover, the Scriptures, which were in many ways so fundamental to Western notions, were translated in the UV using *baihua*, the new literary medium. So, the UV could not have appeared under more favorable circumstances. Western cultural influence gained momentum after the revolution. The fruits of "Western learning" were apparent in most of the new literature. Biblical motifs could be found in the works of many great writers such as: Lu Xun (1881–1936), Mao Dun (1896–1981), Guo Moruo (1892–1978), Wen Yiduo (1899–1946), etc. This shows that the UV was widely read and accepted even in non-Christian circles. However, this was chiefly for its literary, rather than its religious, value.

Did the UV play a role in this radical language change? In his interview by Marshall Broomhall, Cheng Jingyi (1881–1939), the most prominent leader of the Chinese church, answered: "With regard to your question as to whether the widespread use of the Mandarin Bible played any part in making easy the introduction of *Kuoyu* [*guoyu*] as a literary medium, I believe it has . . . While one cannot say that the Mandarin Bible has been the means of introducing the new style of writing in China, it must have played an important part in the matter."[10]

10. Broomhall, *Bible in China*, 7.

How did Chinese intellectuals view this question? Zhou Zuoren, one of the authorities of the New Culture Movement, gave a lecture on "The Bible and Chinese Literature" at Yanjing University in 1920, in which he first pointed out the excellence of the *baihua* style of the translated Bible and predicted the influence of the UV on modern Chinese language:

> We can see from the European Bible translations that they all stood in relation to the development of art in their respective countries, like Wycliffe's translation in England or Luther's in Germany. China has the same hope today. The European Bible translations helped to accomplish the unification and development of the national languages of their respective countries. This was unintentional, because it [Bible translation] was religiously motivated. The time, place, and position of the Bible in China is very different than in Europe, and the result will therefore also be different; nevertheless, the reform of the Chinese language and literature can gain much help and profit from it. . . .
>
> Fourteen or fifteen years ago, in the time of the 'back-to-the-ancient ideology,' I was not very pleased with the classical translation of the New Testament. I considered retranslating the Gospels, not only to correct the mistakes of the *Authorized Version* but also to shape it into the style of great classical elegance comparable to the Buddhist canonical books, for only that would have been suitable. This eventually did not happen . . . Four or five years ago I still planned to retranslate Jesus' parables according to the example of the *Baiyu jing*. But now I think that the Mandarin translation [Union Version] is really quite good, and even has great literary value. Although the requirements of a good model are uncertain, it nevertheless can be said that this is Mandarin of rarely seen quality. This translation, though made with religious goals, and hardly any literary consideration, has preserved, because of its most diligent translation technique, the flavor of the original in many places, thus increasing its value as translated literature. . . .
>
> I am reminded of someone who opposed the new literature, maintaining that these literary productions were not new because they all came from "The Gospel According to Matthew." At the time I felt that his statement was ridiculous, but when I recall it now, I am prepared to admire his insight. "The Gospel According to Matthew" bears indeed the earliest Mandarin in (translated) European literature, and I predict that it will have a very great and very deep relation to the future of new Chinese literature.[11]

---

11. Zhou, "Shengjing yu Zhongguo," 6–7, translated by Zetzsche.

In her study on the UV and the New Literature in China, J. Wickeri states: "The Bible may have briefly been recognized as a model for translation during the early part of the May Fourth movement and, as noted earlier, had some impact as a model for *baihua* prose."[12] But she concluded there was no direct causality, in either direction, between the launch of the *baihua* movement and the production of the UV.

More positive views towards the status of the UV are found among Chinese scholars. Zhu Weizhi (1905–99), professor at Nankai University in Tianjin, is the best-known scholar in the field of comparative studies of the Bible and Chinese literature in China today. In his monograph entitled *Christianity and Literature* (1941), he presented his views concerning the relationship between the Bible and literature: "I think, since the Republic of China, the largest contribution of Christianity in China to the Chinese literature, is firstly, the publication of the Chinese Bible, the Union Version; secondly, is the publication of *Hymns of Universal Praise* [Hymnary]. Although neither is perfect, it can at least be said that they have laid the foundation of Christian literature, moreover they have been pioneers in new literature, which is worth recording in letters of gold."[13]

After 1949, works on the Bible and biblical studies were not printed in China. Zhu's research came to a halt. It was after the Cultural Revolution that he resumed work by reintroducing biblical literature, such as in his *Twelve Lectures on Biblical Literature* (1989). In this series of lectures, he still reckons that the UV was a pioneer in the New Culture Movement.

Subsequent researchers have shared positive comments on the UV. Xu Zhenglin, a professor at Shanghai University, believes the UV had "a distinct influence on the Chinese language and colloquial literature"[14]; Chen Jianming, a professor at Sichuan University, studied the impact of modern Christian publication in China on Chinese society and expressed the same thought that the UV, to some extent, had "a profound impact on the *baihua* movement" and "the emergence of the UV was the promotion of the *baihua* movement."[15]

12. Wickeri, "Union Version," 148.

13. Zhu, *Jidujiao yu Wenxue*, 151.

14. See Xu Zhenglin's viewpoint in Liang, "Twenty Years," 400. In his thesis, Xu attempts to investigate into how the Bible, via Christianity as one aspect of Western culture, has exerted a great influence on modern Chinese literature.

15. Chen, *Jiyang Wenzi*, 208.

It may be true that the *baihua* of the Bible did not form the literary language, because it already existed in novels. But to translate a sacred book into the common speech, which later became the national language, was another thing. The missionaries had begun to publish the scriptures in Mandarin sixty years before Chinese scholars supported this *baihua* movement. The appearance of the UV, a successful translation, displays the church in China as a pioneer in producing literature in the vernacular language. Although the emergence of the literary *baihua* was not the motivating force behind the appearance of the UV, the development of *baihua*, as shown by Zetzsche,[16] contributed to the reception of the UV in the southern provinces where the people spoke distinctly different dialects from Mandarin. This enabled the UV to become a veritable uniform and standard translation for all of Chinese.

The UV had already replaced other translations after a decade of circulation, a fact that must be attributed, to a certain degree, to the development of *baihua* literature, which by that time had attained nationwide acceptance as the new form of Chinese literature. Although one cannot say that the UV played the role of leading the New Culture Movement, its pioneer status must certainly be recognized. The result of these movements adds weight to the influence of the UV and credits the formation of the UV as in some ways authoritative.

On a related note, education was one of the major activities of Protestant missions. A study made in 1923 by James Y.C. Yan, educator and founder of the national Mass Education Movement, showed that by the end of the First World War, 90 percent of Chinese could not read or write. Missionaries gave much attention to "illiteracy education," among other social concerns, such as opium smoking, foot-binding, concubinage, and female infanticide. In 1914, there were 4,388 Protestant primary schools with 118,294 pupils, and 184 middle schools with 12,698 pupils throughout China. Six years later, the number had increased to 6,601 primary schools with 184,487 pupils and 291 middle schools with 15,212 enrolled.[17] Obviously, schools run by Protestant churches developed rapidly in the first twenty years of the twentieth century. Various devices were employed to reduce illiteracy. Many of the first textbooks of this "new learning" were produced by missionaries, and the Mass Education Movement, launched in 1923, was birthed by the YMCA, a Protestant organization.

16. Zetzsche, *Bible in China*, 333.

17. He, *Jidujiao Zaihua*, 39.

Protestant churches made a great effort to enable all members to read the Bible for themselves. The Phonetic Promotion Committee of the National Christian Council had as its motto: "Every Christian a Bible reader and every Christian a teacher of illiterates."[18] The UV in *baihua* enabled learners to master the skill of reading and writing easily, and it gave stimulus and impulse to the art of reading. Many adult Sunday schools in church and literacy classes in the countryside were established by the church to instruct the populace in the rudiments of reading, contributing greatly to the campaign to eliminate illiteracy.[19] A careful record of one missionary in North China showed that at least 90 percent of those who could not read when they became catechumens learned to read before receiving baptism.[20] By the late 1920s, a noteworthy achievement was evident: according to the eminent church historian Kenneth S. Latourette, 60 percent of the men and 40 percent of the women who were church members were sufficiently literate to read the UV New Testament with some degree of fluency, a much higher proportion than in the nation at large.[21]

The Effect of Reference Works

Any translation has to be done well in order to be accepted, and this is one reason why the UV became favored. The version was praised for its great faithfulness to the Greek and Hebrew, its conveyance of meaning with colloquial Mandarin, and its elegance of style. The influence of the UV also gained momentum after the appearance of several biblical reference works.

The Concordance of the Old and New Testament in the Revised Union Mandarin Version UV was produced by the foresighted missionary, Courtenay H. Fenn (1866–1953). He published his New Testament Concordance in 1909, soon after the New Testament Mandarin version appeared in 1906. After the completed UV appeared in 1919, the complete concordance to the UV was published in 1923. It has been one of the standard works of reference that accompanies the UV. This was a tremendous work: dividing verses in which were over one million characters into 22,800 entries, and then classifying them according to over 3,000 subjects. A great achievement!

18. Latourette, *History of Christian Missions*, 781.
19. Chen, "Mantan Heheben Shengjing," 21.
20. Broomhall, *Bible in China*, 8.
21. Latourette, *History of Christian Missions*, 780.

It has become a valuable work of reference, offering a quick and easy means of checking the usage of words in the UV. Looking up a word will show all the main instances of its occurrence throughout the Bible, quoting the surrounding text, and providing references for the book, chapter, and verse. This useful biblical reference work was warmly welcomed by the Chinese church.

After five years of the UV, another useful reference book appeared: *The Concordance of Jesus' Life and Teaching* by F.C. Dreyer, published in 1924. The *Mandarin Bible Dictionary*, published by the Chinese Sunday School Association, first appeared seventeen years before the UV. With great foresight, the editor, G.A. Clayton, began to revise the dictionary according to new usage in the New Testament UV of 1906 so that its revision could be published alongside the completed UV in 1919. Other relevant works are: *Chinese Bible Encyclopedia,* edited and published by the Shanghai Union Publishing House in 1925, based on the *International Standard Bible Encyclopedia* edited by James Orr; and *Dictionary of the Gospels* by J. Hastings, translated by Lin Fuhua, published by Christian Literature for China in 1933. All of these works emerged within fifteen years after the publication of the UV, and all texts quoted therein were those of the UV of 1919. This increased the general acceptance of the UV and had a powerful effect on its popularization. Up to this day, these reference books are still the main tools for Bible study. Even in the late 1990s, *The Concordance of Bible Themes* (1997) and *Baker Encyclopedia of the Bible (Simplified Chinese Version)* (1999) were still compiled from the UV. In view of this, we can readily understand why the UV soon replaced other existing versions and remains in a dominant position.

The Expectation of Chinese Christians towards the Scripture

Eugene Nida (1914–2011), a linguist with the American Bible Society and Executive Secretary for Translations until his retirement, once described the Bible as God's Word in man's language.

Every Bible reader has their own expectations of a translation according to their own knowledge, denomination, experience, and thoughts, which affect their acceptance or rejection of a translation. The expectation may be that Bible translation must be sacred and inviolable; or it could be that a translation's theological viewpoint must be in harmony with theological studies, academic studies, or with the discoveries of archaeol-ogy. What kind of expectation of the Chinese Bible do Chinese Christians have? What is their attitude towards "God's Word in human language"? Generally speaking, Christians believe that the Bible is God's inspired Word. The question is how to interpret "inspired by God."

There are two schools of thought. One views the Bible as the work of humans who were inspired by God. Thus, it is hard to avoid human errors that will need to be revised. As time passes, Biblical language grows out of date and can become an obstacle to the reader. Therefore, Bible transla-tions should be constantly renewed to keep them fresh. Further, revision is necessary to accord with new discoveries in theology, archeology, and other relevant studies.

The other school insists that the Bible is sacred and inviolable. Since the Bible is "inspired" by God, then no word or sentence should be changed, for they come with God's grace and blessing. Zetzsche remarked: "The attitude appears to be very typical for Bible translation in China after the publica-tion of the UV. The UV is viewed by a great majority in the Chinese church as *the* authorized version which should not be changed, lest the Bible itself, the "word of God," be changed."[22] The Bible, as the Word of God, is identi-fied with a particular translation, the UV, which is solemn and dignified, and has surpassing religious authority. In such a case, further translation or revision becomes an almost impossible endeavor. This has proved to be the case for even moderate revision under heavy pressure. Revision has been defended by Shen Cheng'en, director of *Tian Feng*, the national monthly magazine of the Protestant Churches in China:

> Some Christians believe that the words of the Bible should remain exactly the same, nothing added, nothing subtracted; not one dot, not one stroke of a character should be changed. Therefore, the Bible text should not change, not even the topic headings. This is a great misunderstanding. All scripture is inspired by God and is the Word of God; certainly, we should not willfully alter it. But here we are talking about a translation. Although the UV of 1919 is a better translation than those that came before it, and has been used for more than seventy years, yet, it is not a perfect translation. Furthermore, the language and system of writing are developing and changing. A translation which was good seventy years ago may not remain adequate for today.[23]

22. Zetzsche, *Bible in China*, 345.
23. Shen, "Huanhu Hengpaiban Shengjing," 4.

As revealed in the above quotation from Shen, the UV has sacred status in the hearts of Chinese Christians, as does its very name in Chinese, *Shengjing* (Holy Canonical Book), which they believe should not be changed.

Zhuang Rouyu, the first person to present a scholarly study of the phenomenon of authoritativeness in Protestant Chinese Bible translations, expertly analyzed the authority of the UV from the aspects of religion, history, language, and market.[24] The evidence from her analyses confirms that the UV has truly enjoyed an irreplaceable and authoritative position among Chinese Christians. The authority of the UV lies in its unique character. The UV cannot be viewed as an isolated occurrence in the history of the Protestant church and mission in China. Instead, it is the product that built upon missionaries' century-long effort. It was the fruit of a century of the development of Chinese Bible translation. Through suffering, wars, political movements, social reform, and persecution, the Chinese people have learned even more to love and treasure the UV, the Word of God that has comforted and sustained them in all their trials.

Zetzsche proposed a strong thesis regarding the phenomenon of the authoritativeness of the UV when he said, "The result was a majority perception of the *Union Version* as an authorized version—a far broader majority than anyone would have anticipated. The authorization that the *Union Version* experienced in the Chinese Church was not endowed because of its merits as a good translation, but rather through its status as a Chinese 'canonical book' (*jing*), which is viewed as authentic and not to be altered."[25]

In the late 1970s, a heated debate was stirred up by translation work on the *New Chinese Version*. Articles concerning the UV and the NCV were collected in *Yijing Luncong*, edited by Liu Yiling (1979). The pro-UV party praised the UV with one voice and questioned the NCV's principle of translation and authority, while the pro-NCV party endeavored to argue for the advantage of the NCV by comparing it with the UV and criticizing the UV. This phenomenon was analyzed by Zhuang when she wrote, "Behind all these arguments, there was a notion that two versions cannot exist at the same time. This is a strange thought. Why has the relationship between the

24. Zhuang, *Jidujiao Shengjing*, 26–30.

25. Zetzsche, *Bible in China*, 369.

UV and the NCV become a relation of replacement? Obviously, there is the assumption that 'there is only one authorized Bible for all readers.'"[26]

It seemed that Chinese Christians were not quite ready for multiple versions at that time. Cheng Zhiyi once said: "If a re-translation is not more excellent than the current Mandarin version [the UV], it is better to continue using the Mandarin version."[27] The UV's authority partially comes from its uniqueness and its typical "union style" that later translations and revisions feared to lose, dare not to violate, and dare not overstep. It is still true that in evaluating a new version, Chinese Christians expect it to be better than the version it replaces, rather than, as in the English-speaking world, expecting various versions for different readers to choose from. Only if this situation changes radically will the UV's authority be challenged. Until then, it will continue to enjoy its dominant position.

Summary

Since 1919 became the year when the UV appeared, it has been remembered as a remarkable turning point in the history of Chinese Bible translation. The fact that the UV is recognized as an epoch-making version or a "milestone" manifests its unique significance.

For over a century, Western missionaries had made efforts to give China a proper vernacular Bible. The UV was the result of the Chinese church's strong desire for the development of a standard version. It soon replaced the previous versions with its excellent translation. Not only was it accepted, but it has also been embraced as an authorized, canonical book.

The rapid language development in China that followed the New Culture Movement and the subsequent May Fourth Movement increased the use of the spoken language as a standard for written Chinese. The appearance of two union versions coincided with the literary revolution, through which *baihua* displaced classical literary Chinese as the literary language of choice. This explained why the Mandarin Union Version, not the *Wenli* Union Version, became the more popular.

The UV demonstrates that the church in China was a pioneer in producing literature in the national language. The unique significance of the UV can also be seen in its contribution to Chinese literature. The new awareness in the nineteen-twenties of the Bible as literature was in large

26. Zhuang, *Jidujiao Shengjing*, 104.
27. Cheng, "Shengjing zhi Zhongwen Yiben," 27.

measure due to the UV. Its influence gained momentum from the development of language reform and also from the emergence of several biblical reference books that quoted all of their texts from the UV.

The authority that the UV experienced in the Chinese church was endowed partly by its sacred status in the hearts of Chinese Christians. Unlike the Western Protestant church, which appreciates the coexistence of a wide variety of English Bibles serving different purposes, the Chinese church seems to be expecting a supreme version that would surpass the UV in many ways and be good enough for all. Thus, until then, the UV will remain in its dominant position.

7

Contemporary Challenges

To ANALYZE THE CONTEMPORARY challenges facing the UV, it is necessary to explore the versions translated by Chinese that appeared post–UV. Two periods will be considered: from 1919 to 1999 and from 2000 until today.

Account of Translation Works by Chinese (1919–1999)

After the publication of the UV, the history of Chinese Bible translation entered a new era. The responsibility of translating the Bible into Chinese gradually shifted from Western missionaries to native Chinese. Many attempts have been made by Chinese Christians to produce new translations of the Bible. During the first fifty years (1919–69), six translations of the New Testament and some parts of the Bible appeared.[1] These efforts were all made by native Chinese individuals, with the exception of two collaborative New Testament translations: one was Sydenstricker's version, which appeared in 1929, translated by Absalom Sydenstricker and Zhu Baohui. The other was The Bible Treasury New Testament, translated by Heinrich Ruch and Zheng Shoulin, published in 1939. Besides these New Testament translations, some other translations of various parts of the Bible came out. Robert P. Kramers of the Netherlands Bible Society in Hong Kong commented, "None of these versions seems to have had a very wide circulation, nor do they seem to have had backing from the majority of Chinese

1. See appendix 3.

churches."[2] However, they show that Chinese Christians made efforts at translation in the post-missionary period, which is valuable to today's study of the history of Chinese Bible translation.

By the end of the 1990s, three new translations of the whole Bible were produced by different teams in Hong Kong: Chinese Living Bible (1979), Today's Chinese Version (1979), and New Chinese Version (1992).

Translations by both individuals and teams will be considered.

Individual Translations

Three New Testament translations by one-man translators in this new era deserve detailed accounts: the translations of Wang Xuanchen (1933), Zhu Baohui (1936) and Lü Zhenzhong (1946). The former two translations may be considered an indirect result of the preparation of the UV, since Wang was Mateer's assistant in translating the New Testament of the UV, and Zhu was the assistant to Sydenstricker, who was once a member of the UV committee. The third translation, of which the New Testament was published in 1946, retains its influence up to the present as Lü continued his work until the whole Bible translation was completed and published in 1970.

The New Testament by Wang Xunchen

Wang Xunchen (also known as Wang Yuande) was the first Chinese to translate the New Testament into Chinese. The idea of translating the Bible afresh started to bud in his mind while he was working as an assistant to Mateer on the UV project from 1903 to 1908. We learn more about him from Goodrich's high commendation of Mateer's coworker:

> Happily, for the work, Dr. Mateer had another scholar, trained also in his school, Mr. Wang Yuan Teh [Wang Yuande], a young man of keen, incisive, logical mind, who had read all the best books in the Mandarin colloquial. Mr. Wang was quick to see any fault in the structure of a sentence, and insistent on its being put right. He also worked most faithfully in this translation, refusing offers which came to him of a salary several times the amount he received. I think he was held partly by Dr. Mateer's personality, which drew him strongly, and partly by his own love for the work itself. When

2. Kramers, "Some Thoughts," 160.

the chariot of fire came for Dr. Mateer, he left us, much to our regret and loss.[3]

After Mateer's death in 1908, Wang returned home and became a professor at Qilu University, Mateer's former Dengzhou College, where Wang had been a student. He did not immediately engage in re-translating the Bible since he felt himself inadequate to do so without expertise in biblical studies. He eventually enrolled in a seminary, and then started to re-translate the New Testament in 1930.[4] His translation of the New Testament was published in 1933 by the Qingdao section of the Church of Christ in China.

In the preface to his translation, Wang vividly described the working of the UV committee in their meetings, which he had attended for five years without a day's absence:

> In summer time, [translators] came with their translated drafts, gathering in the Dongshan Sanitarium in Yantai. Everybody contributed opinions for mutual criticism. Sometimes it was harmonious and affable; sometimes there was dispute and confusion; occasionally some would raise their voices and pound the table, then angrily walk away. A moment later, coming back with a smile, we would discuss it over again. Each final draft would require energetic discussion for several days without a result being reached, and then the main body of Western missionaries would make the final decision. However, it was difficult to follow the crudeness of the original and to work on the style at the same time. That was the greatest problem. I experienced this without missing a day for a full five years. When the book was completed and published in China (i.e. Mandarin Union Version), it met a half-and-half mixture of praise and blame. I was not fully satisfied.[5]

This is the only known first-hand description of the UV work by a Chinese. From Wang's preface, we also learn about how he worked alone with his new translation. For three years, the translation occupied him so much that he could "neither eat nor sleep." He repeatedly went over every verse and read all of them aloud to himself from fifty to more than a hundred times to see how fluent they sounded. He sought to create a fluent translation which was understandable whether reading it or listening to it,

---

3. Fisher, *Calvin Wilson Mateer*, 259.

4. Cheng, "Shengjing," 24. Zetzsche dated it 1931, while other Chinese writers, such as Yang Senfu, Yu Ligong, are in agreement with Cheng.

5. Wang's preface of the 1933 New Testament.

while at the same time remaining faithful to the original. The basis versions for his translation, listed at the end of his preface, were a 1916 Latin edition, the 1901 American Standard Version, the 1907 and 1919 editions of the Mandarin Union Version New Testament, *Wenli* Union Version, Morrison's translation, and Liu Zhun's translation—a Catholic version.[6] The Greek text was not included.

Wang employed modern punctuation according to the standards issued by the National Department of Education. To distinguish supernatural beings, he first creatively used the third person pronoun *ta* (祂), with the "god" radical (礻) for "God," "Christ," "Holy Spirit," and "angels." He used the pronoun *ta* (牠) with the animal radical (牜) for "demons." The "god" pronoun *ta* is more and more preferred and adopted by Evangelical Chinese Christians nowadays, but it is limited to the three persons of the Trinity. In this way, "God" is not defined with masculine, feminine, or neuter gender, but with a "god" gender instead. This presents a remarkable linguistic phenomenon in the realm of Christian language. However, none of the translations that appeared since the 1970s continued using the "god" pronoun except the Chinese Living Bible (later called the Chinese Contemporary Bible, 2010), which only uses it for the third person pronoun. Identifying "God" with the masculine gender doesn't seem to bother most modern people since God has been addressed as "Heavenly Father," and Jesus, "Son of God."

Wang also noticed that in previous Chinese versions, *gui* had been used to translate three different terms in the original text: demon, devil, and spirit, so he employed *wuling* (unclean spirit) to distinguish from *wugui* (unclean demon).[7]

Wang's translation was never distributed widely but was of great value to Chinese Bible researchers. Zetzsche is surely correct when he states that, "the historical relevance of this version lies doubtlessly in the fact that it was the first complete Protestant NT version done by a Chinese, rather than its great impact on the church or later Bible translations."[8]

---

6. This is an unknown Catholic version. Zetzsche identified this version with *Xinjing Quanji* by Xiao Jingshan (1922) because it was the only available Catholic New Testament at that time. However, the name of the translator, Xiao, was not matched with that on Wang's list.

7. Wang's preface of the 1933 New Testament.

8. Zetzsche, *The Bible in China*, 339.

The New Testament by Zhu Baohui

One cannot mention Zhu Baohui's translation without mentioning Syden-stricker's translation. Sydenstricker once took part in the Mandarin Union Version project. He was elected to fill the vacancy created by the death of Mateer in 1908. In the second meeting the following year, he withdrew from the translation committee due to disagreements with others about the principles of translation.

After leaving the committee, Sydenstricker made his own translation of the New Testament and Zhu Baohui was his assistant. Zhu studied Greek at Nanking Theological Seminary under the Southern Presbyterian missionary John Leighton Stuart, who taught Greek and New Testament in Nanking from 1908–19. In 1918, Zhu became a teacher of Greek at the correspondence school of the seminary, where Sydenstricker had served as dean of the school since 1921. While working together, Zhu Baohui was able to assist Sydenstricker in his Bible translation. With the aid of Zhu, Sydenstricker published the first edition of his translation of the Gospels in 1913. Then they produced the whole New Testament in 1929 at the Nanjing Seminary.

Soon, they wanted to revise it as they were dissatisfied with the im-perfect results due to its hasty publication. The progress of revision was interrupted by the death of Sydenstricker in 1931. Later, Zhu decided to continue this task himself. The revision finally turned out to be retransla-tion. In addition to his teaching duties at Nanking Seminary, he had worked on the retranslation for six years and published it in 1936, with financial support from Sydenstricker's daughter, Pearl Buck.[9]

Zhu employed the term *Shangdi* for "God," unlike Sydenstricker, who had used *Shen*. According to its preface, the principles of Zhu's translation were that it was to be a faithful translation into modern Chinese, with mod-ern punctuation and gender-specific pronouns. Benefitting from serving at the seminary for many years, he had a wealth of sources. The versions that formed the basis for this translation are listed in its preface: they are an 1875 edition of a polyglot Bible,[10] four editions of the New Testament Greek text, and Chalmers/Schaub's version. A clearer distinction between verbs and nouns shows that Zhu's translation relied more heavily on the

---

9. Zhu's preface of the 1936 New Testament.

10. Zetzsche (*Bible in* China, 340) further notes it contains the text of the *Vulgate*, the *Septuagint,* the German translation by Luther, and a Hebrew text.

Greek text. For example, Zhu uses *aixin* as a noun for "love" and *xiang'ai* as verb for "to love."[11]

Sydenstricker's translation ideal was primarily to render the text into colloquial Chinese, while Zhu strove for great faithfulness to the Greek. Critics praised Zhu's fidelity to the original but criticized the style as not as lively and vigorous as that of the UV. Zhu's translation includes brief introductions, an outline of the content of the Scriptures, chapter subdivisions, and a voluminous appendix, which included a short Greek grammar, a concordance with explanations based on Greek terms, and a list of translated names in the New Testament. It was thus considered rather like a study text for students of New Testament Greek. In his translation, Zhu includes a brief story of Sydenstricker to show his respect to his teacher.

The New Testament by Lü Zhenzhong

Lü Zhenzhong (1898–1995) graduated from the University of Hong Kong in 1922. Later, he studied Greek and Hebrew at Yanjing University in Peking and taught for fourteen years at the South Fujian Theological College in Amoy. In 1940, he was called to Yanjing University to translate the New Testament, which was published in 1946 by the Institute of Religion of Yanjing University. At the beginning of the 1950s, he was already working on the translation of the Old Testament after receiving some further training in biblical languages at Union Theological Seminary, New York (1947–48), and Westminster College, England the following year. After he returned to Hong Kong from England, he worked diligently on translating the Old Testament with the help of the United Bible Society, which supplied the Greek and Hebrew texts that he needed. Lü based his New Testament work on Souter's and Nestle's Greek texts, but the Hebrew text he used was not specified. He adopted *Shangdi* for "God" and created the word *Yonghengzhu* (Everlasting Lord), which he used in place of *Yehehua* for the tetragrammaton "YHWH." His principle of translation was an emphasis on faithfulness to modern Mandarin.

In 1970, the whole Bible was, according to its imprint, "published for the Rev. Lü Chen-chung [Lü Zhenzhong] by Hong Kong Bible Society." It is known as *Lü Zhenzhong yiben* (Lü Zhenzhong Version, LZV). In 1973, the University of Hong Kong conferred on him the Honorary Degree of Doctor

---

11. Cheng, "Shengjing," 23.

of Divinity. He received this degree for his rendition of the whole Bible into the Chinese vernacular.

During the first two decades after its publication, the LZV did not find its way into the hands of ordinary Christians, but its great reference value is generally acknowledged by Chinese Bible researchers. With the development of technology, the LZV is now available online for everyone who is interested. The United Bible Society approves its value by including it in The Parallel NT: with Six Versions published in 1997.[12]

Collaborative Translations

The Chinese Living Bible

Dangdai Shengjing, known as the Chinese Living Bible, was created by a committee led by Joseph Chiang, which made an effort to paraphrase the original texts into modern Mandarin on the basis of the English translation known as the Living Bible (1971). The New Testament was published in 1974, and the whole Bible appeared in 1979, published by Living Bibles International (Hong Kong), which merged with the International Bible Society in 1992. This translation has never been broadly accepted since it is a paraphrastic translation, and the Chinese church was not ready to welcome it at the time it was published.

Today's Chinese Version

The year of 1979 saw another publication of a new translation of the whole Bible: Today's Chinese Version (TCV), based on Today's English Version. The TCV was produced by a group of biblical scholars supported by the United Bible Society (UBS): Moses Hsü (Xu Mushi), I-Jin Loh (Luo Weiren), Chow Lien-hwa (Zhou Lianhua), Martin Wang (Wang Chengzhang), and Evelyn Chiao (Jiao Ming). They follow the principle of "functional equivalence" set forth by Eugene Nida with the aim of giving today's readers a maximum understanding of the content of the original text. The work began in 1972 and went through an extensive scholarly review process lasting eight years.

12. They are: Greek New Testament, Chinese Union Version, Today's Chinese Version, Lü Zhenzhong's version, Studium Biblicum Version and New Revised Standard Version.

The TCV was not well received by Mainland Chinese in the 1980s, when the church had just reopened after the Cultural Revolution. Conservative congregations were not ready for "another" Bible. Chinese Christians are Bible lovers, or UV lovers, especially after experiencing a long period without a Bible during the Cultural Revolution. It was a common phenomenon in the early days of re-opening church that during a Sunday service, the congregation will read the passage aloud together instead of listening to one reader. In this situation, the TCV, a functional equivalent version, cannot be used along with the UV. Although the TCV has now been printed and distributed on the Mainland through Amity Printing Press (supported by UBS), it is now also facing the challenge of the New Chinese Version.

The New Chinese Version

The New Chinese Version (NCV) came into being in 1992. The New Chinese Bible Center (NCBC), with more than thirty members, was supported by the Lockman Foundation. Formed in 1972, the Center went through four years of hard work before the New Testament appeared in 1976, and sixteen more years until the publication of the Old Testament. In 2001, the NCBC was transformed into the Worldwide Bible Society (WBS) with the mission of promoting the NCV. The WBS introduced its translation process by highlighting the thorough effort by more than 30 presidents, administrators, professors, and lecturers from theological seminaries, and more than 10 pastors, overseers, elders, and Christians who majored in Chinese. The goals of translation were fidelity, elegance, and expressiveness. Meticulous discussions in three working panels (original language, theological, and Chinese language) were enhanced by input from the general public among Chinese churches.

It is hard to imagine how the work of translation could successfully be carried out since it involved so many people from so many places. Certainly, the diversity and authority of these representatives would add weight to the new translation. Joseph Hong, United Bible Society translation consultant, criticized the NCV: "It claims to be a functional equivalence translation into modern Chinese, but in fact appears to be a modified text of the [C] UV Bible."[13]

The NCV was translated from the Hebrew and Greek with reference to the UV. The Old Testament was based on *Biblia Hebraica Stuttgartensia*

13. Hong, "Revision," 243.

(1977); the New Testament was based on *The Greek New Testament* (2nd edition) and *Nestle-Aland Novum Testamentum Graece* (25th edition).

The above translations, either by individuals or by teams, emerged after 1919. Are any of them a challenge to the UV? Has the dominant position of the UV been weakened because of these coexisting versions?

Assessing the Challenges from a Historical Perspective

It has been over two hundred years since Morrison entered China and produced the first Bible in the vernacular language, and it has been one hundred years since the Union Version appeared. Numerous and various Chinese Bible versions have emerged since then. So, it seems that there has been no shortage of Chinese Bible versions for Chinese Christians to choose from, according to their cultural background, reading interest, or for the purpose of ministry. Among various versions, why has the UV been adopted as the uniform, standard version by Chinese Christians? Is there any version that could be the competitor to the UV?

However, in fact, there were no legitimate alternatives until 1970. The reason is that the UV, since it appeared in 1919, has been accepted by Chinese Protestants worldwide in their different cultural experiences, levels of education, and denominational backgrounds. Versions produced before the UV have been automatically eliminated. Even the *Wenli* Union Version, which emerged at the same time with the same purpose, was last printed in 1934.[14] Pre-UV translations can only be accessed in special archives; there are no opportunities for them to be selected for general use. Thus, only those translations that appeared after the UV could be its challengers.

The translations of Wang and Zhu were not of the whole Bible. They cannot be placed on a par with the UV. If there were financial support for them to be reprinted, Bible researchers might want to have copies, but they would not be read widely. In short, these two New Testament translations have value for study but will never be a challenge to the UV.

Among the four translations of the whole Bible which have appeared since the 1970s, the Chinese Living Bible was not accepted from the start. It is regarded as fine literature with smooth, easy and readable Chinese, but not a formal Bible translation due to its being based on a paraphrase and

14. The result of my questionnaire (appendix 5) shows that 61 percent of respondents do not know that there are *Wenli* versions, 29 percent of respondents have heard of *Wenli* versions and only 11 percent have seen a copy.

perceived as too colloquial. Some scholars do not even mention it in their writings about Chinese Bible translation.[15]

The Lü Zhenzhong version appeared in 1970 but found only a very limited number of readers. The reason for this was not so much the good or bad qualities of translation, but an extraordinary fact: this book had been published, certainly at great financial expense, by the Hong Kong Bible Society, exclusively for the Rev. Mr. Lü and his relatives and friends. During the last three decades, the advance of computer technology has solved the problem of its limited and costly publication. Gaining access to the LZV is now as easy as the click of a button. Side by side with the TCV, NCV, and UV, the LZV can be reached through various Bible software. As a translation by a Chinese pastor who had knowledge of Greek and Hebrew, the LZV has great reference value, and is favored by ministers and theological students. However, there is no sign of it being used in public worship or Bible study.

Today's Chinese Version is the first translation by a group of Biblical scholars and church leaders. It is a new translation which seeks to state clearly and accurately the meaning of the original texts in words and forms that are widely accepted by people who use Chinese as a means of communication. As a translator, Zhou Lianhua stated that this translation avoids using traditional religious vocabulary and style; rather, it attempts in this century to set forth the Biblical content and message in a standard, daily, natural form of Chinese, in order to reach readers with a junior high school education and to reach non-Christians as well. Obviously, it challenged the UV with its intelligibility in modern Chinese and in being a functional equivalent translation. However, an intelligible translation is by no means an acceptable version, as Nida points out:

> One of the greatest surprises for Bible translators is to find that a perfectly intelligible translation of the Scripture may not be acceptable. Though intelligibility and acceptability are closely related factors in communication, they are by no means so interdependent that greater intelligibility inevitably means increased acceptability. In fact, many people prefer a translation of the Scriptures which they only partially understand. For example, the archaic and obscure words and grammatical forms of the King James Version seem to many people to fit the esoteric nature of the contents and to lend authority to the text.[16]

15. Such as Luo Xurong, Wang Weifan, and Zhao Weiben.

16. Nida, "Intelligibility and Acceptability," 301.

Nida indicates that intelligibility is not the rule for measuring whether a translation is acceptable. The same is more or less true of Today's Chinese Version. After its publication (1979), the TCV was advocated by many as *the* new Chinese Bible and the successor to the UV.[17] Even today, however, the TCV, using modern, clear, and readable language, and being supported by the United Bible Society, still does not enjoy the same acceptance as the UV.[18] There are certain readers who prefer the UV not because of the sense of divine authority alone, but because the rhythm of literary texts, and even the partially understood words that may evoke an esoteric feeling, accord with their religious sentiments. The UV is praised as the most beautiful classical literature in Mandarin. Its position in China is generally described as comparable to the KJV in the English-speaking world.

With every day, easily understood Chinese, the TCV finds favor among members of the younger generation. Its bilingual version should appeal to their Bible study groups when "English-fever" is all the rage. However, it has to face the challenge of other bilingual editions: UV/ NIV, published in 1997 by the International Bible Society; and UV/ESV, published in 2003 by the Worldwide Bible Society.

The New Chinese Version is known in Chinese as *Xinyiben* (lit. new translation), but was it a new translation? When Joseph Hong criticized it as a modified text of the UV, he did not stand alone. To ensure that readers would accept the new translation, the NCV retained the style of the UV. Its translators tried to retain as much as possible of the familiar and loved terminology of the UV, unless it needed to be updated, so that readers could readily see how similar it was to the UV. Thus, it gave people a sense of confidence that the new translation was reliable and acceptable.

The UV and the NCV are the only competitors for quality of translation. Promoters of the NCV highlighted its superiority over the UV by giving parallel examples, such as:

> Missing elements.
>
> At times, the [C]UV misses some important elements originating from the source text due to incomplete translation. This can be an obstacle to the accurate interpretation of the translation, or, even worse, can mislead general readers who are unable to read the source languages. For example: Hebrews 11:3
>
> NCV: "The universe was formed at *Shen de hua* (God's word)."

17. See Xiao, *Shangdi de Ai*, 1981.
18. See summary of survey, appendix 5.

[C]UV: "The universe was formed at *Shenhua* (fairy tales)."

The [C]UV Bible translation team used *"Shenhua"* instead of *"Shen de hua"* by omitting the possessive auxiliary word "de," trying to make the language succinct. It so happens that the Chinese characters for *shen hua* mean *fairy tales*. As a result, fairy tales instead of God's word are said to have formed the universe. This has provided a big joke for atheists, for they have always mocked Christians for their faith being a fairy tale. Now they have found evidence in the Bible to prove their stance and it was certainly a tragic mistake.[19]

Through this kind of promotion, the NCV strives to show its strength to win more readers. According to its publisher's (Worldwide Bible Society) declaration, "After publication this Bible has been more and more supported by Chinese believers, and churches switching from the previous version to the New Version have been increasing." In 2004, the WBS published the entire Bible—NCV/[C]UV Parallel.[20]

Is the NCV a challenge to the UV? In my 2006 survey, 70 percent of respondents knew that there were various Chinese versions; 79.5 percent used the UV, 11.5 percent use the TVC, 3 percent used the NCV, and 6 percent used the UV along with either the TCV or the NCV.[21] The answer, at that time, was clear: No. In China, the China Christian Council/Three Self Patriotic Movement controls the publication and distribution of the Bible. Any Bible or Hymnal published outside of the CCC/TSPM in Mainland China is treated as illegal. Since the NCV has no relationship with the CCC/TSPM, it cannot officially be distributed in Mainland China, though the WBS has published many different editions of the NCV Bible to meet the different needs of the Chinese Christians. This could be one of the reasons why the percentage of NCV readers is so low. Acknowledging that reaching people in Mainland China is a challenge to the NCV, J. H. Taylor and Rong Baoluo, the President of WBS, expressed the hope that not only believers from Hong Kong, Taiwan, and Singapore, but also those in the Mainland, would be able to experience the help and the light of the NCV.

In April 2006, the Revised Union Version New Testament was published in Hong Kong. The question remains whether it will be embraced or

---

19. http://www.worldwidebible.net/English/NewLight/index.htm.

20. http://www.worldwidebible.net/English/NCV/history.htm.

21. See Appendix 5.

rejected by Chinese churches. Will the NCV and the RUV be a challenge to each other?

It was hoped that the revision of whole UV could be completed by 2007, the bicentenary of Robert Morrison's arrival in China. That goal placed a considerable challenge before the revision committee. Although there were now modern means of communication and other technological aids to speed the translation and publishing process, Joseph Hong, the chief of the revision committee, was not optimistic about meeting the publication goal of 2007. As early as 2002, he was concerned the goal might be too daunting for the Committee.[22] His worry was not unreasonable. The year 2006 saw the revised New Testament only, and it took another four years for the Old Testament to be completed. In 2010, the whole Revised UV was finally presented to the reader with smooth modern Chinese, rich footnotes, and practical appendices. It was a result of twenty-seven years' effort.

Is a New Translation Necessary?

A Bible translation should eventually be the work of indigenous Christians, and any translation for which the main responsibility lies with foreigners will be considered by many to have only a preliminary usefulness. The UV, with its uniqueness, has maintained this "preliminary" position for almost a century, which was beyond the imagination of the original Western missionaries. The importance of indigenous translation is more and more clearly recognized by Chinese Christians. As the result of Chinese Christians' efforts, some newly published translations have appeared since the 1970s, and translation projects have been ongoing both inside and outside of China. The year of 1995 saw a publication of the New Testament: *Putonghua*[23] *yiben* (lit. Common Language Version). Information concerning translators and publishers is given in general terms, in order to avoid getting them into trouble. They risk being banned because any such activities without the approval of the religious authorities are reckoned as "illegal religious publications" in the Mainland and will be suppressed. So, all we know from its preface is that it is translated by a translation group in Beijing under the guidance of New Testament scholars, based on the Greek text and first published in China in 1995. They claim that they employ modern vocabulary, as its title indicates, to replace archaic, obscure words and

22. Hong, *Revision*, 248.

23. "*Putonghua*" is the contemporary term for "Mandarin" in Mainland China.

to reach out to contemporary Chinese people with a smooth and fluent translation.

Although these ongoing translation projects may be considered "unofficial," they are worthy of mention here as they indicate that Chinese Christians are aware of the responsibility to produce an indigenous translation.

Since the UV already exists, and is "good enough," is a new translation necessary? Four reasons given by Nida for re-translation and revision of the English Bible may cast light on the question:

> One may quite rightly ask why so many revisions required. Are our traditional translations so erroneous as to require such a host of changes? Do so many revisions merely add up to the fact that we cannot be certain about what the Scriptures mean? Are such translations and revisions merely a form of subtle attack upon the traditional tenets of our faith? The answers to these questions are fourfold, including: (1) better knowledge of the original texts, (2) more accurate understanding of the meanings of the Biblical passages, (3) changes which have occurred in the English language through the years, and (4) a revised concept of communication, and hence of translation.[24]

In a similar vein to that of Nida, Xu Mushi, translator of the TCV, gave four reasons for re-translation of the Chinese Bible in 1980, when the TCV was published: (1) the foreigners who translated the Chinese Bible had a limited grasp of a language which was not their mother tongue, (2) the UV appeared in the early days of using *baihua*, which has changed in the last sixty years, (3) the Chinese language has changed through societal shifts, and (4) archaeological discoveries in this century have affected our understanding of biblical times.[25]

From such critical standpoints, Bible translation is a creative activity. Revision may be needed with each new discovery, study, or language change. In this way, the Word of God will be communicated clearly to people in their time and culture.

In light of these expert opinions, a new translation is necessary. In the case of the UV, there are four reasons for this conclusion. Two are general: language change and better knowledge gained from the discoveries of archaeology, etc. The other two relate specifically to the UV: the fact that it had foreign translators and also that it was produced a hundred years ago.

24. Nida, *Message and Mission*, 200.

25. Xu, "Xiandai Zhongwen Yiben," 13–4.

Nida's opinion is that "no Scripture is regarded as fully effective for more than fifty years."[26]

Continuing Efforts of Chinese Translators in the Twenty-first Century (2000–)

What are the goals of those who are producing new versions? Since 2000, several efforts of Chinese Bible translation have achieved their aims.

The Chinese Standard Bible (CSB), produced in 2009 by Holman Bible Publishers and Asia Bible Society, is a new translation directly from Greek and Hebrew. The introduction states that it is committed to being faithful, expressive, and elegant and that the goals of this translation are:

- To provide Chinese-speaking people across the world with an accurate, readable Bible in contemporary Chinese.

- To give those who love God's Word a text that has numerous helps for readers, is visually attractive on the page, and is appealing when heard.

- To equip serious Bible students with an accurate translation for personal study, private devotions, and memorization.

- To affirm the authority of Scripture as God's Word and to champion its absolute truth against social or cultural agendas that would compromise its accuracy.

The CSB New Testament is printed in parallel with the UV, so it is easier for the reader to compare the difference. The Old Testament is still in process of translation.

The Contemporary Chinese Version (CCV) was one of products presented in 2010 by Chinese Bible International, formerly the International Bible Society. It was a new effort inaugurated in 1994 to provide a translation that was accurate, readable, and appealing to Chinese churches. In the preface, the character of this version was summed up as: "a translation that is faithful to the original, written language is close to daily life." At the end of the preface, they humbly said that the CCV was not a final translation of the Chinese Bible, but one translation in the history of Chinese Bible translation, seeking to carry out the mission of passing on the knowledge and experience of Bible translation to the next generation. With many notes,

26. Nida, "Bible Translation," 60.

the CCV aims to help believers to study the Bible. Its Old Testament is still in process of translation.

The year of 2010 also saw *The Chinese Contemporary Bible* (CCB) published by the International Bible Society (Biblica Inc.), which was a revision of the Chinese Living Bible. In addition to Today's Chinese Version, the CCB received official approval in Mainland China, and was published by the China Christian Council and printed by the Nanjing Amity Press in 2016.

The Chinese New Living Translation (CNLT) is another product of Chinese Bible International, published in 2012. This entire Bible is a translation of the English New Living Translation, which is simple to understand and easy to read. The CNLT has the English NLT printed alongside it, with the aim of helping readers to "learn English while reading the Bible." In this way, they also hope to reach non-believers outside the church.

The Worldwide Chinese Bible (WCB) was produced in 2015 by the Worldwide Bible Society (WBS, formerly the New Chinese Bible Center). WBS was established in 2001 to promote this New Chinese Version to Chinese Christians around the world. Seeking to meet the different needs of Chinese churches and individual Chinese Christians worldwide, the NCV appeared in various editions, such as, New Chinese Version / English Standard Version Bilingual (2003); Chinese New Version[27]/New International Version Bilingual (2006); Chinese New Version Study Bible (2008), with notes adopted from the NIV Spirit of the Reformation Study Bible. None of existing translations has as many editions as the NCV. The Worldwide Chinese Bible is a result of a new effort of the WBS based on the NCV. Taking advantage of computer technology to bring God's Word from the ancient world to the world today, they strove to present a new translation that could be understood by Chinese of all ages. They also provided numerous notes adopted from the NIV Study Bible to meet the needs of the twenty–first century Chinese church.

The Chinese New English Translation Bible (CNET) is a free online Chinese version of the New English Translation Bible, translated by *Deren* Culture Exchange Foundation, and published by the Biblical Studies Press in 2011. The preface of the NET Bible states that it is a completely new translation in English, with over sixty thousand translators' notes, done by more than twenty biblical scholars who worked directly from the best

---

27. NCV changed into CNV due to confusion with the abbreviation used for English New Century Version. However, NCV is used throughout this study for consistency.

currently available Hebrew, Aramaic, and Greek texts. The CNET translated almost all of the NET notes, which fall into three categories: translation notes, study notes, and textual and critical notes. For the Bible text, instead of translating from the NET, the CNET adopted the most accepted Chinese version, the UV, and revised it only in three aspects:

1. Revised a sentence whenever its meaning was different from that of the NET, so that it would coincide with the annotation.

2. Updated vocabulary to employ modern usage. Slightly modified some dialogue to reflect a contemporary, lively tone.

3. Changed measurements to the metric system and kept the original system in the annotation.

Thus, the CNET is actually composed of its revision of the UV and its translation of the NET's notes. The CNET aims to provide a source of trustworthy Bible study resources for the Chinese world with copious quality translators' notes in digital from, which enable instant access with just a few clicks. The CNET may soon become one of the most popular versions because of its availability on the internet, ease of use, and free downloads.

From the above, we see that Chinese Bible translation is moving from the stage of the UV only towards that of multiple versions. There is a perception that various versions are needed to serve different demands and interests: one for traditional or public worship; one for academic study; one as easy reading for the less educated to understand; one elegant version for literati to enjoy; one for personal devotion; and, now, one digital/audio version for those who listen more than they read, and use electronics more than paper in this modern age. Early in 1965, Jia Baoluo pointed out that allowing the existence of various versions did not divide the truth of God. The truth of God may enlighten us in various ways.

Today's translators do not face the problem of language style as did early Western missionaries, for written Chinese is now fairly close to the standard spoken language. However, there still exist in the Chinese language certain linguistic features, such as vocabulary, which to some extent, varies from place to place: that of Mainland China differing from Taiwan, Hong Kong, Singapore, and Malaysia. Some of these variations are regional; some are influenced by either cultural backgrounds or political situations. For instance, a Mainland reader feels uncomfortable when Genesis 34:2 "the prince of the land" is translated with the word *shouzhang* in the NCV (which was translated in Hong Kong). This is because *shouzhang* is linked with the revolution, or the Communist Party, for Mainland Chinese. It means the leading cadre of the army or senior officers of high rank in the government.[28] A word with such a modern usage cannot be appropriate to the context of ancient Israel. This is merely one example illustrating that acceptable vocabulary for Hong Kong may not be appropriate for the Mainland. Differences such as this cause problems in practice. As a possible solution, it has been suggested that different versions could be made for the people of Hong Kong and for overseas Chinese. Would this be returning to the beginning, when different versions were being produced? Will history repeat itself? To respond to these questions, it will help to reflect on what the situation was in the past. How did the missionaries of the past come to produce the Union Version?

"Is a new translation necessary?" The answer to the question is positive, but only if there are qualified translators equal to the task, whatever the needs. Otherwise, inferior translation variation would cause not only confusion in the faith but would also result in the demolition of the authority of the Bible.

A new translation is necessary for many reasons. However, the new version should meet what is desired with high quality. To produce the best possible Chinese version of the Scriptures, two essential factors are necessary:

1. Strong scholarship:

   Excellence in the Chinese language, particularly standard Chinese and punctuation.

   Being well versed in Greek and Hebrew, which enables entrance into the biblical world without relying on others.

   Mastery of the skill of translation.

2. Dedication:

   True faith, because the Bible is, in contrast to other literature, the carrier of the Word of Life.

   Selfless devotion.

   Pure motivation without desire for personal fame and wealth, only a single aim to give the Chinese church its best possible version of Scripture.

---

28. See *Dictionary of Modern Chinese*, 1165

Here, it is helpful to repeat again the earnest advice of Harold B. Rattenbury when he delivered the speech for the first review of the complete Bible in 1919:

> The final Chinese version will never come until we have *Chinese* scholars, deeply versed in the original tongues, masters also of Mandarin, translating into their own native tongue. It is for the Church to prepare her Hebrew and Greek scholars.[29]

Summary

In the post-missionary era, the responsibility of translating the Bible into Chinese gradually shifted from Western missionaries to native Chinese.

In the first fifty years, six translations of the New Testament and some other parts of the Bible appeared, most produced by individuals. Although none of these versions seemed to have had a wide circulation, they provide evidence of the great efforts that Chinese Christians made in the realm of Chinese Bible translation.

Four translations of the entire Bible, mostly produced by teams, appeared at different times between 1970 and 2000. Their translators are Chinese theologians and biblical scholars who had aimed to produce versions that were more faithful to the original, using modern Chinese.

These coexisting versions challenged the UV with more idiomatic, intelligible Chinese, greater accuracy in translating the source text, and updated knowledge gained from archaeological discoveries. Yet none of these versions have enjoyed the same acceptance by the Chinese Church as the UV. After more than thirty years, the dominant position of the UV remains unchanged.

Ongoing translation projects are expressions of the translators' zeal to adequately communicate the message of the Bible to Chinese readers, regardless of whether they are Christians. However, the authoritative status of the UV will remain until the mindset that there should be "one authorized version for all readers" changes. Advances in computer technology have opened a new door for Bible translation. Several new translations and revised versions have appeared in the twenty–first century, and Chinese Bible translation is moving from the stage of the UV only towards that of multiple versions. Doubtless, the UV will one day move from the center to

---

29. Murray, "The New Mandarin Bible," 443.

the margin of acceptance, but its historical value and its marvellous contribution to the Chinese Church remain indelible and enduring.

Conclusion

THE HISTORY OF CHINESE Bible translation began in the seventh century when the Nestorian missionary Alopen came to China. He brought with him some 530 volumes of different books in the Syrian language, including the Bible. There is strong evidence in the Nestorian inscription and in the Dunhuang Cave documents that parts of the Bible had been translated into Chinese. Unfortunately, nothing except the names of the Old Testament and New Testament books were preserved. The Nestorian Church disappeared completely with the destruction of the Tang dynasty.

The Franciscan Montecorvino translated the New Testament and Psalms in the thirteenth century when Christianity again arrived in China. This was the first translation of the Bible into Mongolian, the language of the then ruling class of the Yuan dynasty. Once again, the texts did not survive once the Franciscan mission ended in 1368.

These early Christian missions to China failed to achieve a lasting position in Chinese society. One of the reasons that cannot be overlooked is the lack of a complete Bible in the native language and multiple copies of Biblical texts as a support for persecuted remnants through the changes of dynasties, which confirms that the whole Bible translated into vernacular language is very important to mission and to churches' survival in their trials.

The Jesuit missionaries came to China in the late sixteenth century. They translated some parts of the Bible that were necessary for liturgical purposes, preaching and teaching. During the seventeenth and eighteenth centuries, some Roman Catholic individuals translated the entire Bible or parts thereof into classical Chinese, but none of these were published. Jean Basset, for example, translated some parts of the New Testament, but they remained only in manuscript form. Nevertheless, these manuscripts later played an essential role in the history of Protestant Bible translation.

Not a single Chinese translation of the Bible in published form existed at the beginning of the nineteenth century when Protestant missionaries entered China. Among the early translators of published biblical works, Morrison and Marshman were pioneers.

Protestant missionaries came from different mission societies and different countries. Amid various mission activities, Bible translation became the arena in which they could work together. A multitude of Bible translations were produced either by teams or by individuals. The desire for a common, universal version grew stronger. After a hundred years, missionaries' joint efforts, with the aid of their Chinese assistants, eventually presented to the Chinese Church a successful union version, which rapidly became and remains the most widely used Protestant Chinese Bible, the Chinese Union Version, as it is known today.

As a landmark version, the UV divides a 200-year history of Chinese Bible translation into two parts: 1) The history of Bible translation led by Western missionaries; 2) The history of Bible translation by Chinese.

During the earlier history, there were two very controversial topics: one was the definition of language style and the other was the "term question"—how to name God in Chinese. As for language style, missionaries' changing understanding and perception of the Chinese language and its different styles became an important factor in the history of Chinese Bible translation. At first, once the missionary translators fully realized the great potential of classical Chinese, they chose a more exalted form of that style of language, *Wenli*, with the hope of exerting influence on the highly educated classes of Chinese society. Later, the necessity of a Bible not only for the literati but also for the common people was urgent; translations in the commonly used Mandarin and a lower level of classical language began to supplant the *Wenli* versions. Mandarin and Easy *Wenli* Bible translation was very active between 1855–1905, while *Wenli* translation ceased. It was only taken up again during the union versions project.

The union versions project experienced a similar process. The *Wenli* union version fell into disfavor and finally, after fifteen years, ceased to appear in print. This was a result of the New Culture Movement, which elevated spoken Mandarin to a literary medium. Work on an Easy *Wenli*, once thought of as the most appropriate style for a union version, unexpectedly came to an end with its New Testament translation. The Mandarin version was the only one of the three translations that was viewed by all missionaries as a necessity. The style competition among *Wenli*, Mandarin and

Easy *Wenli* was finally settled when Mandarin was accepted as the unified, universal written and spoken language for the whole nation. This process demonstrates the attempts missionary translators made to give the Chinese Church the very best version. Missionary translators achieved what they desired, yet never imagining that the UV influence would last so long.

The Term Question was much more complex and controversial, plaguing both Catholic and Protestant missionaries for centuries. Every effort made by the Protestant missionaries to produce a Chinese version through different teams launched heated debates and no agreement was reached throughout the course of their translation work. The core issue was whether Chinese culture had any knowledge of a monotheistic God and then whether the Christian deity could be equated to the Supreme *Shangdi* (Lord Most High) of the Chinese Classics. In order to find support for adopting the name of a native deity *Shangdi*, or a generic term *Shen* (god or gods), to render God into Chinese, missionaries studied the Chinese Classics and their various commentaries. Some drew on Chinese philosophical and historical works for explanations. Unconsciously, they acted as receivers and annotators of Chinese culture, and served as a medium for cultural exchange between China and the West. However, the controversy was never resolved because each party believed what they advocated was the only appropriate choice. The insistence on using one standardized Chinese term to name God was unworkable. Finally, a "solution" acceptable by all the Protestant churches was for the Bible to be published in both *Shangdi* and *Shen* editions. One may purchase and read a *Shangdi* or *Shen* edition, according to his or her taste.

The Term Question has recently been thoroughly studied and ably summarized by scholars. They either focus on historical surveys of the issue or engage with the theological and hermeneutical issues. As this study has explored, the differences between the terms *Shangdi* and *Shen* increasingly faded into the background. The Cultural Revolution of the 1960s suppressed any discussion of God by denigrating "*Shangdi*" as "foreign" and associating "*Shen*" with benighted superstition in order to downplay their affiliation with traditional Chinese culture.

An unintended result is that both terms, *Shangdi/Shen,* now refer primarily to the God of the Bible in the minds of Chinese. Both terms are now accepted, especially by a new generation, as identical and are used interchangeably: *Shangdi* indicates transcendence, while *Shen* indicates a concept of divine immanence. Pre-existing *Shangdi/Shen* editions make it easier to accept that they are just two different names for the Most High. From the perspective of Chinese surname culture, Chinese are accustomed to have different/alternative names. Multiplicity of names is not as unbearable to Chinese as to Western missionaries. Things change as time passes. The term question that foreign missionaries were incapable of solving in the past no longer perplexes Chinese believers. Chinese Bible readers and interpreters today have accepted both terms with their own understanding.

What part did the Chinese play in the Chinese Bible translation? It is worthy of further study. Throughout the nineteenth century, Bible translation was the story of Western missionaries: they guided or undertook the translations. In order to give Chinese the Bible in their native language, Western missionaries experienced a severe struggle in adopting language styles and addressing the Term Question, together with exploring and defining the principles of translation. Finally, they presented China with an excellent work. It is without doubt that this achievement included the participation of native Chinese scholars, because missionary translators were attempting to render Scripture into a receptor language that was not native to them. Unfortunately, despite the fact that the Chinese participants played a significant and indispensable role in the translation work, their names were rarely known, as the early missionaries seldom referred to them by name in their correspondence. Their value was recognized and appreciated by the UV missionary translators. They were given the same voting rights as the Western missionaries and their full names were recorded in the captions of photos taken while they were working together. In recent years, the role of Chinese assistants in the history of Chinese Bible translation has been well examined and reappraised by scholars. It is proven beyond doubt that the UV is the fruit of the combined efforts of both Western missionaries and their Chinese assistants. The missionaries were dominant in the UV project, but the standard and idiom of the Chinese language in translation indicates that these Chinese assistants made a remarkable contribution.

The Chinese Church and historians should be made aware that Chinese assistants played an important role in the UV translation. However, further identification of individual Chinese coworkers is challenging. On the one hand, there is difficulty in converting from the old Wade-Giles system of Romanizing letters into Chinese characters. On the other hand, there is a lack of impartial materials. For instance, in mainland China, Wang Tao is remembered as a Qing dynasty translator, reformer, political columnist, newspaper publisher, fiction writer; and an excellent figure in the history of cultural exchange between China and the West. However, there is no mention of his contribution to the Delegates' version and the Nanking Version due to religious and political bias. Much work of identification still is needed as scholars realize that the contributions of the individual Chinese assistants and their lives are worthy subjects of further detailed studies.

The UV cannot be viewed as an isolated occurrence in the history of the Protestant Church and mission in China. Instead, as demonstrated by this study, it was the end of a development over a whole century and it concluded the missionaries' efforts in this field of their work. The UV is by no means perfect. The linguistic limitations of the foreigners are recognized, but the defects do not outweigh the merits. The UV has been recognized as an authoritative version by Chinese Christians. The authority of the UV lies neither in the leading role played by Western missionaries, nor in the capability of its translators, nor in the original text it is based on. It lies in the fact that the UV is identified with the "Word of God," the "Word of Life." The life that Chinese have received from the UV cannot be destroyed, including the Life that saved the lives of those severely persecuted during the Cultural Revolution. Through suffering, the Chinese Christians have learned to treasure the UV, the Word of God, that has given them comfort and strength, and has sustained them to go through many ordeals. Protestantism has been able to take root in China and the Church has been able to survive tremendous trials, largely because of the UV—the vernacular Bible that has taken root in the hearts of Chinese. The religious and emotional bonds between the UV and Chinese Christians are deep and strong and will not be easily cut off. The UV's sacred status in the mind of Chinese Christian gives it unshakable authority.

The authority and unique significance of the UV can also be seen in its role as a landmark that proclaims the successful ending of the historical mission of translating the Chinese Bible by the Western missionaries. It also indicates that Chinese Bible translation had moved from pluralism to unification, producing the first Chinese Bible in common use by Chinese. Over the past century, the UV, with its unique character, has enjoyed a solid position in the hearts of Chinese Christians worldwide.

Another major reason that makes the UV unique is its important role in the New Culture Movement. The UV appeared during an era when the nation was experiencing rapid language changes. The New Culture Movement (NCM) replaced Classical Chinese with Mandarin as the primary literary medium, creating a favorable circumstance for the UV. In turn, the

UV in Mandarin came into being just in time for the NCM. As a model for standard Mandarin, its emergence helped promote the NCM. The mutual influence of the two combined to shape modern Chinese language and culture. Scholars from mainland China tend to have a very positive attitude towards the UV. They have concluded that the UV had a distinct influence on the Chinese language and colloquial literature, and to some extent also had a profound impact on the NCM. The UV appeared as the times demanded and emerged at just the right moment. How could such a coincidence occur without God's will and work?

However, the authority of the UV is often questioned by younger generations. They simplistically criticize the quality of its translation. While reading Chinese-English bilingual Bible versions, they find there are "unfaithful" translations in the UV, and many passages where the Chinese and English versions don't match. They don't realize the real problem—the bilingual Bibles published overseas place the UV in parallel either with the New International Version in English or with the English Standard Version. Unfortunately, the UV is not a translation of either. This flawed comparison would be like placing the New International Version in parallel with the King James Version; they are not comparable. No wonder the translation of the UV would have many "errors."

The UV has been criticized for a variety of reasons: as a foreign product based on English sources (though the translators reference Hebrew and Greek), with awkward wording, archaic language, or a mixture of vernacular and classical Styles. Yet, with all these problems, it still remains popular among Chinese Christians. In his article "A Century Later, Still Dominant," Yao Xiyi observed from a historical perspective that "In their long and painstaking process of translating the Scripture into Chinese in the early 19th century, Western and Chinese translators had accumulated a rich repository of theological notions and terms in Chinese languages. The UV inherited and integrated them into its own translation."[1] It is in being "its own translation" that shaped a unique *Hehe* (UV) style that others cannot surpass. A good example is in Isaiah 6:3 "Holy, holy, holy, is the LORD of hosts: the whole earth is full of his glory." where "Holy, Holy, Holy" was translated into "*Shengzai, Shengzai, Shengzai!*" the same as that in Revelation 4:8. The UV's translators creatively combined the vernacular *Sheng* and classical *Zai*. Yet, it sounds so sonorous and powerful, with a

---

1. Yao, https://www.chinasource.org/resource-library/articles/a-century-later-still
-dominant.

majestic momentum that inspires awe in the reader. It is such a wonderful translation that no recent translations and revisions would make a change. No one can find a better rendering.

In the beginning of Chinese Bible translation, Nestorian translators were influenced by terms and concepts from Confucianism, Buddhism and Daoism. Nestorians adopted some usages from these three religious' languages in order to be accepted by the natives. Evidence from the Nestorian inscription confirms this. The impact of Confucianism can be seen in the early Catholic and Protestant translations in classical style. This was the way they hoped to reach the Chinese literati, the best and the brightest of society, who were Confucians. The Bible in Mandarin aims to approach the common people. Certain terms used creatively to serve Christian ends have been accepted over time as Christian terminology. Some other terms have changed meaning due to language development, which has resulted in the need to revise the UV.

The UV is merely a *transitional translation* and is by no means perfect. It needs to be constantly revised for many reasons. This consensus is reflected in a recent change of the title of "RCUV" (Revised Chinese Union Version) into "CUV2010," showing the year when the Chinese Union Version was revised, clearly indicating an expectation of freshly revised versions to come in future years. The Chinese Church is now taking responsibility for its own Bible translation. Efforts to retranslate the Bible into modern Chinese are ongoing in individual as well as collaborative ways. Translators are responding to the needs of the digital age, with emphasis not only on readability but also understandability when texts are read aloud.

Entering the E-era, new translations seem to challenge the UV. Yet, the largest sales volume so far still belongs to the UV. Its dominant position has not diminished. Newly published study Bibles, for example, all choose the verses of the UV as their study text, showing the UV is still in favor. The UV's charm lies in its uniqueness, unique style, and its union flavor, which others cannot surpass.

Looking back on history, the UV has served the Chinese church for a whole century and will continue to serve until the appearance of a thoroughly new version. This needed new union translation must be faithful to the original Hebrew and Greek texts as well as to the reader; apply the latest research in archaeology, linguistic, and textual studies; and have the fewest errors and the most elegant Chinese, all of which are required to meet the current needs of the Chinese Christians.

The history of Chinese Bible translation has gone through the stages of the Nestorians' lost translation, the Catholics' unpublished translation, the Protestants' numerous translations to achieve the UV; and from the stage of Western missionary dominance to Chinese self-determination. At this stage the story of Chinese Bible translation is written by Chinese. With such a precious heritage, this new chapter of the story will be even more splendid than what has preceded it.

With the development of translation practice and technology, and the impact of pluralism, Chinese Bible translation is coming to a stage of multiple versions. Doubtless, one day, the UV may move from the center to the edge of the stage. However, the UV's historical value and its marvelous contribution to the Chinese Church are indelible and enduring, just as the King James Version heritage has been to the English-speaking church.

As its name—Union Version—indicates, the UV united translators from different countries and from different denominations who worked together; it united Western missionaries and Chinese assistants who cooperated to produce an excellent work; it united all Chinese Protestant believers worldwide to worship the One, Living God under a single common version of the Bible—the *Heheben*. It is by the *Heheben* that we Chinese turn away from idle worship to the true God; it is through the *Heheben*, we know the Way, the Truth and the Life. It is in the *Heheben* we have found the meaning of life. Its Chinese name——*Heheben*——indicates, "He" (*hehao*, be reconciled), we were reconciled to God through the death of his son; "He" (*heyi*, be united; be one), we are one in Christ. This is the message of the *Heheben*.

The UV may be criticized as "antiquated" and "inaccurate," in human eyes, yet, in God's hands, the UV is a prepared instrument. God has used it to make his glory known, and still uses it. This is why the UV is so unique and stands strong until today: By celebrating the 100th anniversary of the UV, the history of Chinese Bible translation has been rediscovered and recited; the little-known story of the origin of the UV has been retold; the forgotten contributions of the missionaries and Chinese assistants have been reappreciated. Isn't this marvelous?

APPENDIX 1

Comparison of The Chinese Bible Contents of Protestant with Roman Catholic

English Bible OT	Protestant Bible OT (39)	Roman Catholic Bible OT (46)
Genesis	創世記 *Chuangshiji*	創世紀 *Chuangshiji*
Exodus	出埃及記 *Chuaijiji*	出谷紀 *Chuguji*
Leviticus	利未記 *liweiji*	肋未紀 *Leweiji*
Numbers	民數記 *Minshuji*	戶籍紀 *Hujiji*
Deuteronomy	申命記 *Shenmingji*	申命紀 *Shenmingji*
Joshua	約書亞記 *Yueshuyaji*	若蘇厄書 *Ruosueshu*
Judges	士師記 *Shishiji*	民長紀 *Minzhangji*
Ruth	路得記 *Ludeji*	盧德傳 *Ludezuan*
1 Samuel	撒母耳記上 *Samuerjishang*	撒慕爾紀上 *Samuerjishang*
2 Samuel	撒母耳記下 *Samuerjixia*	撒慕爾紀下 *Samuerjixia*
1 Kings	列王紀上 *Liewangjishang*	列王紀上 *Liewangjishang*
2 Kings	列王紀下 *Liewangjixia*	列王紀下 *Liewangjixia*
1 Chronicles	歷代志上 *Lidaizhishang*	編年紀上 *Biannianjishang*
2 Chronicles	歷代志下 *Lidaizhixia*	編年紀下 *Biannianjixia*
Ezra	以斯拉記 *Yisilaji*	厄斯德拉上 *Esidelashang*
Nehemiah	尼希米記 *Niximiji*	厄斯德拉下 *Esidelaxia*
Tobit	***	多俾亞傳 *Duobiyazhuan*
Judith	***	友弟德傳 *Youdidezhuan*

Esther	以斯帖記 *Yisitieji*	艾斯德爾傳 *Aisideerzhuan*
1 Maccabees	***	瑪加伯上 *Majiaboshang*
2 Maccabees	***	瑪加伯下 *Majiaboxia*
Job	約伯記 *Yueboji*	約伯傳 *Yebozhuan*
Psalms	詩篇 *Shipian*	聖詠集 *Shengyongji*
Proverbs	箴言 *Zhenyan*	箴言 *Zhenyan*
Ecclesiastes	傳道書 *Chuandaoshu*	訓道篇 *Xundaopian*
Song of Solomon	雅歌 *Yage*	雅歌 *Yage*
Wisdom	***	智慧篇 *Zhihuipian*
Sirach	***	德訓篇 *Dexunpian*
Isaiah	以賽亞書 *Yisaiyashu*	依撒意亞 *Yisayiya*
Jeremiah	耶利米書 *Yelimishu*	耶肋米亞 *Yelemiya*
Lamentations	耶利米哀歌 *Yelimiaige*	耶肋米亞哀歌 *Yelemiyaaige*
Baruch	***	巴路克 *Baluke*
Ezekiel	以西結書 *Yixijieshu*	厄則克耳 *Ezekeer*
Daniel	但以理書 *Danyilishu*	達尼爾 *Danier*
Hosea	何西阿書 *Hexiashu*	歐瑟亞 *Ouseya*
Joel	約珥書 *Yueershu*	岳厄爾 *Yueeer*
Amos	阿摩司書 *Amosishu*	亞毛斯 *Yamaosi*
Obadiah	俄巴底亞書 *Ebadiyashu*	亞北底亞 *Yabeidiya*
Jonah	約拿書 *Yuenashu*	約納 *Yuena*
Micah	彌迦書 *Mijiashu*	米該亞 *Migaiya*
Nahum	那鴻書 *Nahongshu*	納鴻 *Nahong*
Habakkuk	哈巴谷書 *Habagushu*	哈巴谷 *Habagu*
Zephaniah	西番雅書 *Xifanyashu*	索福尼亞 *Suofuniya*
Haggai	哈該書 *Hagaishu*	哈蓋 *Hagai*
Zechariah	撒迦利亞書 *Sajialiyashu*	匝加利亞 *Zajialiya*
Malachi	瑪拉基書 *Malajishu*	瑪拉基亞 Malajiya

English Bible NT	Protestant Bible NT (27)	Catholic Bible NT (27)
Matthew	馬太福音 *Mataifuyin*	瑪竇福音 *Madoufuyin*
Mark	馬可福音 *Makefuyin*	瑪爾谷福音 *Maergufuyin*
Luke	路加福音 *Lujiafuyin*	路加福音 *Lujiafuyin*
John	約翰福音 *Yuehanfuyin*	若望福音 *Ruowangfuyin*

Acts	使徒行傳 *Shituxingzhuan*	宗徒大事錄 *Zongtudashilu*
Romans	羅馬書 *Luomashu*	羅馬書 *Luomashu*
1 Corinthians	哥林多前書 *Gelinduoqianshu*	格林多前書 *Gelinduoqianshu*
2 Corinthians	哥林多後書 *Gelinduohoushu*	格林多後書 *Gelinduohoushu*
Galatians	加拉太書 *Jialataishu*	迦拉達書 *Jialadashu*
Ephesians	以弗所書 *Yifusuoshu*	厄弗所書 *Efusuoshu*
Philippians	腓立比書 *Feilibishu*	斐理伯書 *Feiliboshu*
Colossians	歌羅西書 *Geluoxishu*	哥羅森書 *Geluosenshu*
1 Thessalonians	帖撒羅尼迦前書 *Tiesaluonijiaqianshu*	得撒洛尼前書 *Desaluoniqianshu*
2 Thessalonians	帖撒羅尼迦後書 *Tiesaluonijiahoushu*	得撒洛尼後書 *Desaluonihoushu*
1 Timothy	提摩太前書 *Timotaiqianshu*	弟茂德前書 *Dimaodeqianshu*
2 Timothy	提摩太後書 *Timotaihoushu*	弟茂德後書 *Dimaodeqianshu*
Titus	提多書 *Tiduoshu*	弟鐸書 *Diduoshu*
Philemon	腓利門書 *Feilimenshu*	費肋孟書 *Feilemengshu*
Hebrews	希伯來書 *Xibolaishu*	希伯來書 *Xibolaishu*
James	雅各書 *Yageshu*	雅各伯書 *Yageboshu*
1 Peter	彼得前書 *Bideqianshu*	伯多祿前書 *Boduoluqianshu*
2 Peter	彼得後書 *Bidehoushu*	伯多祿後書 *Boduoluhoushu*
1 John	約翰一書 *Yuehanyishu*	若望一書 *Ruowangyishu*
2 John	約翰二書 *Yuehanershu*	若望二書 *Ruowangershu*
3 John	約翰三書 *Yuehansanshu*	若望三書 *Ruowangsanshu*
Jude	猶大書 *Youdashu*	猶達書 *Youdashu*
Revelation	啟示錄 *Qishilu*	若望默示錄 *Ruowangmoshilu*

APPENDIX 2

Three Executive Committees of The Union Version Project

A. Executive Committee of the Easy Wenli Version

Nation	Name	Mission
America	W. Ashmore (1824–1909)	American Baptist Missionary Union
	C. F. Reid (1849–1915)	American Southern Methodist Episcopal Mission
	H. Corbertt (1835–1920)	American Presbyterian Mission
	G. F. Fitch (?–1933)	American Presbyterian Mission
	A. H. Smith (1845–1932)	American Board of Commissioners for Foreign Missions
Britain	D. Hill (1840–1896)	English Wesleyan Mission
	J. W. Stevenson (1844–1918)	China Inland Mission
	J. C. Gibson (1849–1919)	English Presbyterian Mission
	T. Bryson (?–1936)	London Missionary Society
	J. R. Wolfe (1832–1915)	Church Missionary Society
Germany	R. Lechler (1824–1908)	Basel Mission
	F. Hubrig (1840–1892)	Berlin Mission

B. Executive Committee of *Wenli* Version

Nation	Name	Mission
America	C. Goodrich (1835–1925)	American Board of Commissioners for Foreign Missions

	A. M. Pilcher (1838–1909)	American Methodist Episcopal Missionary Society
	J. Wherry (1837–1918)	American Presbyterian Mission
	Y. L. Allen (?–1907)	American Southern Methodist Episcopal Mission
	R. H. Graves (1833–1912)	American Southern Baptist Mission
Britain	J. C. Gibson (1849–1919)	English Presbyterian Mission
	A. Elwin (1846–1922)	Church Missionary Society
	J. W. Stevenson (1844–1918)	China Inland Mission
	F. W. Baller (1852–1922)	China Inland Mission
	T. Bryson (?–1936)	London Missionary Society
Germany	R. Lechler (1824–1908)	Basel Mission
	E. Faber (1839–1899)	General Evangelical Protestant Missionary Society

C. Executive Committee of Mandarin Version

Nation	Name	Mission
America	C. W. Mateer (1836–1908)	American Presbyterian Mission
	C. Goodrich (1835–1925)	American Board of Commissioners for Foreign Missions
	J. R. Hykes (1852–1921)	American Methodist Episcopal Missionary Society
	R. T. Bryan (1855–1946)	American Southern Baptist Mission
Britain	D. Hill (1840–1896)	English Wesleyan Mission
	F. W. Baller (1852–1922)	China Inland Mission
	T. Bryson (?–1936)	London Missionary Society
	A. Elwin (1846–1922)	Church Missionary Society
	J. McIntyre (?–1905)	Scotch United Presbyterian Mission
Germany	E. Faber (1839–1899)	General Evangelical Protestant Missionary Society

APPENDIX 3

Protestant Chinese Bible Translation in Three Stages

A: From the Beginnings to the Union Version

Date & Contents	Name of Version English – Chinese in pinyin	Chief Translators	Language Style	Publisher
1814 NT 1823 OT	Morrison/Milne's *Shen Tian Shengshu*	R. Morrison W. Milne	*Wenli*	BFBS
1816 NT 1822 OT	Marshman/Lassar's *Xin Jiu Yizhao Quanshu*	J. Marshman J. Lassar	*Wenli*	GBMS BFBS
1837 NT 1840 OT	Medhurst/Gultzlaff's *Shen Tian Xin Jiu Yizhao Shengshu*	W. H. Medhurst C. Gutzlaff E. C. Bridgman J. R. Morrison	*Wenli*	BFBS
1840 NT	Gutzlaff's *Xin Yizhao Shengshu*	C. Gutzlaff	*Wenli*	Privately pub
1852 NT 1854 OT	Delegates' version *Weiban Yiben/Daibiao Yiben*	W. H. Medhurst E. C. Bridgman J. Stronach W. Lowrie W. J. Boone	*Wenli*	BFBS
1859 NT 1862 OT	Bridgman/Culbertson's version *Bizhiwen Yiben*	E. C. Bridgman M. S. Culbertson W. J. Boone H. Blodget	*Wenli*	ABS

Date & Contents	Name of Version English – Chinese in pinyin	Chief Translators	Language Style	Publisher
1853 NT 1868 OT	Goddard's Shengjing Xiu Jiu Yizhao Quanshu	J. Goddard E. C. Lord Dean	Wenli	ABS
1857 NT	Nanking Version Nanjing Guanhua Yiben	W. H. Medhurst J. Stronach	Mandarin	BFBS
1866 NT	Peking Version Beijing Guanhua Yiben	J. S. Burdon J. Edkins S. I. J. Schereschewsy H. Blodget W. A. P. Martin	Mandarin	BFBS ABS
1875 OT	Schereschewsky's Mandarin Version Shi Yuese Guanhua Yiben	S. I. J. Schereschewsky	Mandarin	ABS
1878	Schereschewsky's (revision) Shengjing Quanshu	S. I. J. Schereschewsky	Mandarin	ABS
1889 NT	John's Mandarin Version Yang Gefei Guanhua Yiben	G. John	Mandarin	NBSS
1885 NT	John's Esay Wenli Version Yang Gefei Qian Wenli Yiben	G. John	Easy Wenli	NBSS
1889 NT	Burdon/Blodget's Version Bao Yuehan/Bai Hanli Qian Wenli Yiben	J. S. Burdon H. Blodget	Easy Wenli	ABS
1902	Schereschewsky's Version Shi Yuese Qian Wenli Yiben	S. I. J. Schereschewsky	Easy Wenli	ABS
1904 NT	Easy Wenli Union Version Qian Wenli Hehe Yiben	J. S. Burdon H. Blodget R. H. Graves J. C. Gibson G. I. Genahr J. W. Davis	Easy Wenli	ABS BFBS NBSS
1906 NT 1919 OT	Wenli Union Version Wenli Hehe Yiben: Xin Jiu Yue Quanshu	J. Chalmers J. Edkins J. Wherry D. Z. Sheffield M. Schaub T. W. Pearce J. Lloyd	Wenli	ABS BFBS NBSS

Date & Contents	Name of Version English – Chinese in pinyin	Chief Translators	Language Style	Publisher
1906 NT 1919 OT	Mandarin Union Version Guanhua Hehe Yiben: Xin Jiu Yue Quanshu	C. W. Mateer L. Nevius H. Blodget C. Goodrich G. Owen J. R. Hykes T. Bramfitt F. W. Baller S. Lewis S. R. Clarke	Mandarin	ABS BFBS NBSS

B: After the Union Version up to the 1990s

Date & Contents	Name of Version English–Chinese in pinyin	Chief Translator	Publisher
1929 NT	Sydenstricker's Sai Zhaoxiang Yiben	A. Sydenstricker	Presbyterian Mission
1933 NT	Wang Xunchen's Wang Xuanchen Yiben	Wang Xunchen	Qingdao Church
1936 NT	Zhu Baohui's Zhu Baohui Yiben	Zhu Baohui	Privately published
1939 NT 1940 Ps 1958 ed	The Bible Treasury New Testament Guoyu Xinjiuku Yiben: Xinyue Quanshu fu Shipian	H. Ruck Zheng Shoulin	Bible Treasury, Peking
1967 NT	Xiao Tiedi's New Translation Xinyi Xinyue Quanji	Xiao Tiedi	Spirit Food
1946 NT 1970 OT	Lu Zhenzhong's Bible Lu Zhenzhong Yiben: Shengjing	Lu Zhenzhong	HKBS
1974 NT 1979 OT	Chinese Living Bible Dangdai Shengjing	Committee under Joseph Chiang	Tien Dao Publishing House, IBS
1975 NT 1979 OT	Today's Chinese Version Xiandai Zhongwen Yiben	Moses Hsü, I-Jin Loh, Chow Lien-hwa, Martin Wang and Evelyn Chiao	UBS
1976 NT 1992 OT	New Chinese Version Shengjing: Xinyiben	The New Chinese Bible Translation Committee	Lockman Foundation

Date & Contents	Name of Version English–Chinese in pinyin	Chief Translator	Publisher
1995 NT	New Testament: *Putonghua* Version *Xinyue: Putonghua Yiben*	Beijing Translation Team	(unknown)

C: Translation Efforts in Twenty–first Century

Date & Contents	Name of Version English–Chinese in pinyin	Chief Translator	Publisher
2005	The Holy Bible: CUV (Standard Edition) *Shengjing Biaozhunben*	Wang Zhengzhong	Chinese Bible Association
2006 NT 2010 OT	Revised Chinese Union Version NT *Shengjing: Heheben Xiudingban*	I-Jin Loh and Joseph Hong	UBS, HK
2006 2008 2010	The Five Books of Moses/Torah *Moxi Wujing* Wisdom Books *Zhihui Shu* New Testament *Xinyue*	Feng Xiang	Oxford U. Press
2006	The Holy Bible: A Dynamic Chinese Translation *Jianming Shengjing*	Gene Xiao Qingsong	Tucson Chinese Bible Society
2008 NT	Chinese Standard Bible *Xinyue: Zhongwen Biaozhun Yiben*	Asia Bible Society	Holman Bible Publishers
2010 NT	Contemporary Chinese Version *Xinyue Quanshu: Xin Hanyu Yiben*		Chinese Bible International
2010	Chinese Contemporary Bible *Shengjing: Dangdai Yiben Xiudingban*		International Bible Society
2011 NT	New Testament *Xinyue Xin Hehe Yandu Yiben*	Li Guang	Scripture Resource Center
2011	Chinese New English Translation Bible *Xin Yingyu Yiben Shengjing Zhongyiben*	Deren Culture Exchange Foundation	Biblical Studies
2012	Holy Bible – English New Living Translation Chinese New Living Translation *Shengjing: Zhongying Duizhao (Xin Puji Yiben)*		Chinese Bible International

Date & Contents	Name of Version English–Chinese in pinyin	Chief Translator	Publisher
2015 NT	New Testament - Worldwide Chinese Bible Xinyue *Quanshu: Huanqiu Shengjing Yiben*		Worldwide Bible Society

APPENDIX 4

A List of Chinese Assistants in the History of Chinese Protestant Missionary Bible Translation

Western translator	Chinese Assistant			
	Romanized transliteration	Pinyin	Chinese characters	Suggested characters
Morrison	Yong Sam-tak	Rong Sande	容三德	
	Le sëe sang	Li Xiansheng Li Shigong	李先生 李十公	
	Abel Yun Kwanming	Yun Guanming Yin Kunming Yuan Guangming	雲官明	殷坤明 袁光明
	Low-Hëe	Luo Qian/Lou Xian	羅謙	婁憲
	Kō Mow-ho Ko sëe sang	Ge Maohe Ge Xiansheng	葛茂和 葛先生	高先生
		Chen Laoyi	陳老宜	
	Kwei-Une	Gui Youni	桂有霓	
Marshman	An unnamed Chinese assistant mentioned in Marshman's letter to BFBS in 1813.			

199

APPENDIX 4

| Western translator | Chinese Assistant | | | |
	Romanized transliteration	Pinyin	Chinese characters	Suggested characters
Medhurst	Choo Tih-Lang	Zhu Delang	朱德郎	
		Wang Changgui (d.1849)	王昌桂	
	Wang Lan-King	Wang Tao (1828–97) Wang Lanqing (Alternate name)	王韜 王蘭卿 (字)	
Goddard	Kiok Cheng	(assistant during Goddard's time in Bangkok)		
	Chiu Ching Dau	Jiu Jingdao		久京道
	Giu Han Ching	Qiu Hanjing Qiu Hanqing		邱翰景 邱漢卿
Boone		Wong Kongchai	王	王孔財
Schereschewsky	(Unnamed Chinese teacher who accompanied Schereschewsky on a 5-month Yangzi River trip. Two unknown who converted his Romanized manuscript into Chinese characters)			
		Liu	劉	柳
		Wei Jianmin		魏建民
		Jin Shihe		金石禾
		Ye Shanrong Ye Shandang		葉山榮 葉三宕
		You Baoseng Yu Baosheng	尤	尤保森 俞寶生
		Zhang Jiezhi		張傑志
		Lian Yinghuang	連英煌	
Blodget	Lang Yun-shung	Lang Yunsheng		郎耘生
	Su Sien-song	Su Xiansheng	蘇先生	
Burdon		Li	李	黎
(Wenli UV)		Zhuge	諸葛	
		Zhuang	莊	莊/奘
		Zhao	趙	
Wherry	Kuo	Guo (Elder)	郭(長老)	

200

Western translator	Chinese Assistant			
	Romanized transliteration	Pinyin	Chinese characters	Suggested characters
Mateer	Tsou Li Wên	Zou Liwen	鄒立文	
	Wang Yuan Teh	Wang Yuande Wang Xunchen (Alternate name)	王元德 王宣忱 （字）	
Goodrich	Choong His-hsin	Zhang Xixin	張洗心	
	Lee Chihli	Li Qili	李	李齊利
Baller		Liu Dacheng (d. 1918)	劉大成	
Lewis	Li Ch'wen-fan	Li Chunfan (d. 1938)	李春蕃	
		Yan	嚴	彥/閻/晏
Aiken		Wang	王	汪
Owen		Cheng Jingyi	誠靜怡	
Sydenstricker		Zhu Baohui	朱寶惠	

Appendix 5

Questionnaire for Chinese Bible Readers

A SURVEY WAS ADMINISTERED as part of this research. The Questionnaire on Chinese Bible Versions (QCBV) was designed to investigate opinions of Chinese Bible readers about the UV and *Shen/Shangdi* editions. The survey was conducted among Chinese church groups in both North America and Mainland China, and thus provides a unique picture of attitudes towards Chinese Bible translation among these groups. The three sections, below, describe the construction, administration and analysis of the QCBV.

1. Construction: Order of Content and Appearance

The QCBV consists of fourteen questions divided into two sections: A) About you (1–6) which included status (i.e., Christian or non-Christian) age, gender, location, education and years of being a Christian; B) About Chinese Bible versions (7–14). Questions 7–9 were used to provide a comparative analysis of acceptance of *Shen/Shangdi* editions. Questions 10–12 were used to investigate readers' knowledge about various Chinese Bible versions. Questions 13–14 were used to analyze opinions about the UV.

Four special considerations:

- The questionnaire was clearly marked *Bujiming* (confidential), to let respondents give their answers free from unnecessary misgivings.

- A brief note was added to question 7 to indicate that "different editions" meant *Shen* or *Shangdi* editions.

- For question 8, a Bible verse (Gen 1:1) was offered in order to help respondents fully understand the question and mark the right option.

- "Seeker" was distinguished from "non-believer" in Status, because some of them (especially those from House Churches) have been seekers for years but had no chance to be baptized due to shortage of pastors.

2. Administration: Distribution and Response

Two groups were selected to receive questionnaires in North America: group 1 mainly consisted of early migrants on the east coast (including Canada) and group 2 was a Chinese Church formed of new migrants on the west coast. Three groups were selected in Mainland China. They included Seminary, House Church and the Three-Self Church members. Each group had a coordinator who was supplied with the copy of the questionnaire, and then s/he duplicated the form according to the size of their groups. Distribution techniques varied. The seminary group was invited by the coordinator to take a questionnaire after their class. Others were distributed when groups gathered together. Attempted distribution to a group of ministers of the Three-Self Church failed because of a lack of written permission from the church authorities. Most of forms were collected immediately after they were completed. Surveying was conducted in 2005. 102 questionnaires were received back from North America, of which one was invalid, and 248 questionnaires were received back from Mainland, 4 invalids. The total of valid returned forms was 345.

3. Statistical Analysis

The following is a summary of the results of the QCBV:

1. Among 345 respondents, 75.5 percent were laity, 10.2 percent were theologically educated, 6.4 percent were ministers or evangelists, 6.1 percent were seekers, and 1.7 percent were non-believers.

2. 65.8 percent of respondents were female.

3. 75.5 percent of respondents were from Mainland China.

4. 76 percent of respondents were young people and middle-aged (21–60).

5. 53 percent of respondents had received college or university education, 35.4 percent had received middle school education.

6. 58 percent of respondents had been Christians for more than 10 years.

7. 70 percent of respondents knew there were *Shen/Shangdi* editions. The proportion of them among the theologically educated respondents was 100 percent, among the ministers or evangelists was 95.5 percent, and among the laity was 66 percent.

8. 77 percent of respondents used the *Shen* edition, 19 percent used the *Shangdi* edition and 4 percent used both.

9. 36 percent of respondents preferred the *Shen* edition, 10 percent preferred the *Shangdi* edition and 54 percent claimed that it does not matter; both are accepted.

10. 75 percent of respondents affirmed that they knew there were various Chinese Bible versions.

11. 79.5 percent of respondents used the UV, 11.5 percent used the TCV, 3 percent used the NCV. 6 percent claimed that they used the UV together with other translations (the TCV or the NCV or the LZV) at the same time.

12. 39 percent of respondents knew there were *Wenli* versions, 11 percent claimed that they had seen a copy of *Wenli* Bible.

13. On the translation of the UV, 32.3 percent of respondents considered it excellent, 45.3 percent considered it good, 20.8 percent considered it average, three non-believers and one minister considered it fair. One non-believer considered it poor.

14. 44.7 percent of respondents believed the UV needed no revision, 29.4 percent believed revision is needed, 8 percent believed new translation is needed, and 17.9 percent believed that no changes should be made. Most of the theologically educated respondents (83 percent) and ministers (65 percent) believed the UV needed to be revised.

APPENDIX 6

A List of Union Versions Translators with their Chinese Names

This list identifies the significant missionary figures involved in the translation of three Union Versions

Aiken, Edwin E. (1859–1951)	安德文
Allan, C. Wilfred (1870-1958)	林輔華
Baller, Frederick W. (1852–1922)	鮑康寧
Blodget, Henry (1825–1903)	白漢理
Bramfitt, Thomas (1850–1923)	布藍非
Burdon, John Shaw (1827–1907)	包約翰/包爾騰
Clarke, Samuel R. (1853–1916)	柯拉克
Chalmers, John (1825–1899)	湛約翰
Davis, John Wright (1849–1917)	戴維思
Edkins, Joseph (1823–1905)	艾約瑟
Genahr, Gottlieb I. (1856–1937)	葉道勝
Gibson, John Campbell (1849–1919)	汲約翰
Goodrich, Chauncey (1835–1925)	富善
Graves, Rosewell H. (1833–1912)	紀好弼
Hykes, John R. (1852–1921)	海格思
Lewis, Spencer (1854–1939)	鹿依士
Lloyd, John (1850–1931)	盧壹
Mateer, Calvin W. (1836–1908)	狄考文
Nevius, John L. (1829–1893)	倪維思

Owen, George S. (1847–1914)   歐文/文書田
Pearce, Thomas W. (1855–1938)   皮堯士
Schaub, Martin (1850–1900)   沙伯/韶瑪亭
Sheffield, Davello Z. (1841–1913)   謝衛樓
Sydenstricker, A. (1852–1931)   賽兆祥
Wherry, John (1837–1918)   惠志道

Bibliography

American Bible Society Record (1865).

Baller, F. W. "The Revised Mandarin Bible (Union Version)." *China's Millions* n.s. 27 (1919) 57–59.

Bao Huiyuan, ed. "Zhongwen Shengjing Fanyishi Jianbiao (1700–1990)." In *Shengjing: Xin Guojiban Yanduben*. USA: Christian Renewal Ministries, 1996.

The Bible Translator (1960)

Blodget, H. *The Use of T'ien Chu for God in Chinese*. Shanghai: American Presbyterian Mission, 1893.

Bondfield, G. H. "The Bible in China, a List of Versions in Wenli, Easy Wenli, and Mandarin, with Notes." *China Mission Year Book* 6 (1915) 466–73.

Boone, W. J. "An Essay on the Proper Rendering of the Words Elohim and *theos* into the Chinese Language." *Chinese Repository* 17 (1848) 17–53, 57–89.

———. "Defence of an Essay on the Proper Rendering of the Words Elohim and *theos* into the Chinese Language." *Chinese Repository* 19 (1850), 345–85, 409–44, 465–78, 569–618, 624–50.

British and Foreign Bible Society Report (1815), (1939).

Broomhall, M. *The Chinese Empire: A General & Missionary Survey*. London: Morgan & Scott, 1907.

———. *Robert Morrison: A Master-Builder*. London: CMS, 1924.

———. *The Bible in China*. London, Philadelphia: The China Inland Mission, 1934.

Cai Jintu. "Zhongwen Shengjing de Liuchuan." In *Dao Zai Shenzhou*, 239–78. Hong Kong: International Bible Society, 2000.

Camps, A. "The Father Gabriele M. Allegra, OFM (1907–1976) and The Studium Biblicum Franciscanum The First Complete Chinese Catholic Translation of the Bible." *Bible in Modern China: The Literary and Intellectual Impact*. Edited by Irene Eber, S. K. Wan, and Knut Walf. Nettetal: Steyler, 1999.

Charbonnier, J. *Christians in China: A.D. 600 to 2000* San Francisco, CA: Ignatius, 39–51, 2007.

Chen Jianming. *Jiyang Wenzi, Guangchuan Fuyin: Jindai Jidujiao Zaihua Wenzi Shigong*. Taibei: Yuzhouguang Quanren Guanhuai Jigou, 2006.

Chen Zhongdao. "Mantan Heheben Shengjing." *Yijing Luncong*. Edited by Liu Yilin. Hongkong: Fuyin Wenxuan, 1979.

Cheng Zhiyi. "Shengjing zhi Zhongwen Yiben." In *Shengjing Hanyi Lunwenji*, edited by Jia Baoluo (R. P. Kramers), 1–28. First printing 1947. Hong Kong: Fuqiao, 1965.

China Mission Year Book 1 (1910)–13 (1925).

The Chinese Recorder 1 (1867)–50 (1919).

The Chinese Repository 1 (1832)–20 (1851).

Covell, Ralph R. *Confucius, the Buddha, and Christ: A History of the Gospel in Chinese.* American Society of Missiology Series 11. Maryknoll, NY: Orbis, 1986.

Darlow, T. H., and H. F. Moule, eds. *Historical Catalogue of the Printed Editions of Holy Scripture in the Library of the British and Foreign Bible Society* I–II, 181–255. London: British and Foreign Bible Society, 1903.

Dawson, C. *The Mongol Mission: Narratives and Letters of the Franciscan Missionaries in Mongolia and China in the Thirteenth and Fourteenth Centuries.* 1955. Reprint, New York: Sheed & Ward, 1980.

Dictionary of Modern Chinese. Shanghai: Shangwu Yinshuguan, 1997.

Ding, Guangxun. See Ting, K. H.

Dodd, C. H. "The Translation of the Bible: Some Questions of Principle." *The Bible Translator* 11 (1960) 1, 4–9.

Eber, I. *The Jewish Bishop and the Chinese Bible: S. I. J. Schereschewsky (1831–1906).* Studies in Christian Mission 22. Leiden: Brill, 1999.

———. "The Interminable Term Question." In *The Bible in Modern China: The Literary and Intellectual Impact.* Edited by Irene Eber, S. K. Wan, and Knut Walf. Monumenta Serica Monograph Series 43. Nettetal: Steyler, 1999.

Eber, Irene, S. K. Wan, and Knut Walf, eds. *The Bible in Modern China: The Literary and Intellectual Impact.* Monumenta Serica Monograph Series 43. Nettetal: Steyler, 1999.

Feng, Bingcheng. *You zi yin* . Haiwai Xiaoyuan, California: 1996.

Fenn, Eric. "The Bible and the Missionary." In *The Cambridge History of the Bible.* Vol. 3, *The West from the Reformation to the Present Day,* edited by S. L. Greenslade, 383–407. Cambridge University Press, 1963.

Fisher, D. W. *Calvin Wilson Mateer: 45 Years a Missionary in Shantung, China: A Biography.* Philadelphia: Westminster, 1911.

Foster, J. *The Church of the Tang Dynasty.* London: SPCK, 1939.

Galik, Marian. ed. *Influence, Translation, and Parallels: Selected Studies on the Bible in China.* Netherlands: Drukkerij Steijl, 2004.

Garnier, A.J. *Chinese Versions of the Bible.* Shanghai: Christian Literature Society for China, 1934.

Gibson, J. C. "Review of the Various Colloquial Versions and the Comparative Advantages of Roman Letters and Chinese Characters." *Records 1890,* 62–89. Shanghai: Presbyterian Mission, 1890.

Goodrich, C. "The Experience of a Bible Translator." *China Mission Year Book* 4 (1913) 378–81.

Gu Dunrou. "Shengjing Guoyu Ben Yiwen Jiantao." In *Shengjing Hanyi Lunwenji,* , edited by Jia Baoluo (R. P. Kramers), 110–34. Hong Kong: Fuqiao, 1965.

Hai Enbo (M. Broomhall). *Dao Zai Shenzhou,* translated by Cai Jintu. Hong Kong: International Bible Society, 2000.

He Kaili. *Jidujiao Zaihua Chuban Shiye (1912–1949),* translated by Chen Jianming and Wang Zaixing. Chengdu: Sichuan Daxue Chubanshe, 2004.

Hickley, Dennis. *The First Christians of China.* London: China Study Project, 1980.

Hong Fang. "Zhongwen Shengjing *Gongtong Yiben* Fanyi Yanjiuhui." *Jiandao Xuekan* 4 (1995)161–62.

Hong, Joseph. "Revision of the Chinese Union Version Bible: Assessing the challenges from an historical perspective." *The Bible Translator* 53 (2002) 238–48.

Jia Baoluo (R. P. Kramers), ed. *Shengjing Hanyi Lunwenji*. Hong Kong: Fuqiao, 1965.

———. "Zuijin zhi Shengjing Zhongwen Yiben." In *Shengjing Hanyi Lunwenji*, edited by Jia Baoluo (R. P. Kramers), 29–37. Hong Kong: Fuqiao, 1965.

———. "Ping Lü Zhenzhong Mushi Xinyue Xinyi Xiugao." In *Shengjing Hanyi Lunwenji*, edited by Jia Baoluo (R. P. Kramers), 135–47. Hong Kong: Fuqiao, 1965.

———. "Zhongwen Shengjing zhi Xiuding—Qiantu Ruhe?" In *Shengjing Hanyi Lunwenji*, edited by Jia Baoluo (R. P. Kramers), 150–60. Hong Kong: Fuqiao, 1965.

Jia Liyan (A. J. Garnier). "Zhongwen Shengjing Yiben Xiaoshi." In *Xinyue Shengjing Liuchuan Shilue*, 87–146. Hong Kong: Found Treasure, 1999.

John, Griffith. "Leading Rules for Translation." *Chinese Recorder* 16 (1885) 381–86.

———. "The Easy Wen Li New Testament." *Chinese Recorder* 17 (1886) 145–48.

Kramers, R. P. "Some Thoughts on Revision of the Bible in Chinese." *The Bible Translator* 7 (1956) 152–62.

Ku, Tun-jou (Gu, Dunrou). "Notes on the Chinese Version of the Bible." *The Bible Translator* 8 (1957) 160–65.

Latourette, K. S. *A History of Christian Missions in China*. London: SPCK, 1929.

Lee, A. C. C. "Naming God in Asia: Cross-Textual Reading in Multi-Cultural Context." *Quest: An Interdisciplinary Journal for Asian Christian Scholars*, vol.3, no.1 (2004) 21–42.

_____. "God's Asian Names: Rendering the Biblical God in Chinese." *SBL Forum*, November, 2005.

Lees, J. "Letter to a Friend on Wen-li v. Vernacular." *Chinese Recorder* 23 (1892) 178–81.

Legge, J. *The Notions of the Chinese Concerning God and Spirits: with an Examination of the Defense of an Essay on the Proper Rendering of the Words Elohim and Theos into the Chinese Language, by William J. Boone*. Hong Kong: Hong Kong Register Office, 1852.

———. *The Nestorian Monument at Hsi-an Fu*. London: Tribner and Co., 1888.

Li Cheng. See Feng Bingcheng

Li Shiyuan. "Zhongwen Shengjing Fanyi Jianshi." *Jingfeng* 53 (1978) 2–14.

Li Zhigang. *Jidujiao Zaoqi Zai Hua Chuanjiaoshi*. Taibei: Shangwu, 1985.

Liang Gong, ed. *Shengjing Baike Cidian*. Shengyang: Liaoning Renmin Chubanshe, 1990.

———. "Twenty Years of Studies of Biblical Literature in the People's Republic of China (1976–1996)." In *The Bible in Modern China: the Literary and Intellectual Impact*. Edited by Irene Eber, S. K. Wan, and Knut Walf, 383–404. Monumenta Serica Monograph Series 43. Nettetal: Steyler, 1999.

Liang Qianyi. "Guoyu Heheben de Xiuding Gongzuo." *Jinri Huaren Jiaohui* 12 (1986) 26–27.

Liu Yiling. "Gaiyi Zhongwen Shengjing de Yige Jianyi." In *Shengjing Hanyi Lunwenji*, edited by Jia Baoluo (R. P. Kramers), 95–109. Hong Kong: Fuqiao, 1965.

———, ed. *Yijing Luncong*. Babeili: Fuyin Wenxuanshe, 1979.

Loh, I-Jin. "Chinese Translations of the Bible." In *An Encyclopaedia of Translation: Chinese-English~English-Chinese*, edited by Chan Sin-wai and D. E. Pollard, 54–69. Hong Kong: The Chinese University Press, 1995.

London Mission Society Report (1916).

Long Lingguang. "Lun Shengjing Zhongyi." In *Long Lingguang Wenji*, 198–280. Hong Kong: Jidao Shulou, 1984.

Luo Weihong. *Zhongguo Jidujiao*. Beijing: Wuzhou Chuanbo Chubanshe, 2004.

Luo Xurong. "Shengjing Zai Zhongguo de Yiben." *Jinling Shenxuezhi* 8 (1988) 37–39; 9 (1989) 49–51.

MacGillivray, D. ed. *A Century of Protestant Missions in China (1807–1907): Being the Centenary Conference Historical Volume.* Shanghai: American Presbyterian Mission, 1907.

Marshman, J. C. *The Life and Times of Carey, Marshman, and Ward: Embracing the History of the Serampore Mission.* 2 vols. London: Longman, 1859.

McNeur, G. H. *China's First Preacher: Liang A-Fa 1789–1855.* Shanghai: Kwang Hsueh, 1934.

Medhurst, W. H. "Memorial Addressed to The British & Foreign Bible Society on a New Version of the Chinese Scriptures." *Documents 1836.* London, 1836.

———. "Remarks in Favor of *Shangti* and against *Shin,* as the Proper Term to Denote the True God." *Chinese Repository* 16 (1847) 34–37.

———. "Reply to the Essay of Dr. Boone on the Proper Rendering of the Words *Elohim* and *Theos* into the Chinese Language." *Chinese Repository* 17 (1848) 489–520, 545–74, 600–47.

Mo Feite (S. H. Moffett). *Yazhou Jidujiao Shi.* Edited and translated by Zhongguo Shenxue Yanjiuyuan Zhongguo Wenhua Yanjiu Zhongxin. Hong Kong: Chinese Christian Literature Council Ltd., 2000.

Moffett, S. H. *A History of Christianity in Asia.* Vol. 1. American Society of Missiology Series 36. Maryknoll, NY: Orbis, 1998.

Moseley, W. *A Memoir on the Importance and Practicability of Translating the Holy Scriptures in the Chinese Language and of Circulating them in the Vast Empire.* 2nd ed. N.p., 1801.

Moule, A. C. *Christians in China before the Year 1550.* London: SPCK, 1930.

Mu Er (A. C. Moule). *1550 Nianqian de Zhongguo Jidujiao Shi.* Translated by Hao Zhenhua. Beijing: Zhonghua, 1884.

Muirhead, W. "Historical Summary of the Different Versions etc." *Records of the General conference of the Protestant Missionaries of China Held at Shanghai, May 7–20, 1890,* 33–41. Shanghai: American Presbyterian Mission, 1890.

Muller, J.A. *Apostle of China: Samuel Isaac Joseph Schereschewsky, 1831–1906.* New York; Milwaukee, 1937.

Murray, A. H. Jowett. "The New Mandarin Bible." *Chinese Recorder* 50 (1919) 439–43.

Nida, Eugene A. *Message and Mission: The Communication of the Christian Faith.* New York: Harper & Row, 1960.

———. "Bible Translation in Today's World." *The Bible Translator* 17 (1966) 59–64.

———. "Intelligibility and Acceptability in Bible Translating." *The Bible Translator* 39 (1988) 301–08.

Questions and Answers on Important Doctrines of Christian Faith. Shanghai: China Christion Council, 1983.

Records of the General Conference of the Protestant Missionaries of China, Held at Shanghai, May 10–24, 1877. Shanghai: Presbyterian Mission, 1877; referred to as *Records 1877.*

Records of the General Conference of the Protestant Missionaries of China, Held at Shanghai, May 7–20, 1890. Shanghai: Presbyterian Mission Press, 1890; referred to as *Records 1890.*

Records: China Centenary Missionary Conference, Held at Shanghai, April 25 to May 8, 1907. Shanghai: Centenary Conference Committee, 1907; referred to as *Records 1907.*

Saeki, P. Y. *The Nestorian Monument in China.* London, SPCK, 1916.

———. *The Nestorian Documents and Relics in China.* Tokyo: The Toho Bunkwa Gakuin, 1937.

Schereschewsky, S. I. J. "Translation of the Scriptures into Chinese." In *Records of the General Conference of the Protestant Missionaries of China, Held at Shanghai, May 7–20, 1890*, 41–44. Shanghai: Presbyterian Mission, 1890.

Shen Chengen. "Tantan Hengpaiben *Xinyue Fu Shipian.*" *Tianfeng* 8 (1986) 18–20.

———. "Huanhu Hengpaiben Shengjing Quanshu Chuban." *Tianfeng* 7 (1989) 2–4.

Smalley, W. A. *Translation as Mission: Bible Translation in the Modern Missionary Movement.* Macon, GA: Mercer University Press, 1991.

Song, B. A. *Training Laborers for His Harvest: A Historical Study of William Milne's Mentorship of Liang Fa.* Eugene, OR: Wipf & Stock, 2015.

Spillett, H. W. *A Catalogue of Scriptures in the Languages of China and Republic of China.* London: British and Foreign Bible Society, 1975.

Standaert, N. "The Bible in Early Seventeenth Century China." In *The Bible in Modern China: The Literary and Intellectual Impact*, edited by Irene Eber, S. K. Wan and Knut Walf, 31–54. Nettetal: Steyler Verlag, 1999.

Strandenaes, Thor. "Principles of Chinese Bible Translation as Expressed in Five Selected Versions of the New Testament and Exemplified by Mt. 5:1–12 and Col. 1." PhD. diss., Uppsala University, 1987.

———. "Anonymous Bible Translators: Native Literati and the Translation of the Bible into Chinese, 1807–1907." In *Sowing the Word: The Cultural Impact of the British and Foreign Bible Society 1807–1907*, edited by Stephen Batalden, Kathleen Cann, and John Dean, 121–48. Bible in the Modern World 3. Sheffield: Sheffield Phoenix, 2004.

Su Jing. *Zhongguo, kaimen! Malixun ji Xiangguan Renwu Yanjiu.* Hong Kong: Jidujiao Zhongguo Zongjiao Wenhua Yanjiushe, 2005.

Teng Jinhui. "Heheben yu Xinyiben Yiwen Bijiao." *Zhongwen Shengjing Xinyi Weiyuanhui Tongxun* 4 (1976) 1.

Ting, K. H. (Ding Guangxun). "Nüxing, Muxing, Shenxing." In *Ding Guangxun Wenji*, 229–33. Nanjing: Yilin, 1998.

———. *Love Never Ends.* Nanjing: Yilin, 2000.

———. *God Is Love: Collected Writings of K. H. Ting.* Colorado Springs, CO: Cook Communications Ministries International, 2004.

Wang Mingdao. "Xinyue Hanwen Yiben Zhong Dang Gaizheng de Yixie Difang." In *Shengjing Hanyi Lunwenji*, edited by Jia Baoluo (R. P. Kramers), 38–70. Hong Kong: Fuqiao, 1965.

Wang Shenyin. "Jiaoding Hanyi Shengjing Zouyi." *Tianfeng* 2 (1981) 10–13.

Wang Weifan. "Shengjing Yiben Zai Zhongguo." *Jinling Shenxuezhi* 14/15 (1991) 62–73.

Wang Zhengzhong. *Shengjing Hehe Yiben Xiuding Gongzuo de Zhenxiang.* Taizhong: Jinxue Chubanshe, 2000.

Wen Yong. *Shengjing Lice.* Beijing: Jinri Zhongguo, 1992.

Wherry, J. "Historical Summary of the Different Versions of the Scriptures." *Records of the General Conference of the Protestant Missionaries of China, Held at Shanghai, May 7–20, 1890*, 45–58. Shanghai: Presbyterian Mission, 1890.

Whyte, B. *Unfinished Encounter: China and Christianity.* London: Fount Paperbacks, 1988.

Wickeri, J. "The Union Version of the Bible and the New Literature in China." *The Translator* 1 (1995) 129–52.

Willeke, B. H. "The Chinese Bible Manuscript in the British Museum." *Catholic Biblical Quarterly* 7 (1945) 450–53.

Wong, Man Kong. *James Legge: A Pioneer at Crossroads of East and West.* Hong Kong: Educational, 1996.

Wylie, Alexander. *Chinese Researches.* Shanghai: n.p., 1897.

Xiao Min, ed. *Shangdi de Ai: Zhuiwangji.* Taibei: Bible Society, 1981.

Xu Mushi. "*Xiandai Zhongwen Yiben* Shengjing Fengxian Libai Zhengdao Ci." In *Shangdi de Ai: Zhuiwangji,* edited by Xiao Min, 12–15. Taibei: Bible Society, 1981.

———. "Zhongwen Shengjing Fanyi Jianshi." *Jingfeng* 69 (1982) 28–36.

———. *Jing yu Yijing.* Hong Kong: Chinese Christian Literature Council Ltd., 1983.

Xu Yihua. *Jiaohui Daxue yu Ahenxue Jiaoyu.* Fuzhou: Fujian Jiaoyu Chubanshe, 1999.

Yang Senfu. *Zhongguo Jidujiao Shi.* First printing 1968. Taibei: Commercial, Ltd.,1984.

Yu Ligong. "Xinyue Shengjing Yizhe Wang Xuanchen." *Yijing Luncong,* 123–26. Babeili: Fuyin Wenxuanshe, 1979.

Yuan, Zhiming. *Shenzhou Chanhuilu: Shangdi yu Wuqiannian Zhongguo.* First printing 1998. Taiwan: Xiaoyuan Shufang, 2000.

———. *Xinyang Duihua.* Xiaoyuan Shufang Chubanshe, 1997.

Zetzsche, Jost. *The Bible in China: History of the Union Version: Or the Culmination of Protestant Missionary Bible Translation in China.* Monumenta Serica Monograph 45. Netetal: Steyler, 1999.

———. "The Work of Lifetimes: Why the *Union* Version Took Nearly Three Decades to Complete." *The Bible in Modern China: The Literary and Intellectual Impact,* edited by Irene Eber, S. K. Wan, and Knut Walf, 77–100. Nettetal: Steyler Verlay, 1999.

———. "The Missionary and the Chinese 'Helper': A Re-appraisal of the Chinese Role in the Case of Bible Translation in China." In *Jindai zhongguo jidujiaoshi yanjiu jikan,* 2000.

Zhao Tianen. "Cong Huaren Jiaohui Fazhan Shi Kan Jiaohui Zengzhang." In *Jindai Zhongguo yu Jidujiao Lunwenji,* edited by Lin Zhiping, 345–53. Taibei: Yuzhouguang Chubanshe, 1981.

Zhao Weiben. *Yijing Suyuan: Xiandai Wu Da Zhongwen Shengjing Fanyi Shi.* Hong Kong: Zhongguo Shenxue Yanjiuyuan, 1993.

Zhou Lianhua. "Jieshao *Xiandai Zhongwen Yiben* Shengjing: Jianlun Fanyi Yuanze." In *Shangdi de Ai: Zhuiwangji,* edited by Xiao Min, 7–27. Taibei: Bible Society, 1981.

Zhou Zuoren. "Shengjing yu Zhongguo Wenxue." *Xiaoshuo Yuebao* 12 (1921) 1–7.

Zhu Weizhi. *Jidujiao yu Wenxue.* First printing 1941. Shanghai: Shanghai, 1992.

Zhuang Rouyu. *Jidujiao Shengjing Zhongwen Yiben Quanwei Xianxiang Yanjiu,* Hong Kong: International Bible Society, 2000.

About the Author

Dr. Ann Cui'an Peng received her MA and PhD in theology from the University of Birmingham in the United Kingdom. In the early 1980s, she studied at Nanjing Theological Seminary, China, where later she served as a lecturer and vice-principal until 1999. In 2007, Dr. Peng completed her PhD thesis on the history of Chinese Bible translation.

As a Senior Associate with the Global China Center, Dr. Peng serves as Associate Editor for the *Biographical Dictionary of Chinese Christianity*, and was involved in translating for the GCC series *Salt and Light: Lives of Faith that Shaped Modern China.*

Index